TEACHING EMERGENT BILINGUAL STUDENTS

Also Available

Teaching Emergent Bilingual Students

FLEXIBLE APPROACHES IN AN ERA OF NEW STANDARDS

Edited by

**C. Patrick Proctor
Alison Boardman
Elfrieda H. Hiebert**

THE GUILFORD PRESS
New York   London

© 2016 The Guilford Press
A Division of Guilford Publications, Inc.
370 Seventh Avenue, Suite 1200, New York, NY 10001
www.guilford.com

Printed in the United States of America

This book is printed on acid-free paper.

Last digit is print number: 9 8 7 6 5 4 3 2 1

Library of Congress Cataloging-in-Publication Data is available from
the publisher.

ISBN 978-1-4625-2718-2 (Paperback)
ISBN 978-1-4625-2719-9 (Hardcover)

About the Editors

C. Patrick Proctor, EdD, is Associate Professor in the Lynch School of Education at Boston College. Previously he was a third- and fourth-grade bilingual teacher and worked in district, state, and nonprofit settings on issues pertaining to bilingualism and literacy. Dr. Proctor's research is broadly focused on emergent bilingual learners from Spanish-speaking homes in K–8 settings. Within that context, his work targets language use and development, cross-linguistic relations, instructional interventions, and teacher practice. He has published many articles and book chapters, has developed language-based and reading curricula, and has worked in close collaboration with Boston-area schools facilitating the translation of research to practice.

Alison Boardman, PhD, is Assistant Research Professor in the School of Education at the University of Colorado Boulder. A former elementary and middle school special education teacher, Dr. Boardman works closely with teachers and school leaders to study and innovate reading instruction across content areas in classrooms that include emergent bilingual students and students with disabilities. She recently led a project to build school- and district-level capacity to sustain best practices for literacy instruction in language arts, social studies, and science classrooms, and is currently involved in developing a project-based learning curriculum and multimodal composition opportunities for diverse learners in ninth-grade language arts classrooms. She has published numerous articles and books on reading comprehension.

Elfrieda H. Hiebert, PhD, is CEO and President of TextProject, Inc. She has worked in the field of early reading acquisition for more than 40 years as a classroom teacher, teacher educator, and researcher. Her research, which addresses how fluency, vocabulary, and knowledge can be fostered through appropriate texts, has been published in numerous scholarly journals and books. Dr. Hiebert's contributions to research and practice have been recognized with such honors as the Research to Practice Award from the American Educational Research Association and the Oscar S. Causey Award from the Literacy Research Association.

Contributors

Alison Boardman, PhD. See "About the Editors."

Marco Bravo, PhD, is Associate Professor of Education in the Department of Education at Santa Clara University, in Santa Clara, California, where he teaches courses in language and literacy development. A former first-grade Spanish–English bilingual teacher, he was a postdoctoral researcher at the Lawrence Hall of Science, where he contributed to the development of integrated science and literacy curricula through the Seeds of Science/Roots of Reading research program. Dr. Bravo has also coauthored informational science books for children.

María Estela Brisk, PhD, is Professor of Education at Boston College. Her research and teaching interests include writing instruction, bilingual education, bilingual language and literacy acquisition, and preparation of mainstream teachers to work with bilingual learners. She is the author of numerous articles and six books: *Bilingual Education: From Compensatory to Quality Schooling*; *Literacy and Bilingualism: A Handbook for ALL Teachers*; *Situational Context of Education: A Window into the World of Bilingual Learners*; *Language Development and Education: Children with Varying Language Experiences* (with Paula Menyuk); *Language, Culture, and Community in Teacher Education*; and *Engaging Students in Academic Literacies: Genre-Based Pedagogy for K–5 Classrooms*.

Amy C. Crosson, EdD, is Assistant Professor in the College of Education at The Pennsylvania State University, University Park. She has led professional development about literacy development of language-minority students for teachers in urban school districts in the United States. In Chile, she supported the professional development of literacy specialists working in low-income municipalities surrounding Santiago. Dr. Crosson began her career as a bilingual (Spanish–English) education teacher in urban school districts in Massachusetts. In her first year of teaching, she received a Commitment to Quality Bilingual Education Award from the Bilingual Parents' Association, Boston Public Schools.

Anne O. Davidson, MA, is a PhD candidate studying Educational Equity and Cultural Diversity at the University of Colorado Boulder. She works as an instructional coach supporting teachers in their efforts to create equity in their classrooms for all diverse learners. Her interest in educational advocacy grew during her years as a special education teacher, when she saw how extensively schools labeled and segregated students perceived as having a disability or learning difference. Ms. Davidson continues to follow the example of equity and respect with which she was raised by advocating for the students who are continually marginalized in schools, and for the use of best practices in supporting the learning needs of all students in inclusive classrooms.

Amy M. Eppolito, PhD, is an English language development specialist with Adams-50 School District in Colorado, specializing in multi-tiered educational models for English learners (ELs) and culturally responsive teaching practices. She was the project coordinator for a U.S. Department of Education grant titled "RTI Effectiveness Model for ELs" and an instructional coach for Collaborative Strategic Reading–Colorado (CSR-CO). She has experience teaching Spanish, English as a second language (ESL), and literacy classes for K–8 students as well as undergraduate courses in the teacher education program at the University of Colorado Boulder. Dr. Eppolito has published articles and book chapters relating to emergent bilinguals with special needs, supporting emergent bilinguals in content classrooms, and collaborative decision making in response-to-intervention models.

Kathy Escamilla, PhD, is Professor in the Division of Educational Equity and Cultural Diversity at the University of Colorado Boulder. She has been in the field of bilingual/ESL education for over 45 years and has been a classroom teacher, a school administrator, and a professor. Dr. Escamilla does research on Spanish language and literacy development and the assessment of Spanish-speaking Latino children in U.S. schools. She is particularly interested in issues related to the development of bilingualism and biliteracy in this population. She is currently working on Phase III of Literacy Squared®, a longitudinal biliteracy research study designed for Spanish-speaking children who are simultaneously bilingual. The study involves 5,000 children and 350 teachers in six states. Dr. Escamilla is the author of three books and over 50 peer-refereed research articles in the field.

Evelyn Ford-Connors, EdD, is a senior lecturer in the Literacy and Language Program at Boston University's School of Education and Associate Director of the Donald D. Durrell Reading and Writing Clinic. Her primary research interests focus on the literacy learning needs of struggling readers and writers. She has created an after-school literacy intervention for high school students and recently completed a classroom-based study examining middle school teachers' talk during vocabulary instruction. Dr. Ford-Connors's current work investigates teacher coaching, with collaboration to refine teaching practices and strengthen teachers' instructional talk.

Boni Hamilton, EdD, is a PhD candidate in the School of Education and Human Development at the University of Colorado Denver. Her area of concentration is Urban Ecologies and she has been a research assistant on the eCALLMS project since it began. Her dissertation focus will be the use of digital tools in elementary classrooms. Dr. Hamilton has published two books: *It's Elementary!: Integrating*

Technology in the Primary Grades and *Integrating Technology in the Classroom: Digital Tools for Every Student.* Her additional research interests include ethics in doctoral studies and the use of multicultural picture books in elementary mathematics classrooms.

Elfrieda H. Hiebert, PhD. See "About the Editors."

Susan Hopewell, PhD, is Assistant Professor of Education in the Division of Educational Equity and Cultural Diversity at the University of Colorado Boulder. She is interested in issues of language, culture, equity, and identity, especially as they impact—or are affected by—literacy practices. Dr. Hopewell utilizes mixed-methods designs to conduct research focused on strengthening biliteracy education for Spanish–English bilingual children in the United States. She is especially interested in questions about the strategic use of Spanish during literacy-based English language development.

Cristin Jensen Lasser, PhD, is Associate Professor of Teacher Education at Colorado Mountain College. She has worked as a graduate research assistant on the CSR-CO project, specializing in instructional coaching with science and social studies teachers in culturally and linguistically diverse middle school classrooms using Collaborative Strategic Reading in both English and Spanish. Dr. Jensen Lasser's research interests include instructional practices for emergent bilinguals and professional development opportunities for teachers of culturally and linguistically diverse students. She teaches courses in planning, instruction and assessment, how people learn (neuroscience), literacy instruction in the primary classroom, and instruction and assessment for emergent bilinguals.

Yalda M. Kaveh, MEd, is a doctoral student in Curriculum and Instruction at Boston College. Her research interests are in bilingualism, heritage language maintenance in children of immigrants, and language policy. Ms. Kaveh has taught English and Persian to adolescent and adult language learners for several years prior to and during her graduate studies in the United States. She has been working with K–8 teachers in Greater Boston on addressing the needs of emergent bilinguals through literacy instruction.

Christine M. Leighton, EdD, is Assistant Professor of Education at Emmanuel College in Boston. She is interested in better understanding the literacy learning experiences of children and adults who are acquiring English as another language. She is devoted to helping preservice and inservice teachers understand literacy and language development to effectively teach English learners.

Francesca López, PhD, is Associate Professor and Co-Director of the Center for Research in Classrooms in the Department of Educational Psychology at the University of Arizona. Her research, which is focused on the ways educational settings inform Latino student identity and achievement, has been funded by the American Educational Research Association Grants Program, an Early Career Award from Division 15 of the American Psychological Association, and the National Academy of Education/Spencer Postdoctoral Fellowship Program. Dr. López is currently coeditor of the *American Educational Research Journal* and senior associate editor of the *American Journal of Education.*

Susan P. O'Hara, PhD, is Executive Director of Resourcing Excellence in Education at the University of California, Davis, and cofounder of the Academic Language Development Network. She is co-principal investigator on an Improving Teacher Quality grant focused on California districts' development of integrated professional learning systems. Dr. O'Hara is also a member of the leadership team for the Understanding Language initiative at Stanford University. She has coauthored more than 50 publications, including the book *Common Core Standards in Diverse Classrooms: Essential Practices for Developing Academic Language and Disciplinary Literacy.*

Marcela Ossa Parra, MA, is Assistant Professor at the Center for Research and Teaching in Education, Universidad de los Andes, Bogotá, Colombia, and a doctoral candidate in the Curriculum and Instruction PhD Program at Boston College. She has published articles about educational policy, self-regulated learning, thesis supervision, and citizen education in practitioner books and academic journals, including *Reflective Practice, Pensamiento Educativo Revista de Investigación Educacional Latinoamericana,* and *Voces y Silencios: Revista Latinoamericana de Educación.*

Jeanne R. Paratore, EdD, is Professor of Education, Faculty Director of the Literacy and Language Education Cluster, and Program Director of Reading and Literacy Education at Boston University. She also serves as Director of the Donald D. Durrell Reading and Writing Clinic. She has published on issues related to family literacy, classroom grouping practices, interventions for struggling readers, and literacy coaching. Dr. Paratore is an elected member of the Reading Hall of Fame and a recipient of the New England Reading Association's Lifetime Achievement Award and the Ida M. Johnson Award honoring distinguished alumni of Boston University's School of Education.

Robert Pritchard, PhD, Professor of Education in the College of Education at Sacramento State University, is a language and literacy specialist who has worked extensively with schools, school districts, and state departments of education on a wide range of professional development projects. A classroom teacher and reading specialist for over a decade, he has also worked internationally as an ESL teacher, teacher trainer, and curriculum specialist. Dr. Pritchard has authored or coauthored numerous publications related to emergent bilinguals, innovative uses of technology, and professional development for teachers, including *Common Core Standards in Diverse Classrooms: Essential Practices for Developing Academic Language and Disciplinary Literacy.*

C. Patrick Proctor, EdD. See "About the Editors."

Dana A. Robertson, EdD, is Assistant Professor and Executive Director of the Literacy Research Center and Clinic at the University of Wyoming. He has conducted research and written on classroom discourse, comprehension instruction, struggling readers and writers, coaching, and teacher professional development related to literacy. Dr. Robertson is a coauthor of *Talk That Teaches: Using Strategic Talk to Help Students Achieve the Common Core* and has published articles in several leading journals, including *The Reading Teacher, Reading Psychology, Language Arts,* and the *Journal of Adolescent and Adult Literacy.*

Vanessa Santiago Schwarz, MS, is a doctoral student in Educational Equity and Cultural Diversity at the University of Colorado Boulder. She spent 8 years working as an elementary school teacher, primarily with students with special needs in New York City's dual-language programs, and spent 2 years teaching internationally. In addition to teaching in public schools, Ms. Schwarz worked as an adjunct instructor in Bank Street College's Teacher Education Program. She is passionate about working with preservice and inservice teachers to create inclusive learning experiences that meet the needs of all students.

Pat Scialoia, BS, has been a teacher in the Boston Public Schools for 20 years. He has partnered with Dr. María Estela Brisk and the Lynch School of Education at Boston College for the past 7 years. During this time, he has seen drastic improvement in the writing of all his students. Bilingual learners are thriving in his fourth- and fifth-grade classrooms.

Peet Smith, MA, is a doctoral student in Special Education in the Department of Counseling, Higher Education and Special Education at the University of Maryland, College Park. Under the advisement of Dr. Ana Taboada Barber, Ms. Smith is interested in exploring the multidimensional nature of student engagement for struggling readers and emergent bilinguals in upper elementary and middle school.

Ana Taboada Barber, PhD, is Associate Professor in the Department of Counseling, Higher Education and Special Education at the University of Maryland, College Park. Her research focuses on the examination of classroom contexts that support reading engagement for monolingual and second-language learners. She is currently working on the development of frameworks within the engagement model as they apply to second-language learners, and has led the development of United States History for Engaged Reading, a literacy curriculum for middle school students of diverse language backgrounds. Dr. Taboada Barber's research has been published in the *Journal of Educational Psychology, Reading and Writing: An Interdisciplinary Journal,* and the *Journal of Literacy Research,* among others. She was also a classroom teacher in bilingual schools in Buenos Aires before coming to the United States as a Fulbright scholar.

Beverly Timothy, MEd, has been an elementary educator in Boston Public Schools for the past 9 years. She teaches a hybrid class of emergent bilinguals and native speakers of English. Ms. Timothy has been working with Dr. María Estela Brisk and the Lynch School of Education at Boston College for the past 5 years teaching writing, using the systemic functional linguistics approach.

Kara Mitchell Viesca, PhD, is Assistant Professor of Culturally and Linguistically Diverse Education at the University of Colorado Denver. Her research agenda focuses on advancing equity in the policy and practice of educator development for general education teachers of multilingual learners. Dr. Viesca is the lead principal investigator on the eCALLMS grant.

Christopher J. Wagner, MA, is a doctoral candidate in Language and Literacy at the Lynch School of Education at Boston College. He is a former secondary English teacher and founder of an out-of-school writing program. Mr. Wagner's research explores the connections among literacy, bilingualism, and identity in young children.

Jeff Zwiers, EdD, is a senior researcher at the Stanford University Graduate School of Education. He supports the Understanding Language initiative and codirects the Academic Language Development Network, a research and professional development project focused on the education of academic emergent bilinguals. Dr. Zwiers has published articles and books on literacy, cognition, discourse, and academic language. His current research focuses on effective lesson planning and classroom practices that foster academic interactions and literacy.

Preface

The Common Core State Standards (CCSS) and the Next Generation Science Standards (NGSS) are controversial and thought provoking, and raise a host of questions for educators, specifically related to the ways in which standard, "academic" language ought to be infused into content-area teaching and learning. In recent years, the adoption and implementation of these standards have accelerated, leaving many practitioners and researchers wondering who—to use the old expression—is being left behind. As editors, our motivation to pursue this book was rooted in the concern that the language demands that characterize these new standards are particularly onerous for emergent bilingual children and the educators who serve them. Indeed, the evidence is clear that the CCSS were not designed with emergent bilingual students in mind. Thus, the contents of this book reflect principles of policy, pedagogy, and professional learning that privilege the unique and additive skills and resources emergent bilingual learners bring to K–8 classrooms.

This volume had its genesis when one of us (Elfrieda Hiebert) convened a 2014 symposium at the International Literacy Association (ILA) annual conference entitled *English Language Learners in Common Core Classrooms*. Here, many of the chapter authors in this book came together to present converging instructional approaches and programs that were designed *from the outset* to meet the needs of emergent bilingual learners in K–8 settings, and which were also specifically aligned with the demands of the CCSS and/or the NGSS. The session was well attended, and we heard the concerns of practicing educators who were looking for ways to support emergent bilingual learners in their schools and classrooms.

Thus the idea for this book was born with teachers, principals, literacy specialists, and professional development providers intended as the target audiences.

In addition to including those experts who presented at the 2014 ILA symposium, we reached out to other outstanding practitioners and researchers who work with emergent bilingual children to add additional voices to this volume. We asked contributors to describe specific programs and pedagogies that promote instructional flexibility, the central premise being that teaching and learning are situational, and that bilingualism is dynamic. We can no longer afford to offer canned instructional programs that are not adaptable for use with a recently arrived fourth grader from Russia in Boston, a Spanish-speaking Mexican American seventh grader in Denver, and a Tagalog-speaking second grader in Los Angeles. We need flexible instructional approaches that can be adapted to, and evolve with, the variable and unique linguistic and cultural characteristics of emergent bilingual learners across the country. We feel that the chapters in this volume align with this vision.

A Note on Terminology

Throughout the book, all authors use the terms *emergent bilingual* and/or *English learner.* This was a negotiated and deliberate decision. To a certain extent, these terms are synonyms. Yet in this field and at this time in educational history, they carry subtle but important differences with respect to linguistic orientation. García, Kleifgen, and Falchi (2008) eloquently capture the nuance:

> English language learners are in fact emergent bilinguals. That is, through school and through acquiring English, these children become bilingual, able to continue to function in their home language as well as in English, their new language and that of school. When officials and educators ignore the bilingualism that these students can and often must develop through schooling in the United States, they perpetuate inequities in the education of these children. That is, they discount the home languages and cultural understandings of these children and assume their educational needs are the same as a monolingual child (p. 6)

However, one cannot ignore the fact that emergent bilingual children are immersed in a complex and fraught educational policy context. As such, students' language proficiencies drive the instructional categorization of *English learner,* a label that, once assigned, triggers specialized language instruction of one form or another. Thus the terms reflect different realms of awareness relative to the politics and schooling of emergent bilingual learners.

Overview of the Book

This book is divided into three broad sections: Policy, Pedagogy, and Professional Learning. In Part I, Policy, López's and Escamilla and Hopewell's contributions both take the political long view and articulate a set of opportunities and challenges that educators face via the new standards movement. López notes that, in contrast to current federal policies that focus clearly on English development at the expense of promoting bilingualism, state-level policies show marked variation with regard to native language use—policies that have been largely impervious to federal-level pendulum swings, and that are characterized by extreme variability with regard to recommended approaches and the types of training teachers receive to work with emergent bilingual children and youth.

Escamilla and Hopewell underscore the insights raised by López and specifically frame how literacy politics and policies have undermined the appreciation and development of bilingualism and biliteracy among emergent bilingual learners in U.S. schools. Importantly, authors of both chapters call the CCSS developers to task for having designed the standards in a monolingual vacuum. This has resulted in the need for post hoc implementation guidance, which is just now beginning to proliferate, thanks to bilingual educators and advocates across the country (e.g., see Valdés, Menken, & Castro, 2015; Understanding Language, *http://ell.stanford.edu*; Zwiers, O'Hara, & Pritchard, 2014). We offer this book in this same spirit of advocacy.

Eppolito and Santiago Schwarz extend policy recommendations to the response-to-intervention (RTI) framework. They discuss how school leaders can design (or restructure) existing models of RTI with the needs of emergent bilingual learners at the forefront. Eppolito and Santiago Schwarz argue that schools must attend to the quality of assessment and instruction for emergent bilinguals at all tiers (general education, intervention, and special education) in order to increase learning and address the disproportionate numbers of emergent bilingual children in special education programs.

Part II, Pedagogy, comprises the bulk of the chapters. These chapters target classroom-based approaches that can be applied across diverse instructional contexts. In her chapter, Hiebert gives us a sense of the linguistic demands of texts, in the context of thinking about what we expect our children to comprehend in the classroom. Crosson provides guidance on teaching for academic vocabulary, with a focus on word selection and instructional strategies. Boardman and Jensen Lasser address the crucial role of teaching reading comprehension strategies in their overview of Collaborative Strategic Reading. Both Ossa Parra and Brisk, along with their colleagues, take us beyond vocabulary and reading and into speaking and writing for text-based argumentative purposes. Ossa Parra et al. provide a blueprint for implementing small-group discussions that is complemented by the related recommendations from Brisk et al., who delve into the intricacies of one of the most challenging aspects of teaching: writing instruction. Taboada Barber and Smith address the very elusive construct of motivation and engagement, and challenge us to consider how these are not fixed constructs that reside within the student but can be fostered through teacher support of student learning and autonomy. Finally, Bravo provides an illustration of quality elementary science instruction that highlights the synergies across many of the chapters in this section.

In the final section, Part III, Professional Learning, authors address the crucial need for feasible inservice models that support teachers who work with emergent bilingual children and youth. In their description of the ALLIES project, O'Hara, Pritchard, and Zwiers show how principles of design-based research can be used to iterate toward school- and system-wide capacity building to meet the language and literacy demands inherent in the new standards, and how instruction can be designed to leverage the unique contexts, languages, and learning environments in which teaching and learning take place. Viesca, Hamilton, Davidson, and colleagues bring technology and distance learning into the conversation as they describe the e-Learning Communities for Academic Language Learning in Mathematics and Science (eCALLMS) project, an online initiative that uses open-access coursework to draw teachers' attention to the language demands of math and science learning in the new standards to better serve emergent bilingual learners.

This volume provides insight into the political landscape and instructional implications of a standards-driven federal agenda that has largely ignored the needs of emergent bilingual children and youth. Our hope is that educators who read this book take it as a starting point to generate new ideas and approaches to designing learning environments that provide emergent bilingual children and youth with instruction that is engaging, challenging, and culturally relevant across myriad educational settings.

REFERENCES

García, O., Kleifgen, J. A., & Falchi, L. (2008). *From English language learners to emergent bilinguals* (Equity Matters: Research Review No. 1). New York: Campaign for Educational Equity, Teachers College.

Valdés, G., Menken, K., & Castro, M. (2015). *Common Core, bilingual and English language learners*. Philadelphia: Calson.

Zwiers, J., O'Hara, S., & Pritchard, R. (2014). *Common Core Standards in diverse classrooms: Essential practices for developing academic language and disciplinary literacy*. Portland, ME: Stenhouse.

Contents

PART I

POLICY

CHAPTER 1

Language Education Policies
in the Common Core Era

Policy Initiatives That Affect
Emergent Bilingual Youth

Francesca López

The history of emergent bilingual students in U.S. schools is as long as that of U.S. schooling itself. Despite steady growth of the emergent bilingual population since 1965 (Krogstad & Keegan, 2014) and four decades of guidelines decreeing schools' responsibilities to ensure that emergent bilingual students receive equitable instructional access (*Lau v. Nichols,* 1974), the educational experiences of these students remain largely contingent on the widely varying state policies aimed at addressing their English proficiency (for a review, see López & McEneaney, 2012). In some states, a majority of emergent bilingual children and youth are educated in language instruction educational programs (LIEPs) that use the native language to teach content as exposure to English is increased. In these states, policies also require teachers of emergent bilingual students to demonstrate proficiency in those students' native language and to hold bilingual certification. In other states, however, teachers are charged with ensuring emergent bilingual students equitable access to instructional materials with *no* additional training.[1]

State-level policies have been largely resistant to change despite fluctuations in federal policies. Policies that promote bilingualism and biliteracy in the early grades have been around for quite some time, particularly in states with longer immigration histories. However, the omission of

---

[1] For a detailed review of state requirements for teacher certification and training, see López, Scanlan, and Gundrum (2013).

evidence-based policies continues to be found in many states that have experienced dramatic growth in their emergent bilingual populations. Although recent changes in state-level LIEP policies are rare, some states with longer histories of educating emergent bilinguals have indeed dramatically revised their policies. Instead of updating policies to reflect evidence-based practices, however, changes reflect deficiency-based political ideologies (e.g., in Arizona, California, and Massachusetts). Within this context of varying approaches to the acquisition of English, the Common Core State Standards (CCSS) have emphasized "content-rich and language-rich" (Hakuta & Santos, 2012) environments. However, when one considers the numerous LIEPs that reflect wide variation in states' interpretations of federal requirements, it stands to reason that applying the CCSS introduces several challenges to meeting the needs of emergent bilingual students. Namely, although high levels of literacy and language-rich contexts are viewed as ideal for *all* students, it is unclear how various LIEPs might promote or constrain the ideals states are adopting to meet these new standards. The purpose of this chapter is to explore that very issue.

To that end, this chapter is divided into three parts. In the first, I provide a brief overview of federal and state LIEP policies in the United States and review the various LIEPs reported by states to the U.S. Department of Education. In the second, I turn to an overview of contemporary policy issues that include a trend toward the promotion of language-rich standards and that provide a summary of implications for LIEPs to ensure that emergent bilingual children and youth have equitable access to language-rich environments that promote literacy. Within this context, I focus explicitly on implications for teacher training prior to turning to recommendations for practice. Finally, I discuss the ways the unique language learning needs of emergent bilingual students are ignored by CCSS, and the potential role of asset-based practices that could strengthen policies.

Language Education Policy

Prior to the No Child Left Behind Act (NCLB; 2001), LIEPs were delineated by the Bilingual Education Act (BEA; Title VII of the Elementary and Secondary Education Act [ESEA]). From 1968 until 2001, the BEA underwent various changes that ranged from a voluntary program for schools experimenting with ways to address the needs of emergent bilingual students to a preference for programs that ensured that those students received instruction in their native languages as they acquired English. With NCLB, federal support for bilingual programs waned, whereas the focus on assessment and accountability increased. For emergent bilingual children and youth, this focus included assessment of English proficiency and academic outcomes (see López & McEneaney, 2012; López, McEneaney, & Nieswandt, 2015). Although NCLB rescinded the priority for the cultivation of bilingualism among emergent bilingual students at the federal level when it removed all references to bilingual education that had existed in prior authorizations of the ESEA, many states continued to require bilingual education to be compliant with the *Lau v. Nichols* (1974) decision (for a detailed review of all state policies, see López et al., 2015).

Each state is required to submit information regarding the LIEPs they report using to meet the needs of emergent bilingual students to the U.S. Department of Education. Notably, only two LIEPs (and at times three) aim to promote bilingualism and biliteracy: two-way immersion and dual language, as well as developmental bilingual education (depending on the definition used by those implementing the program). What follows is a summary of states' most commonly reported LIEPs (for a detailed overview, see López, 2016a).

Structured English Immersion Programs

Structured English immersion (SEI) programs maximize instruction in English by using second-language acquisition strategies, such as using English at a level deemed appropriate for students as they acquire higher levels of proficiency (Clark, 2009). Fully 37 states report using SEI; however, the version of SEI used in Arizona, California, and Massachusetts is markedly distorted from scholarly recommendations. For example, although SEI has been defined as using and teaching English "at a level appropriate to the class of English learners . . . and teachers are oriented toward maximizing instruction in English and use English for 70% to 90% of instructional time, averaged over the first three years of instruction" (Baker, 1998, para. 5), SEI in Arizona, California, and Massachusetts is not intended to last more than 1 year and does not make provisions for languages other than English in instruction.[2]

English as a Second Language Programs

English as a second language (ESL) programs used in the United States tend to be either (1) pull-out, whereby students are removed from their mainstream (English-only) classroom during a designated time(s) and day(s) and are provided with focused English instruction in a small-group setting; or

---

[2]For a detailed description of the various conceptualizations and inconsistencies reflected in SEI programs, see López and McEneaney (2012) and López et al. (2015).

(2) instruction in a content area (e.g., science) that emphasizes the acquisition of English within the content area. All states except Arizona, Florida, Massachusetts, and Washington report providing one or both types of ESL.

Transitional Bilingual Programs

Transitional bilingual programs are the most prevalent bilingual programs, although not used as frequently as SEI and ESL. These programs require teachers to hold bilingual certification and have fluency in emergent bilingual students' native language (López et al., 2013). Like SEI, many states also report using transitional bilingual programs. These programs are considered either early-exit, whereby emergent bilingual students are transitioned to all-English instruction by middle-elementary grades, or late-exit transitional programs (sometimes referred to as *developmental bilingual education* [DBE]), in which the shift to all-English instruction occurs in late-elementary grades (Ramirez, Yuen, Ramey, & Pasta, 1991). It is unclear from state-reported data the extent to which transitional bilingual programs might include early- and/or late-exit, and whether states differentiate between late-exit and DBE. Although DBE is often considered to be a late-exit transitional program, there are cases where DBE is conceptualized as a dual-language program (see the following section on two-way immersion) for emergent bilinguals that spans grades K through 12. Despite the absence of detailed information regarding the type of transitional bilingual programs reported by states to the U.S. Department of Education, scholars have documented that most transitional bilingual education programs have become early-exit due to the dominance of high-stakes assessments (Menken, 2008).

Two-Way Immersion Programs

Two-way immersion programs group emergent bilingual students and students who are native English speakers (hence, *two-way*) in classrooms where instruction occurs in both English and the native language. That is, the programs are designed to promote bilingualism by bringing together a group of children who speak English as their native language and a group of children who share a non-English native language. Although two-way immersion is often interchangeably referred to as *dual-language* or *two-way* bilingual immersion, some states distinguish between dual-language and two-way bilingual programs. It is unclear whether the discrepancies reflect differences among states that use the terms interchangeably or conceptualize the two programs as distinct in terms of the students who enroll in the classes (even though the programs submitted to the National Clearinghouse for English Language Acquisition [NCELA] are meant to reflect programs for emergent bilingual children and youth). Most states report using two-way immersion and/or dual language, with the exception of Alabama, Arkansas, Kentucky, New Hampshire, Oklahoma, South Dakota, Wisconsin, West Virginia, and Wyoming.

Summary

Although federal policy played a substantive role in the extent to which states implemented transitional bilingual education with the BEA of 1974, it should be noted that most states that continue to report using transitional bilingual programs tend to have a longer history with emergent bilingual children and youth (see López et al., 2015). Accordingly, it may be that the institutionalization of these programs greatly facilitates their continuation, given that implementation involves specific teacher training and coursework. Thus, despite the elimination of bilingual education from NCLB, transitional bilingual programs are a mainstay in U.S. classrooms (although the number of early-exit programs has become far greater than prior to NCLB; see López & McEneaney, 2012). The institutionalization of transitional bilingual education notwithstanding, it is noteworthy that several states have pursued LIEPs that potentially favor native language instruction, as evidenced by the relatively large number of dual-language and two-way immersion programs. Despite this growing trend toward asset-based approaches in developing literacy for emergent bilingual students,[3] it is noteworthy that contemporary standards underscore the importance of rigor in literacy, yet fail to recognize the unique needs of these students.

Contemporary Considerations: Language-Rich Standards

Whereas state LIEPs are in place to meet the federal requirements set forth by the *Lau v. Nichols* (1974) Supreme Court decision, state standards for learning outcomes had not been outlined by the federal government until the CCSS.[4] Unlike language policies that are mandated to meet the needs of emergent bilingual students, states were not required to adopt the CCSS. Initially, 46 states adopted the CCSS between 2010 and 2014. However, three have since repealed the CCSS outright and many others have delayed implementation. Some states, in asserting their sovereignty, have renamed

---

[3] Even though dual-language settings can be viewed as reflecting asset-based beliefs about language-minority youth, there are concerns regarding the potential detrimental consequences for language-minority children in these settings (see Valdés, 1997).

[4] Although the CCSS are not explicit mandates, participation was required to be eligible for federal grant funding.

the CCSS since its adoption. Arizona, for example, removed all references to the CCSS, even though the state standards remain aligned with CCSS.

Despite some wavering of states' commitment to CCSS, the large number of states that have adopted the standards prompts careful consideration of the ways these standards can promote or hinder literacy among emergent bilingual students. Some scholars have raised serious concerns about the lack of "concrete supports, direction, and examples . . . in the Common Core State Standards" (Calderón, Slavin, & Sánchez, 2011, p. 112) that could prove detrimental to emergent bilingual students. Other scholars, however, view the CCSS as an opportunity to refocus standards to reflect the role of *language* in acquiring *content*. In this view, the CCSS have been conceptualized as "affordances" (Bunch, Kibler, & Pimentel, 2012, p. 1) that can help engender a departure from viewing language "as form or even as function, and toward a redefinition of language as a complex adaptive system" (Hakuta & Santos, 2012, p. ii). This new focus hinges on the role of literacy development in the context of subject matter. Accordingly, although the CCSS have not been without serious criticisms that must be reconciled, it is the focus on the explicit use of language as the medium of content acquisition that is lauded by scholars who have dedicated their careers to promoting equitable education for emergent bilingual children and youth (Understanding Language, 2013).

In their recommendations for policy, Pompa and Hakuta (2012) assert that a state's "curriculum, instructional materials, teacher preparation, and professional development systems . . . must be aligned with the Common Core State Standards" (p. 126). Inasmuch as alignment that reflects standards across the multiple dimensions of curriculum delivery is necessary, LIEPs play a critical role in CCSS (or in any state standards, for that matter). For states that do not emphasize LIEPs that use emergent bilingual students' native language, the dilemma of ensuring that teachers have the preparation necessary to support the linguistic and content demands of CCSS will be accentuated. Brisk and Proctor (2012) summarize the issue cogently: "The role of language in the New Standards is profound, which has implications for English learners' access to them, particularly when instruction is in English only" (p. 115). States that provide emergent bilingual students with instruction in their native language, however, also face formidable challenges, given the absence of considerations regarding bilingual language development in the CCSS and the absence of standards reflecting non-English languages.

Addressing the needs of emergent bilingual students in the CCSS is a highly complex matter that involves multiple dimensions. State LIEPs, for example, outline the language(s) of instruction, which directly influences the ways in which the CCSS are delivered. In states where two languages are used, there is the additional consideration of bilingual resources aligned with the CCSS. In all states, teacher training will play a role in how the CCSS can ultimately be implemented, underscoring the importance of preparing teachers for the unique needs of emergent bilingual students.

In examining issues related to teacher preparation, it becomes evident that the wide variation across states is in part an artifact of policy and "institutional will" (García, Jensen, & Scribner, 2009, p. 12), though at times it is influenced by the availability of human capital (López et al., 2015). An examination of the preparation requirements for teachers of emergent bilingual students across states (López et al., 2013) reveals that some states are not ensuring that teachers can meet the higher demands of a rigorous curriculum for these students. Several states (Alaska, Hawaii, Kentucky, Mississippi, Montana, Nebraska, and West Virginia) do not require specialist certification for teachers working with emergent bilingual students, nor do they require all teachers to have at least some knowledge regarding the needs of emergent bilingual students. Moreover, these states have no requirements that teachers possess any level of knowledge regarding language development for emergent bilingual students. For states such as these, although they may not have a long history of having to meet the needs of emergent bilingual children and youth, the ways in which pre-service programs prepare teachers merit revision—particularly when one considers the large growth in the number of emergent bilingual students most of these states have witnessed over the last decade (López et al., 2015). Without training that can assist teachers in delivering language-rich instruction that promotes literacy among these students, teachers will be unable to fully implement the affordances of language-rich standards. The CCSS, however, cannot be left up to individual states' interpretations; explicit consideration of emergent bilingual students' needs is warranted if the CCSS are to be appropriately implemented.

In the sections that follow, I briefly summarize key findings related to teacher training and the achievement outcomes of emergent bilingual students that merit serious consideration by policymakers. I then describe key principles reflected in the CCSS that, if altered, could reflect asset-based practices that serve to address preservice teacher training and state standards.

Teacher Training: Key Practices to Meet the Needs of Emergent Bilingual Students

In a recent study, my colleagues and I (López et al., 2013) examined the relationship between discrete requirements in each state's teacher education programs and fourth-grade Latino emergent bilingual students' reading outcomes on the National Assessment of Educational Progress. We found that training requirements reflecting teachers' knowledge in English language development of emergent bilingual students had a marked effect on students' achievement (approximately a .40 *SD* gain for students in states with stringent requirements, compared to peers in states with the least stringent requirements). We explained that "all teachers, not just specialist teachers, should understand the developmental trajectory of ELLs' [English language learners'] English proficiency as well as how to nurture and support it" (p. 20). We further explained that

> this includes knowledge about explicit English instruction and creating opportunities for students to express themselves, as well as modifying the level of English used to make content comprehensible. Supplementing teaching with visual aids, vocabulary instruction, and graphic organizers, for example, are all ways teachers can help ELLs be successful. Requiring teachers to have knowledge about ESL/ELD [English as a second language/English language development] can ameliorate the lack of preparation often felt by teachers while promoting achievement for ELLs. (López et al., 2013, p. 20)

In our study, we also found that requirements focused on teachers' knowledge about native language/English content assessment was associated with emergent bilingual students' achievement, a finding that has been supported by the extant literature (Black & Wiliam, 1998; Stiggins, 1988, 2002). Unfortunately, there is a paucity of training provided to preservice teachers on formative assessments (López et al., 2013), which is "especially detrimental for ELLs" (p. 19). My colleagues and I asserted that

> all teachers should know how to assess their students' formatively. With an accurate understanding of students' content knowledge, teachers can adjust instruction and attend to gaps in learning. Certainly, this recommendation is not limited to teachers who work with ELLs (Stiggins, 1988) but for teachers of ELLs, formative assessment is essential if they are implementing strategies resulting from their knowledge of ESL/ELD. (López et al., 2013, p. 20)

The findings in the study I carried out with my colleagues suggest that states without LIEPs that fully support emergent bilingual students should revise requirements for teacher preparation to ensure that, at the very minimum, teachers have knowledge of emergent bilingual students' language development and assessment of content knowledge. This is particularly urgent for teachers charged with delivering language-rich instruction to these students.

In contrast to states that do not emphasize LIEPs that use emergent bilinguals' native language, those that do face a distinct set of issues related to teacher training. Brisk and Proctor (2012) explain, "For bilingual education programs, this means that the materials in both languages must follow these criteria. This is a serious challenge, especially for materials in the languages other than English" (p. 119). Indeed, the lack of materials in languages other than English for states that have adopted the CCSS is a salient issue among even the most experienced teachers (e.g., López, 2016b). Accordingly, even the most robust preservice teacher programs are likely to need revising to reflect the new emphasis on language within content, which will often require teachers to supplement materials on their own.

Key Principles to Build on the CCSS

The National Comprehensive Center for Teacher Quality and Stanford University's Understanding Language initiative have compiled evidence that points to effective instruction for emergent bilinguals that is aligned with the CCSS as well as with the NGSS. In the sections that follow, I summarize four key principles in these initiatives that can inform preservice teacher training and state standards. By ensuring that course content reflects the needs outlined by Pompa and Hakuta (2012), existing programs can likely begin to address current limitations in teacher training.

Content-Based English Language Development

The first principle involves the engagement of emergent bilingual learners in discipline-specific practices designed to build both *conceptual understanding* and *language competence*. Here, development of language competence is centered on *academic* language that is contextualized within a content area. Put another way, teachers engage "students in purposeful activities, ensure that students experience multiple examples of language in use, and call students' attention to the ways in which language is used to communicate meaning" (Quinn, Lee, & Valdés, 2012, p. 7). Another way to envision this principle is that for classrooms with emergent bilingual students, teachers address both *content* and *academic language* in instruction in tandem, *not* separately. The undergirding framework is that each content area has its specialized language, and accessing the content successfully is dependent on mastery of that particular vocabulary/language.

To summarize, the first principle is focused on ways teachers build content and vocabulary knowledge, rather than on language as its own outcome (i.e., English language arts). Some of the explicit behaviors in which teachers engage to reflect the first principle involve providing multiple, meaningful (i.e., content-based), and extended opportunities for all students to (1) produce oral output using academic language;[5] (2) produce complex texts to develop and use academic language; and (3) analyze how a text's organizational features, syntax, and word choice combine to create meaning and build disciplinary language, thinking, and comprehension (National Comprehensive Center for Teacher Quality, 2012; O'Hara, Zwiers, & Pritchard, 2012; Understanding Language, 2013).

Scaffolds for Emergent Bilinguals

The next principle involves rigorous, grade-level-appropriate instruction that provides deliberate and targeted scaffolds (Understanding Language, 2013). Here the expectation is that teachers are *amplifying* rather than *simplifying* instruction. Scaffolding in this sense is somewhat distinct from what one would expect for all students. That is, typically, scaffolding in classrooms tends to occur from "macro-to-micro" (Walqui, 2006) and is indeed necessary for all students, not only emergent bilingual students.

Walqui (2006) describes the progression of scaffolding as going from planned to improvised, involving (1) a planned curriculum progression over time, (2) the procedures used in a particular activity, and (3) the collaborative process of student–teacher interactions. When we consider the complexity of teaching content and academic language to emergent bilingual students, additional scaffolding strategies are necessary. General strategies include focusing students' attention on key ideas before engaging them in interactive tasks to practice, cyclical as opposed to linear curricula, and setting up tasks that will prepare students to be successful at what is required of them (Walqui, 2006). Instructional tasks that can provide scaffolding to emergent bilinuals include *message abundancy* (Walqui, 2006), which allows emergent bilinguals to hear multiple uses of language. *Modeling* is yet another strategy that can provide emergent bilinguals with support to access both content and language, and it can encompass teacher modeling, student work examples, and other templates (Walqui, 2006). Still other instructional strategies involve the use of *contextualizing*, wherein the teacher embeds academic terms in a sensory context, and *schema building*, which builds on prior knowledge though films, adapted texts, and other visual aids (Walqui, 2006).

Teachers can also minimize linguistic obstacles by using English dictionaries and glossaries, as well as delivering instruction in simplified language for accessibility—so long as the simplification of the language does not water down the content (National Comprehensive Center for Teacher Quality, 2012), and serves as a precursor to more advanced language.

---

[5]For a discussion on the various representations of academic language and how it is represented in the context presented here, see Valdés (2004).

Explicit Strategies for Language Use

The third principle reflects the importance of fostering academic interactions by equipping emergent bilinguals with the strategies necessary to comprehend and use language in a variety of academic settings (National Comprehensive Center for Teacher Quality, 2012; Understanding Language, 2013; Walqui, 2006). Recalling that the first principle includes the degree to which teachers provide students with opportunities to engage in academic communication, the third principle deals with teachers' efforts to foster students' abilities to be able to participate in these opportunities by giving them explicit instruction on strategies they can use to decipher and use academic language in different ways. This can include apprenticeship opportunities whereby teachers model a particular strategy, and also strategies that deal with how language is used in particular scenarios—for example, with prompts teachers provide students to engage or elicit an answer from peers. This principle also involves teaching metacognition—that is, teaching students how to monitor their own understanding (Walqui, 2006). In this way, the scaffolds provided can be accessed when needed by students to push them forward in their learning. This involves teaching students how to interpret their formative assessments—what they know and what they still need to know. This also involves teaching students strategies to help them determine what they need for particular activities (e.g., if writing a lab report, whether students can use a template, glossary, or other supportive documentation).

Home Culture Connections

The last principle involves instruction that leverages emergent bilinguals' cultural assets and prior knowledge. Although accessing prior knowledge is not specific to these students' learning, in this principle, it invokes the kind of knowledge teachers find out about students' lives so that they can incorporate students' prior cultural knowledge into instruction and build from that knowledge. Accordingly, in these classrooms, students' cultural backgrounds are viewed as an asset. Students who have access to literature depicting protagonists who share their culture, for example, are exemplars of ways their cultural background can be consistent with schooling. Teachers' incorporation of students' home experiences into classroom instruction also addresses this principle. Here, it requires teachers to design instruction in a way that allows them to learn from students and their families, connecting what students learn about their own families with school. This culturally relevant approach that invokes *funds of knowledge* (e.g., González, Moll, & Amanti, 2005) has been found to have a pronounced impact on students' reading outcomes (López, 2016b).

The Absence of Asset-Based Practices in the CCSS: A Need for Revisions

Although many have lauded the CCSS for its rigor, there is evidence suggesting that rigorous curricula that increase overall student achievement are inadequate to address the educational needs of emergent bilingual students (Rumberger & Tran, 2010). Other serious concerns have been raised specifically regarding the CCSS, including the absence of developmental considerations (e.g., Main, 2011), which, when coupled with the unique linguistic needs of emergent bilingual students, could prove devastating to their educational trajectory. Moreover, whereas the CCSS focus on *literacy within content* is believed to hold promise to address this gap, Bale (2015) warns that

> the Common Core only makes this connection between language and content in English. The CCSS make no reference to linguistic diversity, to culture and its relationship to language, or to the linguistic and cultural resources that emergent bilinguals bring with them to the classroom. Worse still, the standards make no room for applying the language-content model to any language other than English. The standards invoke all the opportunity represented in sociocultural approaches to language learning, only to foreclose on it by focusing on English only. (para. 21)

Accordingly, it is evident that the CCSS merit revision to reflect the needs of emergent bilingual students. To do so, the CCSS must consider the extant evidence supporting asset-based LIEP policies to replace their current "English-only" orientation (Bale, 2015, para. 24).

Although many state LIEPs also merit revisions given the evidence favoring the use of emergent bilinguals' native languages in instruction, there is a national trend supporting biliteracy as an ideal outcome for all students that encourages these changes in both LIEP policies and the CCSS. First, as reviewed earlier in this chapter, most states report using two-way immersion—substantiating the reported growth in delivering education in two languages across the United States (Maxwell, 2012). Additionally, several states have passed policies (with several more in the early stages of considering policies) granting the Seal of Biliteracy to students who demonstrate fluency in at least two languages by the time they graduate from high school (see *sealofbiliteracy.org*). A consortium of various organizations (the American Council on the Teaching of Foreign Languages, the National Association of Bilingual Education, the National Council of State Supervisors for Languages, and TESOL International Association) provided official recommendations for implementing the Seal of Biliteracy. The guidelines state:

Students must demonstrate the state-determined level of proficiency in English, as well as one or more additional languages, be that language a native language, heritage language, or a language learned in school or another setting. Schools, districts, or states are encouraged to provide other forms of recognition prior to high school reflecting progress along the pathway toward achieving the specified level of biliteracy, which may occur earlier (as with immersion, two-way or dual language immersion programs; English language learners; and other populations). The focus is on achieving the level of proficiency required for English and the level of proficiency required for one or more other languages. (TESOL, 2015)

Accordingly, emergent bilinguals in settings with LIEPs that promote their acquisition of English as well as their native language are particularly well suited to meet the guidelines of the Seal of Biliteracy.

Table 1.1 presents the states that either already have or are in the process of attaining a Seal of Biliteracy, along with information that summarizes the kinds of LIEPs reported to the U.S. Department of Education by each state. Notably, most of the states with (or in the process of acquiring) a Seal of Biliteracy also use two-way immersion/dual-language programs, which ensure biliteracy for emergent bilingual and nonemergent bilingual students in the early schooling years. These states are well positioned to promote biliteracy and would be well served to align CCSS rigor in literacy in both English and the non-English language across compulsory schooling. Indeed, all states that have adopted the Seal of Biliteracy noted in Table

TABLE 1.1. State information on the Kinds of Language Instruction Educational Programs Used as Reported to the U.S. Department of Education as Part of the Consolidated State Performance Report for State Formula Grants

LIEP	State													
	CA	FL	IL	LA	MD	MI	MN	NM	NV	OH	OR	TX	WA	WI
Transitional bilingual	X		X	X	X	X	X	X	X	X	X	X	X	X
Developmental bilingual	X	X	X			X	X	X						X
Two-way immersion	X	X	X		X	X	X	X	X	X	X	X	X	
Dual language	X	X	X	X	X	X	X	X	X	X	X	X	X	

Note. Data compiled from state reports available through the National Clearinghouse on English Language Acquisition and Seal of Biliteracy.

1.1 have also adopted the CCSS, with the exception of Texas.[6] However, the CCSS currently require states to augment standards to reflect non-English languages. If the CCSS were to reflect the unique needs of emergent bilingual students, as well as the research base on asset-based approaches, higher levels of biliteracy would be much more likely. Thus, although this intersection of rigorous literacy, asset-based language policies, and the Seal of Biliteracy is currently much more feasible in some states than others, salient policy changes are necessary to address the current limitations in the CCSS that hinder the biliteracy promoted by some state LIEPs and the Seal of Biliteracy.

As reviewed earlier in this chapter, 27 additional states report using two-way immersion and/or dual-language programs for their emergent bilingual student populations, but have not yet pursued the Seal of Biliteracy. Given that these states already promote biliteracy in the earlier grades, it stands to reason that they would consider expanding additive practices throughout compulsory schooling. Finally, although other states may not have the institutionalization of language programs that can promote high levels of biliteracy for emergent bilingual students throughout their schooling experiences, committing to the Seal of Biliteracy and to high literacy standards is a step in the right direction. Accordingly, future research and practice efforts must examine how to extend biliteracy to earlier grades across various contexts, including the kinds of revisions needed to maximize teacher preparation standards in this area.

Conclusion

In this chapter, I have provided an overview of the variation in policies focused on ways to address the federal requirements to meet the needs of emergent bilingual students, the implications for teacher preparation, and the limited potential of the CCSS to leverage high levels of language(s) across content unless revisions are made. As reviewed here, states have distinct challenges associated with delivering language/content-rich context, which limits the extent to which teachers can be successful in implementing higher standards among emergent bilingual students.

In consideration of the empirical evidence that suggests that states should support bilingual LIEPs when feasible (López et al., 2015), it is in

---

[6] It should be noted that although California is included in the table, it is only through parental waivers that emergent bilingual students can access asset-based language programs. Thus, although California utilizes several practices (e.g., Seal of Biliteracy and availability of asset-based programs) that promote biliteracy, policy changes would enhance the educational experiences of its emergent bilingual population.

states' best interests to consider revising policies focused on meeting the needs of emergent bilingual students and the standards for teacher preparation. For many states with the human capital to deliver bilingual education in early grades, revisions to policy should extend beyond LIEPs and reflect the necessary teacher training to deliver rigorous content and languages. For many other states, bilingual education is not feasible. However, it is imperative that teacher training reflect the necessary knowledge to meet the needs of emergent bilingual students in these settings, thus allowing them to leverage the high levels of literacy and content (albeit in one language) reflected by the CCSS.

As mentioned earlier in this chapter, addressing the needs of emergent bilingual students in the context of policies from both the past and present is a highly complex matter that involves multiple dimensions. There are numerous additional considerations that were not reviewed (e.g., funding allocations) that also play an important role in the extent to which emergent bilingual literacy can be leveraged in a particular context. Nevertheless, by understanding the wide variation in policies—some of which have changed to the detriment of emergent bilingual students and others that have remained stagnant despite shifting student demographics—the ability to begin to address limitations in policy and practice is enhanced.

Finally, the content and language-rich emphasis of the CCSS, when considered alongside the large number of states that reflect asset-based LIEPs, has much to gain by revising the standards to reflect the unique needs of emergent bilingual students. By examining the growing trend of biliteracy across the United States, I assert that revisions to the CCSS can result in a much higher level of biliteracy among emergent bilingual children and youth, thus leveraging the assets they already possess.

REFERENCES

Baker, K. (1998). Structured English immersion. *Phi Delta Kappan, 80,* 199–205.
Bale, J. (2015). English-only to the core: What the Common Core means for emergent bilingual youth. *Rethinking Schools, 30*(1). Retrieved from *www.rethinkingschools.org/special/RS30-1_bale1.shtml.*
Bilingual Education Act. Public Law 90-247 (January 2, 1968), 81 Stat. 816, 20 U.S.C.A. 880(b).
Black, P., & Wiliam, D. (1998). Assessment and classroom learning. *Educational Assessment: Principles, Policies, and Practices, 5,* 7–74.
Brisk, M. E., & Proctor, C. P. (2012, April). *Challenges and supports for English language learners in bilingual programs.* Paper presented at the Understanding Language Conference, Stanford University, Stanford, CA.
Bunch, G. C., Kibler, A. K., & Pimentel, S. (2012, January). *Realizing opportunities for English learners in the Common Core English language arts and*

disciplinary literacy standards. Paper presented at the Understanding Language Conference, Standard University, Stanford, CA. Retrieved from *http:// ell.stanford.edu/publication/realizing-opportunities-ells-common-core-english-language-arts-and-disciplinary-literacy.*

Calderón, M., Slavin, R., & Sánchez, M. (2011). Effective instruction for English learners. *The Future of Children, 21*(1), 103–127.

Clark, K. (2009). The case for structured English immersion. *Educational Leadership, 66,* 42–46.

García, E., Jensen, B. T., & Scribner, K. P. (2009). Supporting English language learners: The demographic imperative. *Educational Leadership, 66,* 8–13.

García, O., Kleifgen, J. A., & Falchi, L. (2008). *From English learners to emergent bilinguals* (Equity Matters Research Review No. 1). New York: Teachers College, Columbia University.

González, N., Moll, L., & Amanti, C. (2005). *Funds of knowledge: Theorizing practices in households, communities, and classrooms.* Mahwah, NJ: Erlbaum.

Hakuta, K., & Santos, M. (2012, April). *Summary of commissioned papers on language and literacy issues in the Common Core State Standards and Next Generation Science Standards.* Paper presented at the Understanding Language Conference, Stanford University, Stanford, CA.

Krogstad, J. M., & Keegan, M. (2014.) *From Germany to Mexico: How America's source of immigrants has changed over a century.* Washington, DC: Pew Research Center. Available at *www.pewresearch.org/fact-tank/2014/05/27/ a-shift-from-germany-to-mexico-for-americas-immigrants.*

Lau v. Nichols, 414 U.S. 563 (1974).

López, F. (2016a). Language education policies and youth. In S. L. Nichols (Ed.), *Educational policy and the socialization of youth for the 21st century.* Charlotte, NC: Information Age.

López, F. (2016b). Teacher reports of culturally responsive teaching and Latino students' reading achievement in Arizona. *Teachers College Record, 118*(5).

López, F., & McEneaney, E. (2012). English language learners and state language acquisition policies. *Educational Policy, 26,* 418–464.

López, F., McEneaney, E., & Nieswandt, M. (2015). Language instruction educational programs and academic achievement of Latino English learners: Considerations for states with changing demographics. *American Journal of Education, 121,* 417–450.

López, F., Scanlan, M., & Gundrum, B. (2013). Preparing teachers of English language learners: Empirical evidence and policy implications. *Education Policy Analysis Archives, 21.* Available at *http://epaa.asu.edu/ojs/article/view/1132.*

Main, L. F. (2011). Too much too soon?: Common Core math standards in the early years. *Early Childhood Education Journal, 40,* 73–77.

Maxwell, L. A. (2012). Dual classes see growth in popularity. *Education Week, 31*(26), 16–17.

Menken, K. (2008). *English learners left behind: Standardized testing as language policy.* Bristol, UK: Multilingual Matters.

National Comprehensive Center for Teacher Quality. (2012). Summary of "Expert forum on the evaluation of teachers of English language learners," Center on Great Teachers and Leaders, American Institutes for Research. Retrieved from *www.gtlcenter.org/sites/default/files/docs/ForumSummary_July2012. pdf.*

No Child Left Behind Act of 2001 (NCLB), Public Law No. 107-110.

O'Hara, S., Zwiers, J., & Pritchard, R. (2012). *Framing the teaching of academic language.* Center to Support Excellence in Teaching: ALLIES. Available at *https://cset.stanford.edu/sites/default/files/ALLIES%20Brief%20v8.pdf.*

Pompa, D., & Hakuta, K. (2012, April). *Opportunities for policy advancement for ELLs created by the new standards movement.* Paper presented at the Understanding Language Conference, Stanford University, Stanford, CA.

Quinn, H., Lee, O., & Valdés, G. (2012, April). *Language demands and opportunities in relation to Next Generation Science Standard for English language learners: What teachers need to know.* Paper presented at the 2012 Challenges and Opportunities for Language Learning in the Context of Common Core State Standards and Next Generation Science Standards Conference, Stanford University, Stanford, CA. Retrieved from *http://ell.stanford.edu/papers.*

Ramirez, J. D., Yuen, S. D., Ramey, D. R., & Pasta, D. J. (1991). *Final report: Longitudinal study of structured English immersion strategy, early-exit, and late-exit transitional bilingual education programs for language minority children.* Retrieved from ERIC database (ED330216).

Rumberger, R. W., & Tran, L. (2010). State language policies, school language practices, and the English learner achievement gap. In P. Gándara & M. Hopkins (Eds.), *Forbidden language: English learners and restrictive language policies.* New York: Teachers College Press.

Stiggins, R. J. (1988). Make sure your teachers understand student assessment. *Executive Educator, 10,* 24–30.

Stiggins, R. J. (2002). Assessment crisis: The absence of assessment for learning. *Phi Delta Kappan, 83,* 758–765.

TESOL. (2015, March 10). *Seal of biliteracy guidelines.* Retrieved from *www.tesol. org/docs/default-source/advocacy/seal-of-biliteracy-approved-guidelines--- final-3-10-2015.pdf?sfvrsn=2.*

Understanding Language: Language, Literacy, and Learning in the Content Areas. (2013). *Key principles for ELL instruction.* Retrieved from *http://ell.stanford.edu/sites/default/files/Key%20Principles%20for%20ELL%20Instruction%20with%20references_0.pdf.*

Valdés, G. (1997). A cautionary note concerning the education of language minority students. *Harvard Educational Review, 37,* 391–429.

Valdés, G. (2004). Between support and marginalization: The development of academic language in linguistic minority children. *International Journal of Bilingual Education and Bilingualism, 7,* 102–132.

Walquí, A. (2006). Scaffolding instruction for English learners: A conceptual framework. *International Journal of Bilingual Education and Bilingualism, 9,* 159–180.

CHAPTER 2

Effective Instruction
for Emergent Bilingual Children

Accelerating English Acquisition
While Developing Biliteracy

Kathy Escamilla and Susan Hopewell

Nationally and internationally, there is agreement that all children are entitled to a comprehensive and effective education. In the United States, educational standards have historically been determined by individual states. However, recently, the comprehensive educational movement has been guided largely by the national development and promotion of the Common Core State Standards (CCSS), which outline what children should know and be able to do in language arts and mathematics. With regard to language arts, the standards prescribe only the skills and abilities that must be achieved in English without also providing guidance about how this is to be accomplished when children enter schools with language and literacy foundations that have been established in languages other than English. We agree that developing formidable proficiency in English is a critical need for children growing up in the United States, and we recognize that effective instruction for these children must consider their unique language and literacy needs in order to accelerate this process. Acceleration, however, need not be at the expense of their current or potential bilingual proficiencies. We propose that, in the right contexts for learning, *English acquisition can be accelerated as biliteracy is developed.*

In this chapter, we examine how the population of emerging bilingual students in U.S. schools has changed in recent decades. Then we discuss issues with regard to English literacy instruction for emergent bilingual students with a focus on two specific issues: (1) the failure of the current "good teaching is good teaching" generic literacy programs for emergent bilingual learners that have been adopted by many school districts; and (2) the need to discuss and develop literacy programs specifically designed for bilingual programs that can accelerate English language and literacy acquisition. Finally, we present a framework for biliteracy instruction that is best used in bilingual instructional programs, but that can also be used in English-medium settings.

Emergent Bilingual Learners in the United States

Because they hail from homes in which English is not the primary or sole language, 21% of students attending U.S. public schools carry the label *English learner* (EL) or *emergent bilingual learner* (Armario, 2013).[1] To illustrate the magnitude of this figure, let us examine it in comparison to overall U.S. population figures. In the fall of 2014, according to the U.S. Department of Education (n.d.), there were 49.8 million students enrolled in U.S. public schools at both the elementary and secondary levels. Of these, nearly 10.5 million were emergent bilingual learners. This is more than the combined total populations of Alaska, Delaware, Hawaii, Idaho, Maine, Montana, North Dakota, Rhode Island, South Dakota, Vermont, and Wyoming. In fact, there are only seven U.S. states that have individual populations that exceed this number: California, Florida, Illinois, New York, Ohio, Pennsylvania, and Texas. In other words, the number of emergent bilingual learners attending U.S. public schools across the nation exceeds the individual populations of 43 of our 50 states. These figures are not insignificant and they are predicted to increase by at least 2 million by 2020, when emergent bilingual learners will comprise 25% of all students in U.S. schools (Fry, 2008; Loes & Saavedra, 2010).

Although the linguistic diversity of our schools is vast, with more than 400 languages spoken, it is imperative that we recognize that 80% of these students live in homes in which Spanish is either the primary or the supplementary language (Kindler, 2002). In other words, about 8.4 million students currently enrolled in U.S. public schools speak Spanish in addition to English. According to the Pew Research Center, the number of Spanish speakers residing in the United States is up 233% since 1980, and although this growth is projected to continue, there is evidence that the number of Latinos who speak Spanish may drop from the current estimation of

---

[1]We prefer, and use throughout this chapter, the term *emergent bilingual learner* because it reduces the emphasis on English and acknowledges that these students come to school with a bilingual advantage. It is important to note, however, that *English learners* and *English language learners* are the dominant terms used in U.S. schools to discuss this particular set of children.

three-fourths to only two-thirds by 2020 (López & Gonzalez-Barrera, 2014). This decrease can be attributed largely to a public schooling system that insists on ignoring ample research that indicates that learning in and through two languages confers long-term academic, cognitive, and social advantages (Alladi, Bak, Russ, Shailaja, & Duggirala, 2013; August & Shanahan, 2006a; Bialystok & Martin, 2004). What is even more vexing is that this bias continues in a post-9/11 United States, in which "intelligence-gathering, diplomacy, and national security" require fluency in languages other than English, yet we systematically eradicate our citizens' bilingualism (Baker, 2011, p. 412).

Communities of practice, by definition, should respond to the needs and resources of the community. Although it may be impossible and financially prohibitive to design instructional environments that sustain and are responsive to all linguistic groups, the preponderance of Spanish-speaking students and families compels us to consider how and to what extent we can accelerate English language acquisition while simultaneously fostering bilingualism/biliteracy. In an era of the CCSS, which promotes the development of language arts only in English, it is important that we interrogate current practices to discover the pockets of hope that complement the goals of the CCSS with a concomitant commitment to biliteracy. Although the CCSS appear to have an assimilationist agenda, there is nothing prohibiting their amplification through a pluralistic enactment of bilingualism and biliteracy (de Jong, 2013). A more pluralistic dialogue and approach takes, as a starting point, the recognition of the reality that, internationally, multilingualism is the norm, and that it can and should be nurtured and sustained in service to the global and individual good. Prior to considering the forms this recognition might take, it is imperative that we critically examine how current practices are, or are not, meeting the needs of our emergent bilingual learners.

Examining "Good Teaching Is Good Teaching"

A problematic assumption about teaching and learning is that *good teaching is good teaching,* and that a framework exists that can be applied universally to guarantee student success. There is a plethora of teachers, administrators, and scholars who invoke the statement that *good teaching is good teaching* to suggest that the need to accommodate an individual student's learning profile or demographic characteristics is unnecessary (Ragan, 2000; Lipsky & Gartner, 2009; Wyatt & Pickle, 1993). For emergent bilingual learners, this stance is problematic in both monolingual and bilingual contexts. In English-only contexts, a universalist approach to language and literacy instruction is often based upon a body of research that was conducted with monolingual English-speaking students and then assumed to be applicable to linguistically diverse classrooms. Even if equally effective, such frameworks are not based upon theories of acceleration. Simply achieving equal gains is insufficient to close any real or perceived achievement gaps. In bilingual/dual-language contexts, a second and equally problematic issue is "good teaching" in which literacy is taught in a sequential way and where literacy instruction in a non-English language uses the same methods and materials as literacy instruction in English. By *sequential literacy instruction,* we mean programs that begin instruction solely in Spanish and delay introduction of English literacy for 2–3 years and then often abruptly eliminate Spanish literacy instruction and replace it with English. Such is often the case within Spanish–English sequential programs. In addition to issues with sequential biliterate instruction, these programs also frequently utilize literacy methods and materials in Spanish that are simply translated from English. Moreover, it has historically been the case that English reading instructional frameworks have been applied in Spanish without critical examination of their appropriateness or effectiveness. A notable example is the insistence on teaching phonemic awareness during emergent Spanish reading instruction when we have research that questions the necessity to do so (Goldenberg, Tolar, Reese, Francis, Ray, & Mejía-Arauz, 2014)

Sequential literacy frameworks were appropriate and effective for the bilingual populations of the 1970s to 1990s, because the majority of children were immigrants entering school with little or no English proficiency who also did not have access to preschool or other prekindergarten educational opportunities. This earlier population contrasts with the current population of emergent bilingual students, of which the majority is born in the United States and enter school with diverse life experiences, including preschool experiences that have occurred in both Spanish and English. These 21st-century emergent bilingual children are ready to learn literacy in two languages upon entry into U.S. schools (Escamilla & Hopewell, 2010). In the sections that follow, we examine each of these contexts with the goal of illustrating how and why such approaches are questionable.

Monolingual Contexts

In the United States, what we know about teaching and learning is derived largely from research conducted with monolingual speakers of English. We have no reason to believe, however, that becoming literate, or achieving academically, in languages other than English, or at the intersection of English with other languages, happens in the same way or at the same rate. Still, we use these monolingual pedagogies as proxies for "good teaching," and we measure and interpret the effects of this teaching with monolingual English language assessments.

The proponents of this belief reduce teaching to a set of high-leverage principles and practices intended to reach all learners and to be equally effective regardless of background. Representative of this stance is Daniel Willingham, a noted cognitive psychologist and neuroscientist at the University of Virginia, who, in a video about teaching and learning, says, "Good teaching is good teaching. And teachers don't need to adjust their teaching to individual student's learning styles" (Willingham, 2009). Although Willingham is admittedly making this statement in response to the idea that teachers should not alter their teaching in response to whether or not a student learns best kinesthetically as opposed to linguistically or aurally, we contend that one could easily replace sensory learning modes with any number of learner characteristics and hear the same proclamation. At its core, this argument is reductive and proceeds from the premise that all students learn in the same way at the same rate. The rhetoric implies that if we simply provide teachers with sufficient training in these universal practices and principles, and we ensure that teachers implement them effectively and with fidelity, all students will succeed. Further, it creates the condition that allows us to deflect blame when any one student or group of students is unsuccessful. It is not that the pedagogy is inappropriate or that the teacher is ineffective, but rather that there is something intrinsic to the student that accounts for the differences in learning outcomes. In other words, it provides the umbrella that shields teachers and the educational system as a whole from blame while raining down upon students and families a litany of accusatory shortcomings that reproaches individuals and communities rather than educational systems for disparate outcomes. It casts students and families as deficient.

One example of this universalist approach to teaching and learning is the adoption of the findings of the National Reading Panel (NRP). This panel was charged by the federal government with reviewing and evaluating the extant scientific evidence on reading instruction to determine and report how best to teach children to learn to read. When their findings were released, there was great fanfare regarding the importance of attending to five critical domains of reading: phonemic awareness, phonics, vocabulary, fluency, and comprehension. These became the foundational elements of reading instruction, and they were generalized as being the five key areas of instruction for everyone—despite the fact that the panel made clear that prior to beginning their work, they had debated the inclusion of "several dozen possible topic areas" (NRP, 2000, p. 2) and only restricted themselves to these five to manage the sheer volume of available research on reading. Further, they specifically stated that they "did not address issues relevant to second language learning" (NRP, 2000, p. 3). Several years later, a National Literacy Panel (NLP) was convened to conduct a similar review of research with the specific goal of focusing on studies that included bilingual learners. In their findings, they noted that instruction in the key components previously identified by the NRP was "necessary, but not sufficient for teaching language-minority students to read and write proficiently in English" (August & Shanahan, 2006b, p. 4). Whereas the findings of the NRP were codified through legislative acts that included No Child Left Behind and Reading First, the findings of the NLP remain largely ignored and its publication was not endorsed by its funding agencies: the National Institute of Child Health and Human Development, the National Institutes of Health, or the Department of Health and Human Services.

It is one thing to talk broadly about the influence of research findings on instructional practices, but it is perhaps more illustrative to examine a more concrete programmatic and curricular choice being made by schools across the nation. Accelerated Reader™ (AR) is a research-based, CCSS aligned reading product that has been used widely in classrooms for 25 years. In fact, Renaissance Learning (n.d.), the company that produces, develops, and markets AR, claims that it is used in one-third of U.S. schools and has been adopted for use in 60 countries. AR uses technology to evaluate students' reading levels, determines books that are appropriate in terms of difficulty and interest, and provides quizzes to assess students' comprehension. A core foundational value of the developers of AR is that "education is a basic human right, and that, given the right approach, virtually everyone can be a successful learner" (Renaissance Learning, n.d.). Stated differently, good teaching is good teaching, and AR has packaged this approach to augment instruction by a teacher. Not only do they put forth a one-size-fits-all package, in the very little attention they give to emergent bilingual learners in their promotional materials, they state, "Best practices for ELLs are generally the same as for native speakers" (Renaissance Learning, 2014, p. 12). Given the extent to which it has been adopted and is being used around the world, it is clear that many, many schools and districts see AR as an important component of language and literacy instruction. The problem is this: Dig deeper into these claims and you find that when it comes to bilingual learners, the claims unravel. In the U.S. Department of Education's What Works Clearinghouse Intervention Report (U.S. Department of Education, 2009) regarding the evidence base on the effectiveness of AR for bilingual learners, one finds the following statement:

> No studies of *Accelerated Reader* that fall within the scope of the English Language Learners (ELL) review protocol meet What Works Clearinghouse (WWC) evidence standards. The lack of studies meeting WWC evidence standards means that, at this time, the WWC is unable to draw any conclusions based on research about the effectiveness or ineffectiveness of *Accelerated Reader* on ELL.

And, although AR claims to include "a number of features to support reading practice for ELLs," the sole feature that is named is that quizzes and diagnostic reports are available in Spanish (Renaissance Learning, 2014, p. 12). This is hardly "a number of features," and certainly not representative of what we know about contextualized, meaningful, interactive instruction for emergent bilingual learners. Yet, we regularly witness emergent bilingual students spending significant amounts of the time set aside for language and literacy instruction engaged in silent reading and the independent completion of AR quizzes.

This exemplar is not meant to be exhaustive, but rather indicative of systemic issues that are representative of approaches to language and literacy instruction that are adopted with little regard for whether and how they will impact the language and literacy achievement of emergent bilingual learners. The critiques we have leveled provide a cautionary tale that teachers, parents, and administrators should remember as they make decisions regarding the language and literacy instruction of emergent bilingual learners.

Although most emergent bilingual learners are in English-only educational environments, the "good teaching" approaches are not limited to these contexts. We turn now to a common approach in organizing literacy instruction in bilingual/biliteracy programs.

Bilingual Contexts

Bilingual/dual-language educational models begin from the assumption that these programs can and should be uniquely conceived and implemented differently than mainstream English-only schools, especially in their attention to how language acquisition is intentionally fostered and accommodated throughout the school day. At face value, this seems to be exactly what is required for these learners. Why, then, would we implicate it under the umbrella of *good teaching is good teaching*? To begin, we must return to the current demographics of the students these programs are designed to serve, and keep these demographics present as we evaluate the instructional and theoretical lenses that are invoked to justify particular models of bilingual teaching and learning.

Arguably, the primary goal of education is the generalization of knowledge and skills to a multitude of circumstances through a process known as *transfer*. Transfer theory proposes that a student's cumulative learning experiences, regardless of the original context, language, problem, or audience, are available to that student when faced with novel contexts, languages, problems, and audiences. This educational mainstay was a foundational organizing principle that guided the development of early iterations of U.S. bilingual programs. What is learned in one language will be easily and fully applied to the other. Further, it has been used to justify particular instructional practices in the teaching of Spanish.

Early inceptions of bilingual programs began from the premise that emergent bilingual learners were entering schools as monolingual speakers of Spanish, and that their literacy instruction, therefore, should be exclusively in Spanish until the foundational skills of reading and writing were firmly mastered before introducing English language literacy. This sequential approach to literacy instruction resulted in students learning to read and write exclusively in Spanish with all English instruction being relegated only to the domains of listening and speaking until about second or third grade. These programs were predicated upon sequential bilingualism as a response to a particular demographic of students assumed to have had very little exposure to English prior to schooling or to students who had had prior schooling in others countries before arriving in the United States. Ironically, today most emergent bilingual learners are born in the United States and have lived a life fully exposed to both Spanish and English since birth. In fact, the Urban Institute reports that at the start of this century fully 77% of students labeled *ELL* in grades K–5 and 56% of students labeled *ELL* in grades 6–12 began their lives in the United States (Capp, Fix, Murray, Ost, Passel, & Herwantoro, 2005). For those children fortunate enough to live in a community that supports their bilingual development, many will attend schools that were created under the assumptions associated with sequential language and literacy acquisition—when, in fact, they are simultaneously learning two languages with a knowledge base that deserves to be developed fully in all four literacy domains (reading, writing, speaking, and listening) beginning in kindergarten. For these students, it makes no sense to delay reading and writing until some abstract set of criteria is met in only one of their languages. In fact, given that in the current era of CCSS, theirs skills and knowledge will be measured only via English, it is particularly troubling that many bilingual models delay English reading and writing instruction such that they essentially ensure that these students will not appear satisfactory as measured by these assessments.

Beyond the overall dilemma of sequential language and literacy development versus simultaneous biliteracy development, there are the actual instructional practices and curricular materials that invoke the "good teaching" dilemma. All languages have unique internal structures that should guide how they are taught. The implication, of course, is that materials and practices in bilingual/biliteracy programs should vary by language. In other words, literacy materials in Spanish should not be mere translations of those developed in English. Further, pedagogies developed to facilitate the teaching and learning of English should not be forced upon the Spanish language. Although Spanish and English share an alphabetic principle, their internal structures are quite different. Analytic approaches to teaching literacy need to understand and be based upon the utilization of principles that are specific to each language.

Given the state of the art with regard to creating effective literacy programs for the large and ever-growing population of emerging bilingual learners, it seems imperative to develop, implement, and empirically study innovative programs that enhance academic achievement of emerging bilingual children while allowing them to utilize all of their linguistic resources to learn. The final section of this chapter presents one such innovation.

A Holistic Biliteracy Framework

As discussed above, it is insufficient to impose current literacy practices on emerging bilingual learners without considering how they need to be modified and/or revised. Here, we present a framework for developing biliteracy titled a *holistic biliteracy framework* (Escamilla et al., 2014). This framework is designed to develop and nurture biliteracy in a way that develops Spanish literacy and accelerates the acquisition of English literacy. We consider this framework to be complementary and enhancing, rather than contradictory, to the current CCSS, Our holistic biliteracy framework is presented visually and discussed below and includes an explanation for how it might be adapted for both biliteracy contexts as well as English-medium programs.

Figure 2.1 presents a graphic of a holistic biliteracy framework that was developed for an ongoing research and instructional program known as *Literacy Squared®*. This framework was designed to align with the new demographic reality in the United States in which the majority of emerging bilingual learners comprises simultaneous Spanish-speaking bilinguals. The biliteracy program is a paired literacy model that directly and explicitly develops literacy in two languages for all children, beginning in kindergarten. The framework is broadly indicated in Figure 2.1 (see Escamilla et al., 2014, for more a more detailed explanation of the framework).

As stated above, the framework is unique in that it is a paired literacy model that is not duplicative, but also does not delay the introduction of English literacy until the second or third grade in the way that many sequential transitional bilingual programs currently do. The framework is specific in that it requires that daily literacy instruction include oracy, reading, writing, and the explicit teaching of metalinguistic skills (each icon in the framework represents one of these four domains). The framework suggests that the teaching of these four domains is essential in both Spanish and English to fully develop proficiency in both languages. The model is unique in that it requires that the two language environments (Spanish and

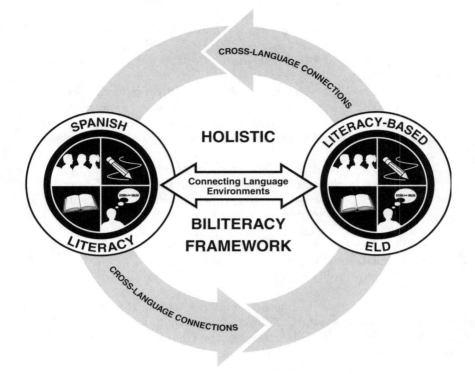

FIGURE 2.1. Holistic biliteracy framework. From Escamilla et al. (2014, p. 6). Copyright 2014 by Caslon Publishing. Reprinted with permission.

English) be connected, but again, not duplicative with regard to instruction. Finally, the model suggests that teachers intentionally and explicitly make cross-language connections.

The framework was created and empirically tested on children in K–5 programs of bilingual education (see Hopewell & Escamilla, 2014; Soltero-González, Escamilla, & Hopewell, 2012; Sparrow, Butvilofsky, Escamilla, Hopewell, & Tolento, 2014); however, we suggest that schools and teachers could also utilize the framework for literacy-based English language development (ELD) if they are teaching in English-medium programs. We would add that nothing about teaching in programs where English is the sole medium of instruction prevents teachers from making cross-language or metalinguistic connections, even if very generally.

The following provides a specific example of the holistic biliteracy framework applied in a bilingual education classroom and highlights a first-grade biliteracy unit developed by Sandra Butvilofsky (2010) of our Literacy Squared team. This biliteracy unit was developed around the focal text *Abuelita llena de vida* (Costales, 2007) in Spanish and an adapted text for the English version titled *Abuelita Full of Life* (adaptation written by Butvilofsky, 2010).

In our framework, bilingual books are excellent texts for developing literacy in two languages and making cross-language connections. However, texts in two languages can also be connected by theme, literacy objectives, or genre. Bilingual books are appropriate for the following reasons:

- Bilingual books deepen understanding of the Spanish text.
- Bilingual books extend linguistic skills and literacy in English.
- Bilingual book lessons reduce the cognitive load of English text comprehension so that focus can be on acquisition of English language skills.
- Bilingual book lessons deepen conceptual knowledge about literacy.
- Bilingual book lessons activate prior knowledge/cultural schema and are culturally relevant.

Abuelita llena de vida is appropriate for this unit in that it is culturally relevant to Spanish-speaking children, is written at a reading level that is accessible in Spanish to first-grade emergent bilingual learners, is adaptable in English, and lends itself well to developing the domains described in the holistic biliteracy framework above. The unit addresses the following standards:

> *Reading:* Describe characters, settings, and major events in a story using key details (CCSS RL1.3). Compare and contrast the adventures and experiences of characters in stories (CCSS RL 1.9).
>
> *Writing:* Write opinion pieces in which they introduce the topic or name the book they are writing about, state an opinion, supply a reason for the opinion, and provide some sense of closure (CCSS W1.1).

In this unit, oracy objectives and activities are detailed. *Oracy,* as defined in Literacy Squared, includes explicit attention to the teaching of language structures in vocabulary and dialogue. Table 2.1 identifies sample oracy objectives and activities in Spanish and English in the *Abuelita* unit and indicates how the two language environments are connected, but not duplicative. For example, in Spanish, students work on their understanding of antonyms, and they do something similar in English. However, in English the lesson also includes activities for learning to use the pronouns

TABLE 2.1. Oracy Objectives and Activities

Oracy Objectives—Spanish:	Oracy Objectives—English:
Understand and create sentences that show an opposite meaning. Acquire and extend vocabulary related to antonyms.	Use descriptive language to express compare–contrast relationships. Ask and answer questions. Use pronouns: *he, she,* and *they.*
Dialogue:	**Dialogue:**
Describe what your grandparents are like.	Where do your grandparents live? When do they visit? What do you do with them?
Language structures:	**Language structures:**
_____ es _____, pero es _____. Aunque sea _____ es _____ _____. Pienso que _____ es _____ porque _____.	She is too old, but _____. He doesn't mind one bit. Abuelita is _____, but/whereas/however José is not.
Example: Abuelita es vieja pero es vivaz (*Abuelita is old but lively*). Aunque su piel está arrugada, es suave para besar. *(Even though she is wrinkled, her skin is soft to kiss).*	
Vocabulary:	**Vocabulary:**
Antonyms: *lively, to mature, to be quiet, to rock, even though, to whisper, incense*	*Grandma/mother, grandpa/father, plant, lively, chase, together*

he, she, and *they* correctly, which is critical in the acquisition of English as an additional language. Further, the oracy structures in English also allow children to learn commonly used phrases in English (e.g., "He doesn't mind one bit").

The unit also includes specific reading and writing activities designed around the approaches that include modeled and interactive read-alouds (and modeled writing), shared reading and writing, collaborative reading and writing, teacher-led small groups, and independent reading and writing. In Literacy Squared, we have focused on shared reading and writing as being more critical to literacy instruction than independent work, and we encourage teachers to design lessons that maximize shared reading and writing activities. We feel that this attention to shared reading and writing is important for several reasons. First, shared activities maximize not only opportunities for repeated reading and writing, but also opportunities for the development of oracy and metalanguage. Next, when children are working in English (a language that may be new to them), they need multiple opportunities to practice with the support of more expert others.

Independent practice, absent guidance, may lead to the fossilization of incorrect language forms, and may impede reading comprehension and writing development.

The *Abuelita* unit consists of Spanish and English reading and writing lessons that span a 2- to 3-week time period. Lessons in Spanish and English are connected and complementary but not duplicative. In the first grade, the unit is planned for a Spanish literacy block that is 2 hours in length and a literacy-based ELD block that is 60 minutes in length. Ideally, the same bilingual teacher delivers the unit, although it can be coordinated between a bilingual teacher and a monolingual English teacher who work in close collaboration with each other. In the *Abuelita* unit in Spanish, the lesson plan calls for reading the text with children, followed by a shared reading activity in which the children and the teacher use the text to examine how the author organized her ideas to describe both *abuelita* and José's reactions to *abuelita*. Children are invited to go back to the text to identify descriptive language. Then the children are asked to pick one phrase that describes *abuelita* that they would like to share with the class and to read this phrase to themselves in preparation for sharing with the class.

When the children read the adapted text in English, they are familiar with the story line because they have already read it in Spanish. The teacher explicitly tells children that they know this text and that they will be reading a summary of it in English. In this way, the language environments of Spanish and English are connected and the learning burden, in English, is reduced for these children as they are reading something in English that they are already familiar with in Spanish. In addition to reading via interactive reading and shared reading, children are given language structures in English to read and respond to that relate to the text. For example, children are given the structure "My favorite character is _____ because _____." In the English shared reading of this text, students engage in a teaching strategy specific to Literacy Squared known as *Lotta Lara*. Lotta Lara is a repeated reading strategy that is accompanied by explicit attention to oracy that includes echo, choral, and partner reading, thereby enabling children to read English text and practice with peers and teachers. The oracy component is critically important in that it aids children in comprehending the text and provides specific attention to oral language development (see Escamilla et al., 2014, for a more detailed discussion of the Lotta Lara activity).

With regard to writing, the *Abuelita* unit, as is true for all Literacy Squared units, utilizes modeled, shared, collaborative, and independent methods to teach writing, and the writing activities are connected to the reading. In addition, Literacy Squared uses a method called the *Dictado* to teach children how writing is connected to discourse and to explicitly teach semantics, phraseology, syntax, spelling, and conventions (see Escamilla,

Geisler, Hopewell, Sparrow, & Butvilofsky, 2009, for a more detailed explanation of the Dictado). In addition to the Dictado, children produce a written product in Spanish and English as a culmination to the unit.

In Spanish, children are asked to bring a picture of a grandparent or an older person they admire, and then to write a descriptive text about that person. They are invited to use the language from the text, in Spanish, to help with their descriptions, and they must use structures that require using antonyms. Children present their final written essays to the class, which gives them more practice reading.

In English writing, the final product involves having students pick a favorite character and write about him or her using at least two descriptive sentences. In preparation for this writing activity, students have learned and used various descriptive vocabulary words and have practiced these words in complete sentences. For example, "My favorite character is _____, because _____. Again, the expectations in Spanish and English are connected to the same text, but are not duplicative.

Finally, the *Abuelita* unit has teaching strategies designed to develop metalinguistic awareness both within and across languages. In our framework, we define *metalanguage* as "thinking and talking about language" (Escamilla et al., 2014, p. 67). Becoming literate in two languages necessitates deep and ongoing development of metalinguistic awareness. The Dictados in the *Abuelita* lesson provide good examples of opportunities teachers can utilize to develop students' metalinguistic awareness. In Spanish first, then English, the following is the unit Dictado:

ABUELITO

El abuelo de Marta es mayor de edad. Abuelito dice que es demasiado viejo para jugar fútbol, aunque zapatea con mucha fuerza cuando baila.

Marta's grandfather is elderly. Grandfather says that he is too old to play soccer, even though he can dance with a lot of energy.

In this Dictado the use of the word *abuelito,* following the first use of *abuelo,* for *grandfather* provides an opportunity for children to learn about the many ways in which the diminutive *ito* is used in Spanish. In this case the use of *abuelito* following *abuelo* indicates endearment. The use of the phrase *mayor de edad* (*elderly*) rather than *old* expands the children's metalinguistic awareness of the variety of ways to describe people's age group.

The English Dictado reads as follows:

ABUELITO SINGS

Marta and Grandpa dance together. Abuelito likes to sing, but Marta does not. He sings "Las mañanitas" to her.

In this Dictado, children can learn the gender-specific nature of pronouns in English (e.g., Marta = *she* and *abuelito* = *he*). This is an example of within-English metalinguistic development. The students can also learn that the conjunction *and* indicates the same, whereas the word *but* indicates a contrast. The direct and explicit way that the teacher draws attention to the metalinguistic language features in the Dictado talk-through is designed to teach metalinguistic awareness.

In this Dictado, students can also engage in cross-language metalinguistic development. For example, students can learn the concept of writing a title that in English requires that each word in the title be capitalized, but in Spanish only requires that the first word of title is capitalized. Similarly, children can learn that some words should not be translated from Spanish to English or they will lose their meaning. In this Dictado, the words *abuelito* and *las mañanitas* should not be translated and for that reason are left as is and, at times, set off by quotation marks in English. These examples represent cross-language metalinguistic development and help children understand how each of their languages is the same as well as different.

Applying the Holistic Biliteracy Framework in English-Only Classrooms

As stated above, the intention of the holistic biliteracy framework, as it is used in Literacy Squared classrooms, is to develop biliteracy in Spanish and English. However, it can also be utilized in English-medium classes because some, though not all, of the basic principles apply. Literacy-based ELD can be an effective stand-alone ELD program if all four language domains are implemented when teachers design and teach lessons. That would include assuring that the ELD program is book-based, that considerations for cultural relevancy are included, and that the English-medium units include oracy, reading, writing, and metalinguistic development. A caveat to these suggestions is that the *book selection is critical*; the book must be one that the children can comprehend without having the Spanish anchor from which to build.

Assessment and Biliteracy Trajectories

To conclude this chapter, we must restate our continuing concern with not only the monolingual and monocultural nature of the CCSS, in general, but also and more problematically, with the English-only assessment system that determines whether or not children and schools are meeting the mandates of the CCSS. Emergent bilingual children who have the opportunity to develop bilingualism and biliteracy must be assessed in both of their emerging languages (in this case, Spanish and English) and results of this assessment must be counted in a school's accountability framework. The current and proposed monolingual assessment systems in literacy are sure to provide an incomplete and inaccurate picture of the biliteracy development of all children in bilingual and dual-language programs and an equally inaccurate picture of the English literacy development of these same children. A monolingual assessment system can never shed light on biliteracy development.

Our work in Literacy Squared has included the development of a trajectory toward biliteracy that is designed to allow schools and teachers to observe and record children's developing biliteracy. We suggest that teachers and schools use this trajectory as an additional source of evidence to determine whether or not emergent bilingual learners are meeting high standards. In the development of Literacy Squared, we hypothesized that because the path to biliteracy is uniquely singular, varying by languages, contexts, age of acquisition, etc., an individual's trajectory would be better measured using a two-language continuum that allowed for a student's reading achievement to be interpreted in comparison to a range of levels rather than a fixed cut score (Hopewell & Escamilla, 2014). Further, biliterate development is not always a linear process and ranges of levels better reflect the complexity that becoming biliteracy entails (Moll, Sáez, & Dworin, 2001). We recognize that a true biliterate trajectory should include attention to more than just reading. However, to date, our work is limited to a reading trajectory.

Using the Evaluación del desarrollo de la lectura (EDL2) and Developmental Reading Assessment (DRA2)—informal reading assessments in Spanish and English (Weber, 2001)—we created a bilingual reading trajectory (see Table 2.2). This trajectory requires that all emerging bilingual children be assessed in both Spanish and English annually, and it enables educators to see children's progress as developing biliterate readers. The reader will note that often children's outcomes in Spanish (EDL2) are higher than in English. However, it is the cumulative nature of the trajectory that indicates that emerging bilingual children are more than their English outcomes, and that when one combines Spanish with English, the results often supersede what monolingual children acquiring literacy in only one language could attain.

In our most recent research with regard to this trajectory, we found that the vast majority of students in our Literacy Squared schools, who might be viewed as low performing if only their scores in English were considered, are actually performing at grade-level competence in Spanish and are in zones of biliteracy. Further, we found that the percentage of children in biliteracy zones increases across grade levels. Table 2.3 illustrates

TABLE 2.2. Bilingual Reading Trajectory

EDL2 level (Spanish)	DRA2 level (English)
A–3	A–3 (exposure)
4–6	A–3
8–10	4–6
12–16	8–10
18–28	12–16
30–38	18–28
40	30–38
50–60	40+

the biliterate achievement of students in our most recent research projects (Hopewell & Escamilla, 2015). If we are ever going to value biliteracy achievement, it is imperative that we couple bilingual/biliterate school programs with a valid bilingual/biliterate assessment system.

Table 2.3 illustrates concretely the application of the biliterate trajectory. For example, in this particular study, at the end of the first grade 170 students (81%) are at the Spanish benchmark. In and of itself, this is evidence of good achievement in literacy, but it shows only one language (Spanish). However, in our work we also consider how students are progressing in English literacy. In this study, when we consider student progress in Spanish literacy and combine it with progress in English literacy, we find that at the first-grade level 78% of our students are in the biliteracy zone. This means that they are making good academic progress in both Spanish and English. The same is true for all the grade levels represented in Table 2.3.

TABLE 2.3. Students Reaching Grade-Level Benchmark and in Biliteracy Reading Zone

Grade	EDL2 goal	Numbers reaching EDL2 (Spanish) benchmark	% reaching EDL2 (Spanish) benchmark (N/209)	% of students at benchmark in Spanish and in biliteracy zone
1	Level 12 or higher	170	81	78
2	Level 18 or higher	190	91	88
3	Level 30 or higher	178	85	92
4	Level 40 or higher	139	68	96

Conclusion

We end where we started. All children are entitled to a comprehensive and effective education that prepares them for college and careers. It is axiomatic that in the 21st century, a comprehensive education ideally includes the opportunity to become bilingual, biliterate, and cross-culturally competent. In this chapter, we have proposed that comprehensive schooling ideally should include opportunities to become biliterate for the nation's large and growing population of emergent bilingual children. We have also proposed that even in the absence of opportunities to become biliterate, emergent bilingual children still need a different pedagogy with regard to the acquisition of literacy. This pedagogy is one that is better tailored to emergent bilingual children's strengths and needs as emerging bilinguals. We believe that the nation has the linguistic and material resources to improve literacy instruction for emergent bilingual children. The question is, do we have the political will?

REFERENCES

Alladi, S., Bak, T. H., Russ, T. C., Shailaja, M., & Duggirala, V. (2013). Bilingualism delays age at onset of dementia, independent of education and immigration status. *Neurology, 81*, 1938–1944.

Armario, C. (2013). U.S. bilingual education challenge: Students learning English as second language at risk. *Huffington Post*. Retrieved from *www.huffingtonpost.com/2013/04/14/us-bilingual-education-_n_3079950.html*.

August, D., & Shanahan, T. (Eds.). (2006a). *Developing literacy in second-language learners: Report of the National Literacy Panel on language-minority children and youth*. Mahwah, NJ: Erlbaum.

August, D., & Shanahan, T. (2006b). Executive summary: Developing literacy in second-language learners: Report of the National Literacy Panel on language-minority children and youth. Retrieved from *www.bilingualeducation.org/pdfs/PROP2272.pdf*.

Baker, C. (2011). *Foundations of bilingual education and bilingualism* (5th ed.). Bristol, UK: Multilingual Matters.

Bialystok, E., & Martin, M. M. (2004). Attention and inhibition in bilingual children: Evidence from the dimensional change card sort task. *Developmental Science, 7*(3), 325–339.

Butvilofsky, S. (2010). Bilingual book lesson: Lecto-escritura en español & literacy based ELD. Retrieved from *www.literacysquared.org*.

Capp, R., Fix, M., Murray, J., Ost, J., Passel, J. S., & Herwantoro, S. (2005). *The new demography of America's schools: Immigration and the No Child Left Behind Act*. Washington, DC: Urban Institute.

Costales, A. (2007). *Abuelita: Full of life/Llena de vida*. Flagstaff, AZ: Luna Rising Books.

de Jong, E. (2013). Policy discourses and U.S. language in education policies. *Peabody Journal of Education, 88*(1), 98–111.

Escamilla, K., Geisler, D., Hopewell, S., Sparrow, W., & Butvilofsky, S. (2009). Using writing to make cross-language connections from Spanish to English. In C. Rodriguez-Eagle (Ed.), *Achieving literacy success with English language learners: Insights from assessment and instruction* (pp. 143–158). Worthington, OH: Reading Recovery Council of North America.

Escamilla, K., & Hopewell, S. (2010). Transitions to biliteracy: Creating positive academic trajectories for emerging bilinguals in the United States. In J. Petrovic (Ed.), *International perspectives on bilingual education: Policy, practice, controversy* (pp. 69–93). Charlotte, NC: Information Age.

Escamilla, K., Hopewell, S., Butvilofsky, S., Sparrow, W., Soltero-González, L., Ruiz-Figueroa, O., et al. (2014). *Biliteracy from the start: Literacy Squared in action*. Philadelphia: Caslon.

Fry, R. (2008). *The role of schools in the English language learner achievement gap*. Washington, DC: Pew Hispanic Center. Retrieved from *http://pewhispanic.org/reports/report.php?ReportID=89*.

Goldenberg, C., Tolar, T., Reese, L., Francis, D., Ray, A., & Mejia-Arauz, R. (2014). How important is teaching phonemic awareness to children learning to read in Spanish? *American Educational Research Journal, 51*, 604–633.

Hopewell, S., & Escamilla, K., (2014). Struggling reader or emerging biliterate student?: Reevaluating the criteria for labeling emerging bilingual students as low achieving. *Journal of Literacy Research, 46*(1), 68–89.

Hopewell, S., & Escamilla, K. (2015, March). *Complementing the Common Core with holistic biliteracy*. Paper presented at the annual conference of the American Applied Linguistics Association, Toronto, Ontario, Canada.

Kindler, A. (2002). *Survey of the states' limited English proficient students and available educational programs and services: 2000–2001 summary report*. Washington, DC: National Clearinghouse for English Language Acquisition and Language Instruction Programs.

Lipsky, D. K., & Gartner, A. (2009). Factors for successful inclusion: Learning from the past, looking toward the future. In S. J. Vitello & D. E. Mithaug (Eds.), *Inclusive schooling: National and international perspectives* (pp. 98–112). New York: Routledge.

Loes, K., & Saavedra, L. (2010). *A new vision to increase the academic achievement for English language learners and immigrant students*. Washington, DC: Urban Institute. Retrieved from *www.urban.org/UploadedPDF/412265-A-New-Vision-to-Increase-Academic-Achievement.pdf*.

López, M. H., & Gonzalez-Barrera, A. (2014). What is the future of Spanish in the United States? Retrieved from *http://hispanicmarketinglibrary.org/RESOURCES/PEW/Lopez_2013.pdf*.

Moll, L. C., Sáez, R., & Dworin, J. (2001). Exploring biliteracy: Two student case examples of writing as social practice. *Elementary School Journal, 101*, 435–449.

National Reading Panel. (2000). Teaching children to read: An evidence-based assessment of the scientific research literature on reading and its implications for reading instruction. Retrieved from *www.nichd.nih.gov/publications/pubs/nrp/Documents/report.pdf.*

Ragan, L. (2000). Good teaching is good teaching: The relationship between guiding principles for distance and general education. *Journal of General Education, 49*(1), 10–22.

Renaissance Learning. (n.d.). About us. Available at *www.renaissance.com/about-us.*

Renaissance Learning. (2014). *Getting results with Accelerated Reader™.* Wisconsin Rapids, WI: Author.

Soltero-González, L., Escamilla, K., & Hopewell, S. (2012). Changing teachers' perceptions about the writing abilities of emerging bilingual students: Towards a holistic bilingual perspective on writing assessment. *International Journal of Bilingual Education and Bilingualism, 15*(1), 71–94.

Sparrow, W., Butvilofsky, S., Escamilla, K., Hopewell, S., & Tolento, T. (2014). Examining the longitudinal biliterate trajectory of emerging bilingual learners in a paired literacy instructional model. *Bilingual Research Journal, 37*(2), 24–42.

U.S. Department of Education. (2009). What Works Clearinghouse intervention report: Accelerated Reader. Retrieved from *http://files.eric.ed.gov/fulltext/ED507570.pdf.*

U.S. Department of Education, National Center for Education Statistics, Institute of Education Science. (n.d.). Fast facts. Retrieved from *http://nces.ed.gov/fastfacts/display.asp?id=372.*

Weber, W. (2001). Developmental Reading Assessment and Evaluación del desarrollo de la lectura: A validation study. Available at *www.pearonlearning.com.*

Willingham, D. (2009). Learning styles don't exist [Video]. Available at *www.teachertube.com/video/learning-styles-dont-exist-119351.*

Wyatt, M., & Pickle, M. (1993). Good teaching is good teaching: Basic beliefs of college reading instructors. *Journal of Reading, 36*(5), 340–348.

CHAPTER 3

Response to Intervention for Emergent Bilingual Students in a Common Core Era

Guiding Principles for Distinguishing between Language Acquisition and Learning Disability

Amy M. Eppolito and Vanessa Santiago Schwarz

Many schools and districts are moving toward using a multi-tiered instructional and assessment model such as response to intervention (RTI) in their programming to implement instruction, monitor academic progress, and refer students for potential learning disability (LD) identification and special education placement. RTI provides an accessible framework for the Common Core State Standards (CCSS). The key components of RTI models include (1) high-quality instruction matched to the needs of students, (2) evidence-based interventions of increasing intensity, (3) ongoing progress monitoring, and (4) data-driven decision making (Hoover, 2008; Klingner, Hoover, & Baca, 2008). This multilevel prevention system includes three "tiers" of intensity (see Figure 3.1). The first level (Tier 1) includes high-quality core instruction that is administered to all students in the general education setting. It is expected that 80–90% of students' needs will be met with high-quality Tier 1 instruction. The second level (Tier 2) includes evidence-based intervention approaches of moderate intensity. About 5–15% of students will likely need Tier 2 support that is targeted, supplemental to Tier 1, and often offered in small-group settings. At the third level (Tier 3), students who show minimal response to the secondary prevention instruction receive individualized instruction with increased intensity (see *www.rtinetwork.org* for further information).

RTI is an instructional approach supported by the Individuals with Disabilities Education Act (IDEA) because of its efforts to educate students

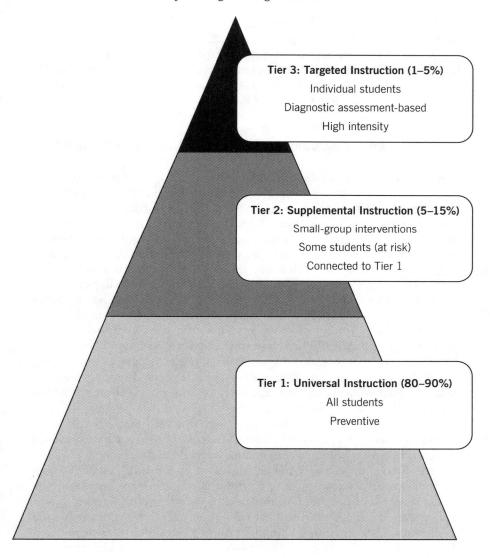

FIGURE 3.1. The RTI model.

in the least restrictive environment (Hehir, 2009). In this chapter, we explore how the model is especially beneficial for emergent bilingual students. We present research and theories that explain how and why a multitiered approach can benefit this unique and diverse group of learners. We focus on elements of high-quality instructional and assessment practices for teachers working with emergent bilingual children.

RTI for Emergent Bilingual Students: What Makes It Work?

In order for RTI to be successful, especially for emergent bilingual students, practitioners must have a deep knowledge of the individual learner's life experiences and how these experiences influence learning. This includes understanding the unique cultural and linguistic background of each student and providing instruction that is culturally and linguistically responsive. The RTI model encourages educators to consider student background in relation to instruction and to the response to that instruction. Furthermore, RTI allows for a comparison of students to other similar classmates rather than to national standards. Ideally, RTI is collaborative in nature, and brings teachers and related service providers together to provide opportunities for early intervention for students who need additional support (Brown & Doolittle, 2008). If administered with adequate consideration for individual student learning and linguistic needs, educators can collaborate with various school professionals to provide optimal support for emergent bilingual students through the three tiers of intervention articulated in Figure 3.1.

Furthermore, RTI provides the means by which teachers can better address the needs of emergent bilingual students who do not have disability labels and thus do not receive mandated special education services. IDEA requires a free, appropriate public education in the least restrictive environment for all students with special needs. On the very broad average, national data indicate that Latino students are not overrepresented in special education (U.S. Department of Education, 2012); however, individual studies of specific emergent bilingual groups in specific states suggest that this "non-finding" may be due to the significant over- and underrepresentation of emergent bilingual students in special education, produced by bimodal distributions (Baca & Cervantes, 2004; Figueroa, 2005; Hosp & Reschly, 2003).

Indeed it is often challenging to distinguish students who have general issues with school-based academics and those who face the challenges of language acquisition from those whose difficulties are associated with disabilities (Baca & Cervantes, 2004; Ortiz et al., 2011). Consequently, emergent bilingual students have historically been referred and identified with disabilities inappropriately, especially in the speech–language impairment (SLI) and LD categories (Artiles & Ortiz, 2002; Dray & Vigil, 2014). By structuring a multi-tiered approach that aims to meet student needs within the general education classroom, emergent bilingual students are more likely to receive an education appropriate to their needs in the least restrictive environment and are less likely to be misclassified with a disability and placed in separated self-contained education settings.

Implementing RTI with emergent bilingual students also facilitates a shift toward assessment that "provides diagnostic information and also functions to guide instruction" (Hamayan, Marler, Lopez, & Damico, 2013, p. 60). Orosco and Klingner (2010) conducted a qualitative study of one urban elementary school with a high percentage of emergent bilingual students and examined how practitioners implemented RTI. Their study showed how an overreliance on standardized measures contributed to deficit beliefs and misunderstandings about the abilities, needs, and progress of emergent bilingual students with special needs.

For RTI to be successful with emergent bilingual students, teachers should use instruction and assessment practices that have been validated with similar populations, including targeted language supports and activities that connect to students' prior knowledge. Thus, although there are potential benefits for using RTI with struggling emergent bilinguals, the advantages are contingent upon high-quality instruction that is culturally and linguistically appropriate, authentic assessment, and meaningful collaboration with school practitioners.

Although there is no magic bullet that distinguishes learning disabilities from language acquisition processes, there are some key guidelines that can provide a strong blueprint for that distinction within the RTI model. We developed these guiding principles by applying research-based principles to our work with practitioners. They include (1) ensuring effective, high-quality instruction for emergent bilingual students in Tier 1 (general education); (2) incorporating tiers of instructional support (Tiers 2 and 3) for emergent bilinguals that are high quality and aligned with Tier 1; and (3) establishing data-based decision-making processes that include considerations for emergent bilingual students. Next we provide an overview of how our work has converged on a set of RTI approaches and practices that align with effective models for teaching emergent bilingual students.

Effective Instruction for Emergent Bilingual Students in Tier 1

When we talk about high-quality, culturally responsive instruction for emergent bilingual students, we need to consider what that instruction would look like in all tiers of the RTI model and how high-quality core instruction must be verified for this population as a foundation to the process. Some emergent bilingual students are inappropriately identified as having LDs because they have not received an adequate opportunity to learn. Federal and state special education laws (e.g., IDEA, 2006) specify that a lack of opportunity to learn must be ruled out before a disability determination can be made. Therefore, looking at the quality of instruction to which emergent bilingual students have access is a necessary first step when deciding whether to pursue an evaluation for possible special education placement. High-quality instruction for emergent bilingual students is interactive, meaningful, and develops both content knowledge and language skills. To determine whether instruction is appropriate, we must look into classrooms and ensure that (1) there is an explicit focus on language and (2) that practices are culturally and linguistically responsive (Klingner, Sorrells, & Barrera, 2007; Ortiz et al., 2011).

Use Instructional Models That Address Language Development

Research has shown that for emergent bilingual students, practices that explicitly focus on language, such as native language instruction and English as a second language (ESL), generally support oral language proficiency and vocabulary development—components deemed necessary for academic and linguistic growth (Hamayan et al., 2013). Further, when emergent bilingual students receive literacy instruction in their home language, they are more likely to succeed academically and linguistically (August & Shanahan, 2006; Krashen, 2003).

Table 3.1 provides a nonexhaustive overview of Tier 1 literacy interventions that explicitly address language development and thus are beneficial for emergent bilingual students. The Language Experience Approach (LEA) is a reading method based on individual students' language abilities. Students take on the role of authors and dictate a story about an actual experience to a scribe, who may be a teacher, a teaching assistant, a parent or community volunteer, or a tutor. Next the students are asked to copy the story (or trace it), illustrate it, and read it again and again. For emergent bilingual students, this approach allows for vocabulary development and word study in context, based on interests and prior knowledge. It can be culturally responsive while also supporting students to make connections between oral and written language.

The Dictado (Escamilla, Hopewell, Butvilofsky, Sparrow, Soltero-Gonzalez, et al., 2014) is a cross-language method that addresses receptive and expressive language skills among emergent bilinguals. The teacher purposefully creates a meaningful text as the focus for teaching spelling, grammar, and language arts. He or she dictates the sentence(s) to the students as they write in pencil or blue/black pen. Then, the teacher and students collaboratively create a corrected model of the text while the students self-correct using red pencil and standard markings. This approach is beneficial for emergent bilingual children because it draws their attention to similarities and differences across languages, thus allowing them to draw from both languages as they utilize their native language.

Collaborative Strategic Reading (CSR; Klingner & Vaughn, 1999) is another beneficial literacy approach for meeting the needs of emergent bilingual students in Tier 1 settings. This multicomponent reading comprehension strategy teaches students metacognitive awareness when reading complex texts. It can be used with both narrative and expository text. Students work in groups of four with assigned roles to interact with a text. Teachers lead students through a brief text preview that includes predicting, brainstorming, and reviewing key vocabulary. Then students lead each other through the process of implementing reading strategies, including word work and finding the main idea. After finishing the short text, students work together to implement after-reading strategies, including questioning and summarizing. After students have completed the reading and analysis in groups, the teacher then leads a wrap-up section. This approach is beneficial for emergent bilingual students because each student has a role with scaffolded materials to support participation, and there is explicit focus on word work. (See Boardman & Lasser, Chapter 6, this volume, for more information about CSR.)

Improving Comprehension Online (ICON; Dalton, Proctor, Uccelli, Mo, & Snow, 2011; Proctor et al., 2011) is a web-based student-directed activity that includes reading comprehension strategies and vocabulary supports embedded in highly engaging and culturally responsive electronic texts. Through this approach, teachers introduce reciprocal reading strategies (Palinscar & Brown, 1985) offline with print text that students are then able to apply in a digital setting. After reading a screen of text, students are prompted to apply a reading comprehension strategy, such as making a prediction, asking a question, or summarizing, or to provide a personal response. Before reading, students work with key vocabulary to make personal connections, create a caption for an image, and complete a word web. During reading, students add words to their glossary and explain why they included the word.

Lastly, Academic Language Instruction for All Students (ALIAS; Lesaux, Kieffer, & Faller, 2010) involves sustained text-based vocabulary instruction that uses explicit instruction in vocabulary and word-learning strategies for 45 minutes each day. This includes eight to nine academic vocabulary words from informational or persuasive text weekly. Strategies in this approach include the use of word charts to show the meaning of words across different contexts, word parts, and how the word is used in the text. This is a useful approach for emergent bilingual students because

TABLE 3.1. Tier 1 Literacy Interventions

Intervention	Frequency	Primary targeted reading area	Description/targeted areas for EBs
Language Experience Approach (LEA)	One story weekly; (working with the same text for 1 week)	Emergent skills; readiness	A reading method based on students' own language. Students as authors dictate a story about an actual experience to a scribe, who may be a teacher, a teaching assistant, a parent or community volunteer, or a tutor. Next, they copy the story (or trace it), illustrate it, and read it again and again. *For EBs: Allows for vocabulary development and phonemic awareness in context, based on interests and prior knowledge; therefore, it can be culturally responsive, helps make connections between oral and written language.*
Dictado (Escamilla et al., 2009)	15–20 minutes a day; at least three times a week		A cross-language method addressing receptive and expressive language skills. • The teacher purposefully creates a meaningful text as the focus for teaching spelling, grammar, and language arts. • The teacher dictates sentence(s) to the students. • The students write in pencil or blue/black pen. • Talk through: The teacher and students collaboratively create a corrected model of the text while students self-correct using red pencil and standard marking to draw attention to errors. *For EBs: Helps students attend to similarities and differences across languages; cross-language transfer; allows students to draw from both language and utilize their native language.*
Collaborative Strategic Reading (CSR; Klingner & Vaughn, 1999)	One or two times a week	Comprehension; vocabulary	A multicomponent reading comprehension strategy that teaches students metacognitive awareness when reading complex texts. It can be used with both narrative and expository text. Students work in groups with assigned roles to interact with a text. The teacher leads students through text preview (predicting, brainstorming, key vocabulary), then students lead each other through during reading activities (word work, main idea) and after reading (questioning and summarizing). The teacher then leads a wrap-up section. *For EBs: Promotes oral language development, interacting with text in meaningful context, and use of native language.*

Program	Time	Focus	Description
Academic Language Instruction for All Students (ALIAS; Lesaux et al., 2010)	45 minutes a day for 18 weeks	Vocabulary and comprehension	Sustained text-based vocabulary instruction that implements explicit instruction of vocabulary knowledge and word-learning strategies. • Eight or nine academic vocabulary words from informational or persuasive text. • Strategies include the use of word charts to show, for example, (1) the meaning words across different contexts, (2) word parts, and (3) How the word is used in the text. *For EBs: Authentic use of vocabulary and explicit teaching of word strategies*
Modified Guided Reading (Avalos et al., 2007)	2–3 or more days (20–30 minutes)	Vocabulary, fluency, and comprehension	Uses the same structure as guided reading but makes modifications that benefit EBs. Emphasizes the importance of text selection and anticipating common stumbling blocks for EBs. • The teacher presents culturally relevant text through a guided discussion connecting the content and language structure to students' personal lives (e.g., picture walk, predicting). • The teacher reads guided reading text aloud to model fluency and generate discussion regarding comprehension and vocabulary guided by the teacher and students. • EBs with higher L2 oral proficiency vocalize softly as they read the text. • The teacher observes and coaches students by reinforcing correct strategies and using word recognition prompts to problem-solve. • Word work focuses on morphological awareness, phonological awareness, connected to guided reading text. • Vocabulary journals and writing assignments connect to guided reading text. *For EBs: Authentic use of language rather than isolated, detailed vocabulary instruction; targets EBs' needs, culturally relevant text.*
Improving Comprehension Online (ICON; Dalton et al., 2011)	2–3 or more days	Vocabulary and comprehension	A web-based student-directed activity that varies reading comprehension strategies and vocabulary supports embedded in highly engaging and culturally responsive electronic texts. • The teacher introduces reciprocal reading strategies offline with print text that students then apply in a digital setting. • After reading a screen of text, student prompted to apply reading comprehension strategy (predict, question, clarify, summarize, visualize) or personal response (feeling). • Before reading, students work with power words to make personal connection, caption an image, complete a word web, and listen to a language alert. During reading, students add words to glossary and explain why. • Includes eight multimedia texts with corrective feedback.

of the authentic use of vocabulary and explicit teaching of word strategies. See the chapters in Part II of this book for additional instructional approaches for emergent bilingual students.

Accurately Assess Knowledge across Languages

The strategies described in the preceding material address the language needs of emergent bilingual students by specifically addressing vocabulary development and reading comprehension strategies. In order to ensure opportunities to learn for emergent bilingual students, educators need to develop a certain subset of skills to make appropriate instructional and assessment decisions. Educators working with emergent bilingual students should have a good understanding of the complex factors that influence bilingualism and learning. For example, bilingual students may be simultaneous or sequentially bilingual, or they may be considered long-term emergent bilinguals with many gaps in their education. Their educational history and exposure to language and literacy development in their native language must be considered. Therefore, when possible, teachers should use valid assessments and assessment procedures that provide accurate information about what students know in each language and what they know across both (Ortiz et al., 2011). These comparisons can help determine if language proficiency is contributing to any challenges in Tier 1, and help inform teachers' instructional plans.

Use Culturally and Linguistically Responsive Teaching

As Ortiz et al. (2011) explained in their overview of RTI, the multi-tiered approaches to intervention have the potential to be effective for identifying and meeting the needs of emergent bilingual students with LD *if implementation is culturally and linguistically responsive* to ensure that students have access to meaningful instruction to which they can relate. This approach uses cultural references to empower students intellectually (Ladson-Billings, 1992) and centers instruction on the strengths that emergent bilingual students with special needs bring to the classroom (Obiakor & Green, 2014).

Classrooms with emergent bilingual students should reflect their cultural and linguistic background to create meaningful connection and instruction (Gay, 2002; Klingner, Boelé, Linan-Thompson, & Rodriguez, 2014). This is true as well for emergent bilingual students with special needs. The goal is to provide instruction that is comprehensible according to each student's language proficiency *and* academic strengths and needs. Dray and Vigil (2014) explained that the learning environment should build on the experiences of students and position any cultural and linguistic differences as *assets*. They stated that when working with emergent bilingual students who have special needs, it is more important for educators to "develop authentic relationships with students in a manner that not only validates and respects their students' hybrid identities but also embeds such information or experiences during instructional activities" (p. 58). Honoring the backgrounds and experiences of students is critical to ensure quality instruction for emergent bilingual students who might require additional learning supports.

García and Tyler (2010) offered a helpful framework for instructional planning and collaboration between content area, ESL, and special education teachers geared toward emergent bilingual students with LD in general education settings. The authors explored the common barriers that prevent meaningful instruction for these students in English-medium content-area classes, and recognized the sociocultural factors involved in the education of certain groups of emergent bilinguals and the worldviews that may vary considerably from those valued at school. They maintained that in order for teachers to implement "meaningful and comprehensible instruction" for emergent bilingual students with LD, instruction "must be culturally and linguistically relevant, and also responsive to their disability" (p. 114). The linguistically responsive portion of this approach includes "language objectives and language supports and [it] develops linguistic competence through purposeful classroom dialogue and frequent opportunities to learn and use academic language" (Klinger et al., 2014, p. 93). Thus, when implementing Tier 1 instruction for emergent bilingual students, teachers should include strategies that target both the culture and language of the students in order to avoid inappropriate referrals to special education.

Conduct a Needs Assessment of Instructional Quality in Tier 1

One way in which schools can ensure the quality of instruction for emergent bilingual students is through the use of a needs assessment. Whether just starting out with RTI or with an existing RTI process, a needs assessment can be a useful tool to guide and improve professional practices and serve as a document of evidence that culturally responsive best practice for emergent bilingual students have been provided at Tier 1. The needs assessment can be in the form of a guide for observing classroom instruction or a schoolwide self-assessment based on the aforementioned principles of good instruction—with its actionable items integrated into current observation protocols or into a separate guide. During our work with three rural elementary schools serving student populations of 40% emergent bilinguals, we collaborated with school leadership teams to develop an observation

guide called the Core ESL Instructional Practices (CEIP) guide that could
be used as part of their RTI model (Hoover, Hopewell, & Sarris, 2014).
The guide was intended for instructional coaching, action planning during
grade-level meetings, and as a document to be referenced when making
instructional and placement decisions for emergent bilingual students. The
themes with observable items from this guide are listed in Table 3.2.

This guide includes the following themes with observable items: (1)
connections, (2) cultural relevance, (3) native language utilization, (4) English language development, (5) materials, (6) differentiation, and (7) using
assessment to inform instruction. We found that integrating the use of this
guide with the districts' current practices and expectations for instructional
coaching and teacher observations facilitated its use in the other areas as
well (grade-level meetings and decision-making meetings).

Effective Instruction
for Emergent Bilingual Students in Tier 2

Schools and districts implement supplemental support for students who
require Tier 2 instruction in a variety of ways. Some choose to establish
small-group, pull-out classes, and some send literacy specialists and interventionists into the classroom to flood the room with supplemental support.
Regardless of the structure of the support being provided, the same guiding
principles for effective Tier 1 instruction for emergent bilingual students
hold true for Tiers 2 and 3 interventions. In fact, many instructional strategies can be used in Tier 1 or Tier 2 (e.g., modified guided reading, LEA;

TABLE 3.2. Core ESL Instructional Practice Guide (CEIP)

Theme	Example of observable item
Connections	Brainstorming, concept mapping
Cultural relevance	Using funds of knowledge
Native language utilization	Cognates, preteaching in L1
English language development	Language frames, structured dialogue
Materials	Graphic organizers, sensory supports
Differentiation	Sheltered instruction, multiple opportunities for guided practice
Using assessment to inform instruction	Authentic assessments, frequent monitoring and feedback

see Table 3.1). In Tier 2, these methods are used to target specific skills or strategies, or they may simply be implemented with smaller groups of students as a means to provide more frequent feedback.

Additionally, schools are often faced with the challenge of limited resources. As a result, school leaders sometimes choose boxed intervention programs because these provide progress monitoring tools and a plethora of resources. However, many times these programs focus only on isolated literacy skills that are difficult for most students, including emergent bilingual students, to transfer when they are out of context. Teaching specific skills in isolation is sometimes necessary, but these skills need to be integrated into the curriculum in a meaningful way.

Baker et al. (2014) offer the following recommendations for providing intervention support to emergent bilingual children:

1. *Spend time on basic foundational reading skills (e.g., decoding) but also include vocabulary development and listening and reading comprehension support.* Ideas for providing vocabulary development include teaching a set of academic vocabulary words intensively across several days using a variety of instructional activities (e.g., teaching word-level strategies; using short, engaging informational text to study academic words in depth).

2. *Provide scaffolded instruction with frequent opportunities for students to practice and apply new concepts across multiple contexts and multiple lessons.* These contexts and lessons include offering opportunities for students to discuss and write in the content areas, such as strategically using instructional tools (e.g., short videos, visuals, and graphic organizers) to anchor instruction and help students make sense of content, and providing daily opportunities for students to talk about content in pairs or small groups.

3. *Provide targeted language and literacy interventions to small groups of students that are tied to assessment and data.* These interventions should be provided to small groups of students (three to five students) who have been identified through data as sharing common literacy learning needs. Intervention support can be focused on basic foundational reading skills but should also include vocabulary development and listening and reading comprehension strategies.

In sum, regardless of the setting in which Tier 2 instruction is delivered, practices utilized should be geared toward individual language and learning needs, offered in small groups with greater intensity than in Tier 1, and student progress should be monitored frequently so that instruction can be adjusted as needed.

Establishing Data-Based Decision-Making Practices for Emergent Bilingual Students

Since most students who are referred for special education consideration are eventually placed in special education (Hosp & Reschly, 2003), determining whether making a referral is appropriate is essential. There is a natural progression of steps that can help educators decide whether an official referral is warranted. To begin this process, the quality of Tiers 1 and 2 instruction for emergent bilingual students should be considered through (1) analysis of class datasets and (2) observation of Tiers 1 and Tier 2 instruction. Specific to Tier 2 instruction, it is necessary to distinguish responders from nonresponders. These topics are addressed below.

Analyze Class Datasets

To determine whether a student should be referred for a special education evaluation, the first step is to consider many students are struggling in a class or across classes at a particular class or grade level. If the majority of emergent bilingual students are making little progress, then it can be assumed that the needs of these students are not being met and the focus should be directed toward improving instruction and making sure it is appropriate for them. Examining class datasets can reveal if there are patterns across groups of students, or if a few students are struggling due to other factors. If most emergent bilingual students are doing well and only a few are struggling, even with intervention support, it is appropriate to look more closely at what is going on with those individual students and consider that they may need further intervention. Analyzing these datasets can not only help teachers determine which subsets of students are struggling or succeeding with grade-level instruction, but also can help teachers make instructional adjustments for whole-class and intervention instruction.

Practitioners and researchers who have been implementing multi-tiered instruction models for many years have developed tools for analyzing data and making data-informed decisions as a foundation for tiered instruction (Kovalski & Pedersen, 2008). Figure 3.2 shows an example of a document from our research project that we use for classwide data analysis. We worked with groups of classroom teachers to analyze class datasets and make instructional adjustments. This tool groups students by their proficiency on designated benchmarks and grade-level goals. An assigned instructional coach helped organize the data on an excel file so it was easily accessible for teachers to discuss during collaboration meetings. They then disaggregated the students by their level of language proficiency on the WIDA (Wisconsin, Delaware, Arkansas) ACCESS test (Gottlieb,

Data Content Area (check one): ____ Reading Fluency ____ Vocabulary		
____ Oral Reading Comp ____ Silent Reading Comp ____ Word Analysis		

Examining Disaggregated Data for EBs and Non-EBs	EBs		Non-EBs
	(Levels 1–2)	(Levels 3–5)	Non-EBs
1. What patterns/trends are emerging from the data?			
2. What is surprising or unexpected from the data?			
3. What are some instructional inferences that can be drawn about these data?			
4. What are some instructional implications based on these inferences?			

FIGURE 3.2. Form for analyzing class data.

Cranley, & Cammilleri, 2007; i.e., Levels 1–2 and Levels 3–5). Students were grouped along a continuum to see which students needed the most intensive support and compared to which previous goals were or were not met.

Specifically, this form was used by third-grade teachers using Dynamic Indicators of Basic Literacy (DIBELs) (Dynamic Measurement Group, 2008) data to group students by their scores on the Oral Reading Fluency (ORF) scale. When they saw a subset of Levels 3–5 students in need fluency support, teachers across that grade implemented a well-known strategy, Reader's Theater, over a period of 6 weeks and saw DIBELS ORF scores improve. Another very common data source teachers used was the Developmental Reading Assessment (Beaver, 2004) to measure reading comprehension. For example, a group of first-grade teachers analyzed the data and found a subset of emergent bilingual students in Levels 1 and 2 in need of support in listening comprehension and oral expressive language. The teachers provided some structured oral language support in both the students' native language (Spanish) and in English over 6 weeks and saw improvement on that data point. This type of analysis allows for documentation of specific instructional strategies and adjustments with direct links to data and evidence.

When organizing class datasets and considering academic benchmarks, it is helpful to identify the language proficiency levels of emergent bilingual students across a classroom or grade level. Consider the following questions:

1. How many emergent bilingual students are in a class/grade level?
2. What are their proficiency levels for each language domain (speaking, listening, reading writing)?
3. Are there significant gaps in their oral language and literacy proficiency scores?
4. Is there a disproportionate number of emergent bilingual students identified as at risk?
5. With which items are emergent bilingual students succeeding or struggling the most?
6. Which research-based modifications were made to support these students?
7. What was the time frame for implementing modifications?

Observe Emergent Bilingual Students in All Instructional Contexts

School leaders must consider how they will incorporate systematic observations of core instructional settings as well as tiered intervention settings. It cannot be simply assumed that all teachers are implementing effective culturally and linguistically responsive practices for emergent bilingual students. Some schools integrate observations of instructional contexts into their teacher development or evaluation programming and designate specific items toward meeting the needs of this student population. Other schools may have a separate observation established once a student is beginning to struggle in the classroom. Either of these procedures can and should be used as documentation of adequate opportunity to learn. The CEIP guide mentioned previously is a good tool with which to accomplish this goal.

The next step is to collect individual student data and, ideally, to observe a target student in multiple settings. Individual student data collection should include the student's strengths as well as struggles across all contexts and instructional settings. The following questions should be considered:

1. What is the student's educational background? For example, are there native language literacy skills that can be transferred to English? Are there educational gaps?
2. Is there a body of evidence using multiple assessments to represent the student's academic and language performance?
3. Is consideration given to cultural, linguistic, socioeconomic, and experiential factors?
4. Does the student differ from true peers in rate and level of learning?
5. Are the child's parents involved as valued partners? What are their perspectives?

When comparing emergent bilinguals with other students, they must be compared to their *true* peers—not only students with similar cultural backgrounds, but also students who share similar educational experiences and language proficiency levels (Brown & Doolittle, 2008). When grouping students by language proficiency, consider the various domains of language and not only students' oral language proficiency or overall scores. It might be more productive to establish true peers via reading or writing proficiency levels in addition to educational and home experiences. Similarly, educators must consider whether the student has received sufficient and adequate intervention support. Teachers need knowledge of when and how to adapt interventions, specifically for emergent bilingual students. Educators should ask the following: If the student is not responding to the intervention, does it need to be adapted or sustained? Does the student have opportunities to apply skills of intervention in meaningful ways? Was the skill taught in isolation without opportunities to practice and get feedback? If a student continues to struggle even with supplemental Tiers 2 and 3 supports, there are some guiding questions to ask at this point (Brown & Doolittle, 2008):

1. How many rounds of supplemental instruction has the student received?
2. Is there evidence of progress from previous interventions?
3. Is the student successful with a different curriculum, teaching approaches, and/or an individualized setting?
4. Does the student differ from true peers?
5. Has the student received continuous instruction? For example, consider absences and changes in schooling environments.

Distinguish Responders from Nonresponders

One of the pervasive questions in implementing an RTI model to identify students with potential learning disabilities is how to know when students should be evaluated for special education or when they need more or different intervention support. Essentially, how do we identify nonresponders (i.e., students who are not responding to instruction and intervention)? This is a problem that is still being researched, but some promising guidelines do exist. Research has shown that most emergent bilingual students, when provided with high-quality interventions, responded to those interventions and were no longer considered at risk (Linan-Thompson, Vaughn, Prater, & Cirino, 2006; O'Connor, Bocian, Beebe-Frankenberger, & Linklater, 2010). From the research, we also know that responsiveness to instruction and intervention for emergent bilingual students is related to (1) teacher effectiveness across the tiers, (2) educators' abilities to adapt and change instruction for nonresponders, and (3) fidelity of implementation of high-quality instruction (O'Connor & Klingner, 2010). Once we ensure that these qualities are met, then we can consider some emerging characteristics of nonresponders:

1. Does the student continue to display characteristics of "summer loss"? For example, does he or she make progress but seem to regress when not receiving instructional support?
2. Does the student demonstrate poor phonological awareness and sometimes poor rapid naming, attention, or spelling (Nelson, Benner, & Gonzalez, 2003)?
3. Does the student demonstrate problem behavior, poor knowledge of the alphabetic principle, or poor memory (Al Otaiba & Fuchs, 2002)?

Determining decision rules for interpreting progress monitoring and other assessment data is often left up to the school district. Currently there is no real consensus on which measures most accurately determine response to instruction and intervention for emergent bilingual students. Districts and school teams must decide on which process they are going to follow and provide teachers with opportunities to accurately interpret data. The following measures are recommended for determining adequate progress for emergent bilinguals:

- *Cut score:* The minimum proficiency level score, below which the learner is considered at risk or struggling (e.g., 25%)
- *Rate of progress:* The rate at which the learner should improve to maintain acceptable progress
- *Gap/discrepancy analysis:* The difference between expected and actual proficiency levels/progress rates

The rate of student progress needs to be considered in relation to true peers in addition to monolingual learners. Additionally, many struggling emergent bilingual readers can achieve at least average levels of performance if they are provided with supplemental, high-quality interventions during early stages of reading development (Lesaux & Siegel, 2003; Vaughn, Mathes, Linan-Thompson, Cirino, Carlson, et al., 2006).

Conclusion

RTI provides schools and districts with an instructional framework for meeting the academic needs of all students. As our field shifts toward

Common Core standards, it is ever more imperative that schools ensure that emergent bilingual students have access to increasingly rigorous standards and that decisions are based on what high-quality instruction looks like specifically for emergent bilinguals across all instructional tiers. Teachers are being asked to integrate language and academic content in a systematic way that hasn't been done before. Schools and districts are wise to build the capacity of educators so that they can meet the demands of the standards and who have the pedagogical knowledge to make instructional decisions for emergent bilingual students. Distinguishing learning disabilities from language acquisition requires an extensive knowledge of the RTI process and how to ensure opportunity to learn for emergent bilingual students before considering a special education referral.

REFERENCES

Al Otaiba, S., & Fuchs, D. (2002). Characteristics of children who are unresponsive to early literacy intervention: A review of the literature. *Remedial and Special Education, 23*(5), 300–316.

Artiles, A. J., & Ortiz, A. A. (Eds.). (2002). *English language learners with special education needs: Identification, assessment and instruction.* McHenry, IL: Center for Applied Linguistics.

August, D., & Shanahan, T. (Eds.). (2006). *Developing literacy in second-language learners: A report of the National Literacy Panel on language-minority children and youth.* Mahwah, NJ: Erlbaum.

Baca, L. M., & Cervantes, H. T. (2004). *The bilingual special education interface* (4th ed.). Upper Saddle River, NJ: Merrill.

Baker, S., Lesaux, N., Jayanthi, M., Dimino, J., Proctor, C. P., Morris, J., et al. (2014). *Teaching academic content and literacy to English learners in elementary and middle school* (NCEE 2014-4012). Washington, DC: National Center for Education Evaluation and Regional Assistance (NCEE), Institute of Education Sciences, U.S. Department of Education. Retrieved from *http://ies.ed.gov/ncee/wwc/publications_reviews.aspx.*

Beaver, J. (2004). *Developmental reading assessment.* Parsippany, NJ: Celebration Press.

Brown, J. E., & Doolittle, J. (2008). A cultural, linguistic, and ecological framework for response to intervention with English language learners. *Teaching Exceptional Children, 40*(5), 66–72.

Dalton, B., Proctor, C. P., Uccelli, P., Mo, E., & Snow, C. (2011). Designing for diversity: The role of reading strategies and interactive vocabulary in a digital reading environment for fifth-grade monolingual English and bilingual students. *Journal of Literacy Research, 43*, 68–100.

Dray, B. J., & Vigil, P. (2014). Educating Latino/a students with special needs. In F. E. Obiakor & A. F. Rotatori (Eds.), *Multicultural education for learners with special needs in the twenty-first century.* Charlotte, NC: Information Age.

Dynamic Measurement Group. (2008). *DIBELS 6th edition technical adequacy information* (Tech. Rep. No. 6). Eugene, OR: Author. Available at *http:// dibels.org/pubs.html.*

Escamilla, K., Hopewell, S., Butvilofsky, S., Sparrow, W., Soltero-Gonzalez, L., Ruiz Figueroa, O., et al. (2014). *Biliteracy from the start: Literacy squared in action.* Philadelphia: Caslon.

Figueroa, R. (2005). Dificultades o Desabilidades de Aprendizaje? *Learning Disability Quarterly, 28*(2), 163.

García, S. B., & Tyler, B. J. (2010). Meeting the needs of English language learners with learning disabilities in the general curriculum. *Theory Into Practice, 49*(2), 113–120.

Gay, G. (2002). Culturally responsive teaching in special education for ethnically diverse students: Setting the stage. *International Journal of Qualitative Studies in Education, 15*(6), 613–629.

Gottlieb, M., Cranley, M. E., & Cammilleri, A. (2007). *WIDA ELP standards and resource guide.* Madison: Wisconsin Center for Education Research.

Hamayan, E. V., Marler, B., Lopez, C. S., & Damico, J. (2013). *Special education considerations for English language learners: Delivering a continuum of services* (2nd ed.). Philadelphia: Caslon.

Hehir, T. (2009). Policy foundations of universal design for learning. A Policy Reader in Universal Design for Learning. Retrieved from *www.udirector. org/sites/udicenter.org/files/Hehir_Policy_Foundations_of_Universal%20 Design_for_Learning.pdf.*

Hoover, J. (2008). *Differentiating learning differences from disabilities: Meeting diverse needs through multi-tiered response to intervention.* Upper Saddle River, NJ: Pearson.

Hoover, J., Hopewell, S., & Sarris, J. (2014). Core ESL Instructional Practices (CEIP). Available at *http://buenocenter.org/wp-content/uploads/2014/04/ CEIP-Teacher-Self-Assessment-Guide.pdf.*

Hosp, J. L., & Reschly, D. J. (2003). Referral rates for intervention or assessment: A meta-analysis of racial differences. *Journal of Special Education, 37*(2), 67–80.

Klingner, J. K., Boelé, A., Linan-Thompson, S., & Rodriguez, D. (2014). *Essential components of special education for English language learners with learning disabilities.* Arlington, VA: Council for Exceptional Children Division for Learning Disabilities.

Klingner, J. K., Hoover, J., & Baca, L. (2008). *Why do English language learners struggle with reading?: Distinguishing language acquisition from learning disabilities.* Thousand Oaks, CA: Corwin Press.

Klingner, J. K., Sorrells, A. M., & Barrera, M. (2007). Considerations when implementing response to intervention with culturally and linguistically diverse students. In D. E. Haager, J. E. Klingner, & S. E. Vaughn (Eds.), *Evidence-based reading practices for response to intervention* (pp. 223–244). Baltimore: Brookes.

Kovaleski, J. F., & Pedersen, J. (2008). Best practices in data analysis teaming. In A. Thomas & J. Grimes (Eds.), *Best practices in school psychology V* (pp. 115–130). Bethesda, MD: National Association of School Psychologists.

Krashen, S. (2003). Three roles for reading for minority-language children. In G. G. Garcia (Ed.), *English learners: Reaching the highest level of English literacy* (pp. 55–70). Newark, DE: International Reading Association.

Ladson-Billings, G. (1992). Liberatory consequences of literacy: A case of culturally relevant instruction for African American students. *Journal of Negro Education, 61*(3), 378–391.

Lesaux, N., Kieffer, M., & Faller, S. (2010). The effectiveness and ease of implementation of an academic intervention for sixth graders in urban middle schools. *Reading Research Quarterly, 45*, 198–230.

Lesaux, N., & Siegel, L. (2003). The development of reading in children who speak English as a second language. *Developmental Psychology, 39*, 1005–1019.

Linan-Thompson, S., Vaughn, S., Prater, K., & Cirino, P. (2006). The response to intervention of English language learners at risk for reading problems. *Journal of Learning Disabilities, 39*(5), 390–398.

Nelson, J. R., Benner, G. J., & Gonzalez, J. (2003). Learner characteristics that influence the treatment effectiveness of early literacy interventions: A meta analytic review. *Learning Disabilities Research and Practice, 18*, 255–267.

Obiakor, F. E., & Green, S. L. (2014). Educating culturally and linguistically diverse learners with special needs: The rationale. In F. E. Obiakor & A. F. Rotatori (Eds.), *Multicultural education for learners with special needs in the twenty-first century* (pp. 1–14). Charlotte, NC: Information Age.

O'Connor, R., Bocian, K., Beebe-Frankenberger, M., & Linklater, D. (2010). Responsiveness of students with language difficulties to early intervention in reading. *Journal of Special Education, 43*(4), 220–235.

O'Connor, R., & Klingner, J. (2010). Poor responders in RTI. *Theory Into Practice, 49*, 297–304.

Orosco, M. J., & Klinger, J. (2010). One school's implementation of RTI with English learners: "Referring into RIT." *Journal of Learning Disabilities, 43*(3), 269–288.

Ortiz, A. A., Robertson, P. M., Wilkinson, C. Y., Liu, Y.-J., McGhee, B. D., & Kushner, M. I. (2011). The role of bilingual education teachers in preventing inappropriate referrals of ELLs to special education: Implications for response to intervention. *Bilingual Research Journal, 34*(3), 316–333.

Palincsar, A. S., & Brown, A. L. (1985). *Reciprocal teaching: Activities to promote read(ing) with your mind. Reading, thinking and concept development: Strategies for the classroom.* New York: College Board.

Proctor, C. P., Dalton, D., Uccelli, P., Biancarosa, G., Mo, E., Snow, C. E., et al. (2011). Improving Comprehension Online (ICON): Effects of deep vocabulary instruction with bilingual and monolingual fifth graders. *Reading and Writing, 24*(5), 517–544.

U.S. Department of Education Institute of Education Sciences. (2012). [Table displaying students served under Individuals with Disabilities Act (IDEA), by race/ethnicity and type of disability in 2011–2012]. *Digest of Education Statistics.* Retrieved from *https://nces.ed.gov.*

Valencia, R. R. (1997). Conceptualizing the notion of deficit thinking. *Evolution of Deficit Thinking: Educational Thought and Practice, 19*, 1.

Vaughn, S., Mathes, P., Linan-Thompson, S., Cirino, P., Carlson, C., Pollard-Durodola, S. D., et al. (2006). Effectiveness of an English intervention for first-grade English language learners at risk for reading problems. *Elementary School Journal, 107*(2), 153–181.

PART II

PEDAGOGY

CHAPTER 4

English Learners and Instructional Texts

Evidence, Current Practice, and a Call to Action

Elfrieda H. Hiebert

A cryptic message on a smartphone, a sign on a road, directions on an app—these examples illustrate texts in the 21st century. But no matter how central new forms of texts are in the lives of individuals, full participation in the workplace and the global digital community also requires proficiency in comprehending conventional text—newspapers, instruction and operating manuals, and books. Indeed, the advent of the digital world has increased the levels of literacy required to be successful in college and careers, leading to recommendations for accelerated levels of text within the Common Core State Standards (CCSS; National Governors Association Center for Best Practices & Council of Chief State School Officers [NGA & CCSSO], 2010).

The gap between Hispanic and white students stretches from 21 points for fourth graders to 26 for eighth graders on the reading portion of the National Assessment of Educational Progress (Hemphill, Vanneman, & Rahman, 2011), where text levels were presumably less rigorous than on next-generation assessments. Such results call for vigilance in designing literacy experiences for English learners (ELs), especially at a time when literacy demands are escalating in both school assessments and in the larger digital world.

To address appropriate learning experiences for ELs in the face of escalating literacy levels, a starting point is to ask how current programs address ELs' needs and strengths. In this chapter, I view the literacy learning opportunities provided for ELs through the lens of textbooks. The components of school literacy instruction are many and go well beyond textbooks, such as learning tasks, the amount of time spent reading and writing, and the nature of teacher–student interaction. Even in considering the content of textbooks—the focus of this study—such factors are important to keep in mind. Teachers choose from among the texts and tasks offered in textbooks. They can choose to have students read a text aloud in a round-robin style, or they can ask students to read texts as homework. Textbooks can be used in myriad ways.

Yet the content of textbooks can provide insight into the expected content for grade levels. Often, in the schools most in need, textbooks serve as the de facto curriculum (Schmidt & McKnight, 2012). Further, in a subject area where the intent is to improve students' reading capacity, the features and content of the available texts create parameters for students' reading experiences. Often, especially in schools serving students from low-income families (which many EL students are), funding for materials is scarce. The textbooks provided through state or district funds serve as the primary source for reading material.

The current focus is on textbooks for ELs in middle school, which is a period when many U.S. students fail to sustain their gains in reading (Spichtig, Hiebert, Vorstius, Pascoe, Pearson, & Radach, 2016). An increasing gap in middle school may be particularly consequential for ELs in that choices to drop out of high school can often be traced to middle school (Rumberger & Rotermund, 2012). The texts of middle school English language arts (ELA) programs may be especially critical in ensuring that ELs are successful in middle school, thereby laying a foundation for success in high school and beyond.

This examination of ELA textbooks—specifically those designated for interventions with ELs—moves through three steps. The first step involves a review of research on elements that contribute to effective literacy experiences, in particular, the three elements that can be influenced by textbook: the amount of available text, the vocabulary within the texts and the concepts or knowledge that underlie the selections in the text. In the second part of the chapter, I summarize the results of an empirical examination of current textbooks offered for ELs from the vantage point of the three elements. In the third and final section of the chapter, I identify ways in which ELA textbooks and their use can be reconfigured to ensure that students participate in literacy experiences that increase their capacity and engagement as readers.

Elements of Effective Literacy Experiences for ELs

Many elements go into effective literacy experiences for ELs, as the chapters in this volume attest. Including, but not limited to, these experiences are opportunities for dialogue and the acknowledgment of students' cultural capital. Although not all of the elements in effective instruction are driven or influenced by textbooks, several critical ones can be traced to them: (1) the amount of text, (2) the progression and repetition of vocabulary, and (3) the topics and knowledge in the texts.

A Sufficient Amount of Text

There is little argument that, as in other domains in life, developing reading proficiency results from practice. Discussions have often attended to the types of reading that are appropriate, such as the criticisms of sustained silent reading by the National Reading Panel (NRP; National Institute of Child Health and Human Development, 2000), rather than on the amount of reading that underlies successful reading at different grade levels. Evidence from several lines of work confirms that classrooms where students spend more time reading see higher reading achievement (Fisher et al., 1980; Foorman et al., 2006). Kuhn and Schwanenflugel (2009) found that classrooms with higher levels of success devoted 7 more minutes every day to reading than classrooms with lower levels of achievement. Opportunities to read in classrooms may be especially important for less proficient readers (e.g., beginning readers, learning-disabled readers, ELs), as suggested by patterns in a meta-analysis of opportunity-to-read studies (Lewis, 2002). Most of the studies in Lewis's meta-analysis showed positive effects, but in the few studies that reported no effect or negative growth, students were fourth graders or higher. Lewis speculated that, because older students have a modicum of reading proficiency, the typical 10- to 15-minute reading periods in research projects are insufficient to influence performance significantly. For students who were less proficient readers, even such short periods typically produced benefits.

Just because a textbook program has either a substantial or an inconsequential amount of text is not evidence that students will spend more, or conversely, less time reading in their classrooms. Although numerous instructional decisions mediate the use of texts, the amount of texts in a program can be an indication of the opportunities for reading that are available at particular grade levels.

Support for Vocabulary

Both automaticity with the majority of words and skill in understanding the meaning of unfamiliar words are essential for meaningful reading experiences. The two proficiencies are closely connected and involve similar processes, but the experiences and instruction that lead to success in the two proficiencies can vary, especially when students have moved beyond the early stages of word recognition. Often distinctions in these two proficiencies are not recognized, however, and a one-size-fits-all solution that emphasizes word recognition (typically phonics) is offered for students failing to meet ELA standards, regardless of whether students are in first grade or middle school (e.g., California State Board of Education, 2008, 2015).

Evidence from several sources suggests that, at least by fourth grade, all but a small percentage of students (1–2%) read grade-level texts with high levels of accuracy (e.g., Daane et al., 2005; Dewey, Kaminski, & Good, 2014; Pinnell et al., 1995). However, at least a third of a fourth-grade cohort reads slowly, a relationship that correlates with lower levels of comprehension (Daane et al., 2005; Roehrig, Petscher, Nettles, Hudson, & Torgeson, 2008; Daniels et al., 2015; Pinnell et al., 1995). These students lack automaticity with the majority of the words in texts.

Approximately 2,500 morphological word families account for about 90% of the words in typical texts, including the texts identified by CCSS writers as exemplifying appropriate complex texts for middle schoolers (Hiebert, 2014). This vocabulary—which I describe as foundational in this chapter—goes much beyond high-function words (e.g., *than, through*). It includes a significant group of general academic words (e.g., *argument, predict*) that are ubiquitous in content-area texts. Words that convey content but take on meanings in different domains (e.g., *manual, launch*) are also present in the foundational vocabulary, as are verbs (e.g., *attracted, invited*) and adjectives (e.g., *bitter, violent*) found in literary texts. For ELs, foundational words cannot simply be designated as *Tier One* words that middle school students are assumed to know. Many of these words are polysemous, and their changing meanings across content areas and in phrases can create challenges for ELs.

The words beyond this foundational vocabulary account for only a small portion of a text, but the size of the rare vocabulary is significant—estimated at about 300,000 words (Leech & Rayson, 2014). Many rare words can be comprehended from the context of text, provided students are facile with the foundational vocabulary (i.e., the 2,500 morphological word families). Further, the approximately 300,000 rare words belong to morphological word families—approximately 88,500 in all (Nagy & Anderson, 1984). Even when viewed as morphological word families, however, rare vocabulary can be challenging. The concepts represented by rare words may be new to ELs and, especially when rare words are also multisyllabic (which is often the case), can be challenging to figure out. Whether textbooks for ELs repeat and/or limit rare vocabulary and provide enhanced opportunities with the polysemous words of the foundational vocabulary is a question of interest in this chapter.

The Topics and Knowledge in Texts

Knowledge about the world (often referred to as *background knowledge*) is a powerful predictor of readers' comprehension of texts, both narrative and informational (Alexander, Murphy, Woods, Duhon, & Parker, 1997). The critical role of background knowledge in comprehension often has led educators to emphasize prereading activities wherein teachers present the main content prior to students' reading. But one of the CCSS themes is that simply providing specific information on a particular text will not develop the bodies of background knowledge required for proficient reading.

An objective of the ELA curriculum is to support students in developing background knowledge that will facilitate comprehension across numerous topics. A single body of knowledge will not suffice because general world knowledge, not simply knowledge specific to a text, aids in comprehension (Best, Floyd, & McNamara, 2008). Relevant background knowledge is especially influential for students who comprehend less well than their peers (Miller & Keenan, 2009). For ELs who come from communities with oracy and literacy traditions that differ from those of the mainstream culture, a strong emphasis on developing background knowledge is especially critical (García, 2000).

Elements of Effective Literacy Experiences: Current ELA Textbooks for ELs

This section of the chapter presents an empirical investigation of the opportunities presented by ELA textbooks for (1) a sufficient amount of text, (2) the breadth of and attention to foundational and new vocabulary, and (3) topics and knowledge represented in texts. I begin with a description of the textbooks that were examined through the lenses of these three elements.

The Sample of Textbooks

The textbooks were those adopted by the California Board of Education (2008) for use with ELs. California's EL population is substantial, with 22.7% of the total enrollment in public schools designated as ELs and an additional 20% of students who speak a language other than English in their homes (California Department of Education, 2013–2014). The California Board of Education has identified two different types of textbooks for use with ELs: (1) the basic language development textbook for use in ELA classrooms (or core programs) and (2) a textbook that is intended for intervention with ELs. Presumably, ELs will be involved with the core textbook in their ELA class and the intervention textbook in a separate instructional period.

Textbooks are voluminous; the typical core textbook for a single grade is approximately 1,000 pages long. The length of the intervention texts varies (260–600 pages). But the heft of these texts, especially those of the core programs, made it necessary to focus on a portion of a single grade-level text in this chapter. Sixth grade was chosen because it represents the beginning of students' experience in middle school, a critical point in students' school development (Rumberger & Rotermund, 2012; Spichtig et al., 2016). For each of the 10 (three core; seven intervention) textbook programs on the list of textbooks approved by the California State Board of Education (2008) for purchase with state funds, 10% of the selections from the middle of each of the sixth-grade textbooks were scanned and the digitized selections were used in subsequent analyses. For a 180-day school year, 10% of a program equates to 18 school days of learning and instruction. I randomly chose a program to represent core and intervention programs for illustrative purposes in this chapter: Holt (core) and Longman (intervention).

A Sufficient Amount of Text

Table 4.1 provides information on the amount of text provided by programs for an 18-day period and the average length of selections. Core programs had more and longer selections than intervention programs. Across core programs, the amount of text available per day was around 841 words. Average speeds of readers, from available data (Spichtig et al., 2016), suggest how long it would take students of different proficiency levels to read the texts: about 5 minutes for students in the 50th percentile and 7 minutes for students at the 25th percentile. The volume of text is not extensive for a 50- to 60-minute ELA period but it provides adequate reading opportunities, especially if sections of text are reread as part of discussions.

Available text in intervention programs was considerably less than in the core program: an average of 291 words daily compared to 1,512 words daily. Further, intervention programs differed substantially in the amount of text provided. The program with the most text (Longman) had 3.37 times as much text as the program with the least amount of text (Scholastic). Even in the Longman program (the intervention program with the most text), students at the 25th percentile could read available text in slightly less than 5 minutes on a daily basis, and those in the Scholastic program could read available text in 1.25 minutes daily. Providing a substantial amount of

TABLE 4.1. Features of Core and Intervention Texts*

	Number of selections	Total words	Lexile	MSL	MLWF	Core vocabulary (%)
Core programs						
McGraw-Hill/ Glencoe	10	12,597	850	12.74	3.49	92.0
Pearson	12	16,160	858	13.11	3.53	95.0
Holt	10	16,606	780	11.53	3.53	91.8
Core program total		15,121	829.3	12.46	3.52	92.9
Intervention programs						
Gateway	4	3,893	825	11.73	3.44	92.5
HMH Portals	4	1,852	713	10.51	3.53	94.0
Longman Keystone	4	5,311	860	12.35	3.45	89.6
Milestones	4	3,488	897	13.14	3.47	88.7
National Geographic	4	1,930	728	11.72	3.63	92.8
Scholastic	3	1,382	653	9.3	3.47	87.0
Sopris West	4	2,514	530	7.9	3.35	88.4
Intervention program total		2,910	743.7	10.95	3.48	90.4

*Based on 10% of the selections in a program.

text for reading within intervention programs does not appear to be viewed as a primary mechanism for increasing ELs' capacity as readers.

A simple count of the words in texts does not indicate how much students will read in an ELA or intervention session. Students may be asked to reread selections, thus increasing their opportunities to read. By the same token, the presence of text does not mean that students will read it, as was evident in results of a recent observational study of high school social studies and ELA classes (Swanson et al., 2016). In social studies classrooms, time spent reading accounted for around 10% of class time, and the percentage was around 15% in ELA classrooms. These averages mask the considerable variation in reading experiences in classrooms. Students in the classes of six of the 11 social studies teachers spent less than 5% of class periods engaged in text reading, while the students of five of the nine ELA teachers engaged in text reading less than 10% of the observed time.

An examination of student texts made it apparent that the literary selections are only part of both intervention and core ELA textbooks. Both types of textbooks also contain many pages of guidance on strategies and skills as well as background on topics and authors. The following excerpt illustrates the content of this guidance in the core and intervention programs:

> A consonant blend is the sound that two or three consonants make when they come together in a word. You can hear the sound of each consonant in the blend. Identifying s-blends can help you spell new and unfamiliar words. Read the s-blends and examples in the chart below [*swept, swim, special, space, stay, stomach, stranger, strong*]. (Chamot, De Mado, & Hollie, 2010, p. 139)

To examine the nature of what I will describe as "instructional machinery," this material from the two illustrative programs, Holt and Longman, was digitized. Slightly more space in the core textbooks was devoted to instructional machinery than to selections, as is evident in the ratio of 1:1.3 for selections to instructional machinery. Text complexity was established with the Lexile framework, using the overall Lexile and the two measures that underlie a Lexile: (1) the mean sentence length (MSL) and (b) the mean log word frequency (MLWF), which assesses vocabulary load. A lower mean on the vocabulary measure indicates more challenging vocabulary. The text complexity of the instructional machinery was higher than for literacy selections, as is evident from the following data: (1) instructional machinery: Lexile = 1010, sentence length = 13.7, and word frequency = 3.27; and (2) literary and informational selections: Lexile = 829, sentence length = 12.46, and word frequency = 3.52.

The ratio of words in selections to instructional machinery was similar in the intervention program: 1:1.3. Further, Lexiles were fairly similar for the two kinds of texts (818 for the instructional machinery; 860 for the literary selections). The word frequency average, however, was higher in the instructional machinery as represented by a lower word frequency mean (3.35) for the instructional texts than for the reading selections (3.45).

Support for Vocabulary in Texts

Capturing the vocabulary demands of different texts would seem an area in which analytic schemes from research and practice would be extensive. After all, knowledge of vocabulary in a language is the essential component in communicating messages and in comprehending texts. Differences in syntax can create challenges in comprehension and in production of academic text, but without knowledge of the vocabulary in a language, communicating or comprehending messages is nigh to impossible. For example, without knowledge of the words *cuscini di schiuma* or *skum kuddar*, I have had a challenging time getting non-down pillows in Italy and Sweden, respectively.

Despite the critical role of vocabulary in comprehension of both oral and written language, schemes for understanding vocabulary demands are few. For the present analysis, I used two indices: (1) the Lexile and its two constituents (MSL and MLWF) and (2) the percentage of rare vocabulary from the Word Zone Profiler (Hiebert, 2011).

The Lexile Framework

The information on Lexiles that appears in Table 4.1 shows that, overall, the texts of the core reading programs had longer sentences and higher Lexiles than intervention texts. But when vocabulary as measured by word frequency is considered, texts of core and intervention programs are similar: an average of 3.50 for the vocabulary/word frequency measure in core programs and 3.49 for intervention programs. It may seem surprising that easier texts, according to the Lexile framework, can have vocabulary that is as challenging—or even more so—than text designated to be more complex. But this finding is not surprising when correlations between Lexiles and sentence length ($r = .94$) and Lexiles and vocabulary/word frequency ($r = -.54$) are compared (Hiebert, 2012). Lexile ratings are more strongly influenced by sentence length than by vocabulary/word frequency.

The Word Zone Profiler

The Word Zone Profiler (Hiebert, 2011) provides a form of information that a Lexile analysis does not: the percentage of rare words within texts. Information in Table 4.1 shows that the rate of rare vocabulary is somewhat higher in intervention than in core selections: 10 new words for every 100 words in the intervention texts relative to 8 new words per 100 in core selections. Further, across the intervention programs, the percentages of rare words vary from a low of 7 rare words per 100 words (National Geographic) to a high of 12 rare words per 100 (Sopris West).

Summary

After considering the results of the analyses of texts for ELs (both the core and intervention texts), a viable conclusion is that program developers view shorter texts with shorter sentences but with similar (if not higher) vocabulary demands to be the means of increasing the capacity of ELs in reading English language texts. These patterns of shorter sentences and less texts contradict research that shows that shorter sentences can require additional inferencing on the part of readers (McNamara, Kintsch, Songer, & Kintsch, 1996), and that less text can have the effect of perpetuating patterns of poor reading (Stanovich, 1986).

The Topics and Knowledge in Texts

The analyses of the knowledge in texts had two levels: (1) identification of the theme of the unit and (2) examination of the content of passages within the focus core and intervention programs. The themes identified by publishers in the core and intervention programs appear in Table 4.2.

Two of the core programs focused on genre as the basis for text selection, whereas the third core program and one intervention program presented text selections around a "big" question (e.g., "How are relationships with others important?" in the Longman program). The remaining intervention programs took a third direction, which was to select texts around a specific topic which, in turn, took one of two forms: (1) conventional academic topics such as the history of the European conquest of North America or (2) contemporary topics such as censorship of music.

TABLE 4.2. Themes of the Core and Intervention Programs

Publisher	Stated theme	Guiding question(s) or subcategories
	Core programs	
Holt	Forms of fiction	In what ways are stories an important part of your life?
McGraw-Hill	What's fair and what's not?	Seeing another side: Freedom and equality
Pearson	Types of nonfiction	What is important to know?
	Intervention programs	
Gateway	Seeking the New World	What reasons did people have for coming to the New World?
HMH Portals	How have we explored the universe?	It came from outer space. Life in zero gravity.
Longman	How are relationships with others important?	No additional
Milestones	Cultures and traditions	None
National Geographic	Creepy classics	How can a powerful character inspire a range of reactions?
Scholastic	When music offends	No additional
Sopris West	Cheer an athlete	No additional

No similar themes or patterns of content were evident within either the core or the intervention programs. Neither was there shared content between the core and intervention texts. If a district had selected the Holt program for its core instruction, students would be reading stories and asking the question as to how stories are important to their lives. The content would be quite different if the district has purchased either the McGraw-Hill or Pearson programs. At another time of the day, when ELs go to their intervention, they might read about topics that, depending on the program chosen by the district, range from colonization of the United States to exploration of outer space.

The call for ELA textbooks in California, as with other states, specifies skills to be included in their adopted programs, but guidelines are not given as to the content of the texts. The knowledge that students acquire from reading will vary considerably, depending on a district's choice of programs. Further, the lack of specification of knowledge domains in ELA programs means that the content of the ELA and intervention classrooms is disparate. Students are picking up bits and pieces of knowledge in their core and intervention programs, but these bits and pieces are not cohesive within either program or between programs.

The second examination of content considered the selections in the two illustrative programs: Holt and Longman. Table 4.3 provides synopses of the selections in the two programs. Selections in both programs have been chosen to support broad themes: the importance of stories in Holt and the importance of relationships in Longman.

In addressing the importance of stories, the Holt program presents an assortment of texts. In the fables, particular animals or individuals take on traditional roles, such as a poor but wise man outwitting a king. Two of the realistic fiction selections deal with situations that students are likely to understand: a boy trying to impress his peers and family in "La Bamba" or a boy working hard to win a basketball championship in "Game." The demands change substantially in the third piece of realistic fiction, "The Gold Cadillac," where the excitement of a girl for her father's new car changes to fear as the family drives the car from Ohio to Mississippi and confronts racial prejudice. The informational articles move from a history of storytelling to the looting and recovery efforts of historical treasures in Baghdad after the 2003 invasion. How precisely these selections assist young people in understanding the stories or story arcs of human lives is not readily apparent.

In the intervention program, an article presents information about relationships between different species and even different kingdoms. The next informational article reports on a camp for individuals from warring groups. One fiction selection is about a girl visiting a nursing home, and

TABLE 4.3. Synopses of Focus Texts in Illustrative Core and Intervention Programs

Title	Synopsis
Core program: In what ways are stories an important part of your life?	
"La Bamba"	A realistic story about a boy who, despite limited dancing skills, is a hit at the school talent show because of his quick thinking during an equipment malfunction.
"The Gold Cadillac"	A realistic story about an African American man in Ohio who, in the 1950s, buys a gold Cadillac and, against the advice of his wife, drives his family in it to the South, where he encounters harassment.
"He Lion, Bruh Bear"	A folk tale in which a lion will not stop waking other animals, forcing a bear and rabbit to take action.
"The Fox and the Crow" and "The Wolf and the House Dog"	Two Aesop's fables.
"Do or Die"	Part of the epic of Gilgamesh in which he and Enkidu go to Cedar Mountain and defeat Huwawa.
"An Interview with Walter Dean Myers"	An interview with the writer of young adolescent articles and books.
"Game"	A realistic story about a teenager who gives his all to basketball, including when hopes of living his dream fade.
"The Golden Serpent"	A fable of how a wise man tricks a king.
"Making It Up As We Go Along"	A magazine article about the history of storytelling.
"Iraqi Treasures Hunted"	A magazine article about the looting of, and subsequent hunt for, historical Iraqi treasures after the invasion of Baghdad in 2003.
Intervention program: How are relationships with others important?	
"Aguinaldo"	A realistic story of a girl who reluctantly visits a nursing home, where she connects deeply with a blind woman.
"Sowing the Seeds of Peace: Cultivating Friendships"	An informational article on a camp for teens from groups at war with one another.
"Blue Willow"	A tale of two star-crossed lovers in ancient China who appear to reunite after death in the form of swallows.
"Partnerships in Nature"	A description of symbiotic relationships between different organisms such as barnacles and whales.

the other is a tale of two star-crossed lovers. What the underlying message students are to garner about relationships from these texts is uncertain.

The knowledge that students will gain (or be expected to draw upon as background knowledge) is dramatically different from program to program within a textbook strand (i.e., core or intervention). Further, selections within a program are loosely configured around themes in ways that are difficult to understand. At best, students will gain bits and pieces of information in the core program and another set of bits and pieces of information in the intervention program. The demands for background knowledge are high for students; the opportunities within these programs to develop connected bodies of knowledge are limited.

Redesigning ELA Textbooks to Support ELs' Literacy Proficiency

Whether the resources of school districts and states are best used to purchase programs with the characteristics of texts in the core and intervention programs reviewed in this chapter can be questioned. In the intervention programs, the text selections are few and relatively short. ELs are not receiving many opportunities to read, nor are they receiving vocabulary instruction that is likely to reduce the vocabulary gap. Further, the textbook programs, whether core or intervention, provide snippets of information rather than supporting students in becoming facile or knowledgeable about particular topics.

The finding about the amount of text devoted to instructional machinery rather than to selections may be the most critical outcome of this analysis. If students are still grappling with *s*-blends as sixth graders (Chamot et al., 2010), they will likely be unable to process the 120 rare words in the selection that follows this excerpt—a selection with words such as *coquettish, mischievous,* and *serenade* (none with an *s*-blend). Further, if such descriptive statements are sufficient for acquisition of the skill, then the difficulties of ELs and other challenged readers should be short-lived.

The shortcomings of current intervention programs do not mean ELA textbooks or intervention programs for ELs should be eliminated. A textbook program provides ready access to a range of selections—a boon in schools where teacher turnover is high (Ingersoll, 2001). However, the template apparent in current programs needs to be dramatically changed with an eye on providing more text, attending to capacity with foundational vocabulary, introducing rare vocabulary strategically, and developing content coherently.

Provide Sufficient Opportunities to Read

Intervention programs with only enough text to add a handful of minutes of reading are unlikely to be the basis for substantial improvements in the reading proficiency of ELs. Intervention programs should provide sufficient text to ensure that students spend at least 10–12 minutes of reading daily. Within the intervention programs, the number and length of selections could be increased dramatically by eliminating much, if not all, of the instructional machinery. If ELs and other challenged readers can gain facility in reading with statements such as the illustration from the intervention program on s-blends, intervention materials are hardly necessary. This material needs to be substituted with additional passages that coherently support bodies of knowledge about both genres and critical topics.

Ensure That Students Are Facile with the Core Vocabulary

ELs who are not fluent readers need opportunities to become facile with the core vocabulary. In instruction of English as a second language (ESL) and English as a foreign language (EFL), sets of selections that systematically emphasize foundational vocabulary are common (Waring & McLean, 2015). Similar sets of texts are available for interventions with challenged readers (e.g., Vadasy & Sanders, 2008). To date, texts that emphasize foundational vocabulary and background knowledge remain uncommon in interventions for ELs in the United States. This genre of texts merits attention as part of the ELA experiences of ELs.

Provide Instruction on Language Systems and Connections across Vocabulary

The intervention programs included a broad gamut of information on the structure and content of vocabulary, typically presented in statements such as that on the s-blend (Chamot et al., 2010). Such guidance has dubious value. Alternative structures for expanding ELs' English vocabulary are needed. One is the use of pictures and illustrations (August, Branum-Martin, Cardenas-Hagan, & Francis, 2009) that permit ELs to connect known concepts with new labels. A feature of intervention programs should be access to organized libraries of photographs and illustrations that have been curated from the vast repositories available digitally.

   Second, explicit guidance on the linguistic sources of English should be provided. Graphics such as Calfee and Drum's (1986) vocabulary pyramid make explicit the differences in the Anglo-Saxon, Romance, and Greek systems that contribute to English. English–Spanish cognates should be prominent in core and intervention programs, not only as a means for recognizing the competence that native Spanish speakers bring to academic and literary English where these words are prominent, but also for native speakers of other languages to understand how the Romance layer of English functions (Lubliner & Hiebert, 2011).

Third, ELs need to be exposed to clusters of words that have semantic connections, especially those that are used widely in narratives and informational texts. Certain concept clusters pertain to specific content areas (e.g., electromagnetism, differences between parliamentary and federal forms of government). But there are concept clusters, such as the roles and jobs of characters (e.g., mayor, judge, juror, engineer, scientist), which appear in both narrative and informational texts.

Develop Bodies of Knowledge and Emphasize the Importance of This Knowledge

At present, ELA texts within a unit give students haphazard and disconnected information. The disjointedness of texts in core and intervention programs is substantial. If ELs are to develop lifelong reading habits and attain college and career readiness, they need to be engaged in acquiring knowledge and experience through text. Unlike mathematics, science, or social studies, there are no stipulations on the topics or themes to be covered in particular grades within the ELA curriculum. Similar to other states and the CCSS, California's call for textbooks gives no guidance on what the content of ELA should be (although guidance on strategies and skills is extensive). States and districts need to make explicit the expected content to be taught and learned in ELA classes. Until such information is provided, I offer three guidelines for teachers to use in emphasizing the content of currently available texts.

First, existing bodies of students' knowledge need to be recognized. ELs are intimate with their native languages and cultures. Many also have experiences and contact across countries. Their knowledge of culture, language, and transnational experiences needs to be firmly recognized and built upon in ELA programs

Second, knowledge needs to be strategically presented from an underlying vision of critical content. Whatever the content, students need to be assisted in seeing connections across texts and in how content coalesces to build bodies of knowledge. Third, students need mechanisms for recording and recognizing their existing and developing bodies of knowledge. As well as the generation of maps and summaries created as a group, individual students need systems to document what they are learning. Their records of knowledge acquisition need to be revisited across a school year and a school career.

Conclusion

The perspective on increasing capacity that appears to underlie current core and intervention ELA programs at the middle school level stands in sharp contrast to existing research. The emphasis is on teaching phonics and structural skills rather than on increasing reading volume and developing bodies of knowledge. Accommodation for ELs is insubstantial, even when texts seem to have been chosen to make connections to students' experiences or languages. Some mechanisms within the intervention texts are surprising, especially the instructional machinery that presumes students who ostensibly have yet to attain facility with basic word patterns will become proficient in that skill by reading instructional guidance that contains substantially more complex words than in the target words.

Dimensions other than texts, such as discussions, are critical in classes for ELs. But texts are an important element when the aim is to bring students to proficient levels of reading. Texts are a vital source of information in the global digital world, and proficiency with texts is essential for full participation in college, careers, and communities. Alternative models of selections and instructional guidance need to be explored for ELs, especially the development of digital programs where selections can be matched to students' word recognition and vocabulary. In such programs, students can be guided in ways much more supportive and adaptive than the snippets of advice now presented in their textbooks. In the face of both increasing numbers of ELs and escalating demands for proficient reading in the digital age, the design and implementation of alternative models are desperately needed. In particular, if ELs are to develop the literacy proficiencies that lead to college and career readiness and full participation in the communities of the 21st century, the role of texts as a source for knowledge building needs to be bolstered considerably.

REFERENCES

Alexander, P. A., Murphy, P. K., Woods, B. S., Duhon, K. E., & Parker, D. (1997). College instruction and concomitant changes in students' knowledge, interest, and strategy use: A study of domain learning. *Contemporary Educational Psychology, 22,* 125–146.

August, D., Branum-Martin, L., Cardenas-Hagan, E., & Francis, D. J. (2009). The impact of an instructional intervention on the science and language learning of middle grade English language learners. *Journal of Research on Educational Effectiveness, 2*(4), 345–376.

Best, R. M., Floyd, R. G., & McNamara, D. S. (2008). Differential competencies contributing to children's comprehension of narrative and expository texts. *Reading Psychology, 29*(2), 137–164.

Calfee, R. C., & Drum, P. (1986). Research on teaching reading. In M. C. Witrock (Ed.), *Handbook of research on teaching* (3rd ed., pp. 804–849). New York: Macmillan.

California Department of Education. (2013–2014). *Fingertip facts on education in California*. Sacramento, CA: Author. Retrieved from *www.cde.ca.gov/ds/sd/cb/ceffingertipfacts.asp*.

California State Board of Education. (2008, November 5). *State board adopted instructional materials*. Sacramento, CA: Author. Retrieved from *www.cde.ca.gov/ci/rl/im/rlaadoptedlist.asp*.

California State Board of Education. (2015, November 5). *2015 English language arts/English language development instructional materials adoption (K–8)*. Sacramento, CA: Author. Retrieved from *www.cde.ca.gov/ci/rl/im*.

Daane, M. C., Campbell, J. R., Grigg, W. S., Goodman, M. J., Oranje, A., & Goldstein, A. (2005). *The nation's report card: Fourth-grade students reading aloud: NAEP 2002 special study of oral reading* (NCES 2006-469). Washington, DC: U.S. Department of Education, Institute of Education Sciences.

Dewey, E. N., Kaminski, R. A., & Good, R. H. (2014). *DIBELS Next national norms 2012–2013* (Technical Report No. 17). Eugene, OR: Dynamic Measurement Group.

Fisher, C. W., Berliner, D. C., Filby, N. N., Marliave, R., Cahen, L. S., & Dishaw, M. M. (1980). Teaching behaviors, academic learning time, and student achievement: An overview. In C. Denham & A. Lieberman (Eds.), *Time to learn* (pp. 7–32). Washington, DC: U.S. Department of Education.

Foorman, B. R., Schatschneider, C., Eakin, M. N., Fletcher, J. M., Moats, L. C., & Francis, D. J. (2006). The impact of instructional practices in grades 1 and 2 on reading and spelling achievement in high poverty schools. *Contemporary Educational Psychology, 31*, 1–29.

García, G. (2000). Bilingual children's reading. In M. L. Kamil, P. B. Mosenthal, P. D. Pearson, & R. Barr (Eds.), *Handbook of reading research* (Vol. 3, pp. 813–834). Mahwah, NJ: Erlbaum.

Hemphill, F. C., Vanneman, A., & Rahman, T. (2011). *Achievement gaps: How Hispanic and white students in public schools perform in mathematics and reading on the National Assessment of Educational Progress* (NCES 2011-459). Washington, DC: U.S. Department of Education, Institute of Education Sciences.

Hiebert, E. H. (2011). *The word zone profiler*. Santa Cruz, CA: TextProject.

Hiebert, E. H. (2012, November 30). *Readability formulas and text complexity*. Paper presented at the annual meeting of the Literacy Research Association, San Diego, CA.

Hiebert, E. H. (2014, July 19). *Development and application of a morphological family database in analyzing vocabulary patterns in texts*. Paper presented at the annual meeting of the Society for the Scientific Study of Reading, Santa Fe, NM.

Ingersoll, R. M. (2001). Teacher turnover and teacher shortages: An organizational analysis. *American Educational Research Journal, 38*(3), 499–534.

Kuhn, M. R., & Schwanenflugel, P. J. (2009). Time, engagement, and support:

Lessons from a 4-year fluency intervention. In E. H. Hiebert (Ed.), *Reading more, reading better* (pp. 141–160). New York: Guilford Press.

Leech, G., & Rayson, P. (2014). *Word frequencies in written and spoken English: Based on the British National Corpus.* New York: Routledge.

Lewis, M. (2002). *Read more—Read better?: A meta-analysis of the literature on the relationship between exposure to reading and reading achievement.* Doctoral dissertation, University of Minnesota, Minneapolis, MN.

Lubliner, S., & Hiebert, E. H. (2011). An analysis of English–Spanish cognates as a source of general academic language. *Bilingual Research Journal, 34*(1), 76–93.

McNamara, D. S., Kintsch, E., Songer, N., & Kintsch, W. (1996). Are good texts always better?: Interactions of text coherence, background knowledge, and levels of understanding in learning from text. *Cognition and Instruction, 14,* 1–43.

Miller, A. C., & Keenan, J. M. (2009). How word decoding skill impacts text memory: The centrality deficit and how domain knowledge can compensate. *Annals of Dyslexia, 59*(2), 99–113.

Nagy, W. E., & Anderson, R. C. (1984). How many words are there in printed school English? *Reading Research Quarterly, 19,* 304–330.

National Governors Association Center for Best Practices & Council of Chief State School Officers. (2010). *Common Core State Standards for English language arts and literacy in history/social studies, science, and technical subjects,* Appendix A. Washington, DC: Author. Retrieved from *www.corestandards. org/the-standards.*

National Institute of Child Health and Human Development. (2000). *Report of the National Reading Panel: Teaching children to read—An evidence-based assessment of the scientific research literature on reading and its implications for reading instruction* (NIH Publication No. 00-4769). Washington, DC: U.S. Government Printing Office.

Pinnell, G. S., Pikulski, J. J., Wixson, K. K., Campbell, J. R., Gough, P. B., & Beatty, A. S. (1995). *Listening to children read aloud: Data from NAEP's integrated reading performance record (IRPR) at grade 4.* Washington, DC: Office of Educational Research and Improvement, U.S. Department of Education; Princeton, NJ: Educational Testing Service.

Roehrig, A. D., Petscher, Y., Nettles, S. M., Hudson, R. F., & Torgeson, J. K. (2008). Accuracy of the DIBELS oral reading fluency measure for predicting third grade reading comprehension outcomes. *Journal of School Psychology, 46*(3), 343–366.

Rumberger, R. W., & Rotermund, S. (2012). The relationship between engagement and high school dropout. In S. L. Christenson, A. L. Reschly, & C. Wylie (Eds.), *Handbook of research on student engagement* (pp. 491–513). New York: Springer.

Schmidt, W. H., & McKnight, C. C. (2012). *Inequality for all: The challenge of unequal opportunity in American schools.* New York: Teachers College Press.

Spichtig, A. N., Hiebert, E. H., Vorstius, C., Pascoe, J. P., Pearson, P. D., & Radach, R. (2016). The decline of comprehension-based silent reading efficiency in the

United States: A comparison of current data with performance in 1960. *Reading Research Quarterly, 51*(2), 239–259.

Stanovich, K. E. (1986). Matthew effects in reading: Some consequences of individual differences in the acquisition of literacy. *Reading Research Quarterly, 21*(4), 360–407.

Swanson, E., Wanzek, J., McCulley, L., Stillman-Spisak, S., Vaughn, S., Simmons, D., et al. (2016). Literacy and text reading in middle and high school social studies and English language arts classrooms. *Reading and Writing Quarterly: Overcoming Learning Difficulties, 32*(3), 199–222.

Vadasy, P. F., & Sanders, E. A. (2008). Repeated reading intervention: Outcomes and interactions with readers' skills and classroom instruction. *Journal of Educational Psychology, 100*(2), 272–290.

Waring, R., & McLean, S. (2015). Exploration of the core and variable dimensions of extensive reading research and pedagogy. *Reading in a Foreign Language, 27*(1), 160–167.

INSTRUCTIONAL TEXTS ANALYZED IN THIS CHAPTER

Anderson, N., O'Sullivan, J. K. Trujillo, J., Lenz, K., McTighe, J., & Marzano, R. J. (2009). *Milestones (California edition).* Boston: Heinle Cengage Learning.

Beers, K., Jago, C., Appleman, D., Christenbury, L., Kajder, S., & Rief, L. (2010). *Holt literature and language arts.* Orlando, FL: Holt, Rinehart & Winston/HMH.

Chamot, A. U., De Mado, J., & Hollie, S. (2010). *Longman keystone.* White Plains, NY: Pearson Longman.

Greene, J. F. (2009). *Language!: The comprehensive literacy curriculum* (4th ed.). Longmont, CO: Sopris West Educational Services.

Hasselbring, T., Goin, L., Kinsella, K., & Feldman, K. (2010). *Read 180* (Enterprise edition). New York: Scholastic.

Houghton Mifflin Harcourt. (2010). *Portals to reading.* Boston: Author.

Moore, D. W., Short, D. J., Tatum, A. W., & Tinajero, J. V. (2009). *Inside language, literacy, and content.* Carmel, CA: National Geographic School Publishing/Hampton-Brown.

Scarcella, R., Rivera, H., Rivera, M., Beck, I. L., McKeown, M., & Chiappe-Collins, P. (2010). *California gateways.* Boston: Steck Vaughn/HMH.

Wiggins, G., Anderson, J., Ball, A. F., Buehl, D., Balderrama, M. V., Blau, S., et al. (2010). *Pearson literature, reading, and language (California).* Upper Saddle River, NJ: Pearson.

Wilhelm, J. D., Fisher, D., Hinchman, K. A., O'Brien, D. G., Raphael, T., & Shanahan, C. H. (2010). *Literature: California treasures.* Columbus, OH: Glencoe/McGraw-Hill.

CHAPTER 5

Supporting Linguistically Diverse Students to Develop Deep, Flexible Knowledge of Academic Words

Amy C. Crosson

In the following exchange, Emela, a native Bosnian speaker enrolled in an advanced English as a second language (ESL) seventh-grade class at a public school in Pennsylvania, considers some contexts in which the academic word *foundation* appears.[1] For each, she is asked to share her thinking about whether the word *foundation* would make sense in that context. Emela's explanations provide insight into the challenge that English learners (ELs) face as they work to develop deep, flexible understandings of word meanings in English—the kind of word knowledge students are expected to develop in the Common Core State Standards (CCSS).

Before presenting the sentences, the interviewer reviews the meaning of *foundation,* a general academic word that Emela and her ESL classmates studied in a vocabulary program:

> INTERVIEWER: So do you remember what *foundation* means?
>
> EMELA: I think *foundation* means, um, something for support.

Next the interviewer presents Emela with a context that requires understanding of the physical meaning of the word:

> INTERVIEWER: Go ahead and read the first sentence and tell me what you think.
>
> EMELA: "We planted flowers around the *foundation* of the building."

---

[1] All names referring to teachers and students in this chapter are pseudonyms.

INTERVIEWER: Do you think that works with *foundation?* Does that make sense or not?

EMELA: Yeah . . . because if you, like, plant flowers around the support of the building . . . around it . . . they'd be pretty.

Finally, the interviewer presents a context that requires understanding of the mental connotation of *foundation:*

EMELA: "His childhood vacations at the beach were the *foundation* of his love for the ocean."

INTERVIEWER: What do you think?

EMELA: No!

INTERVIEWER: Why not?

EMELA: Because his childhood vacation at the beach . . . it doesn't say, like, how to like support it, but it just says, like, what he likes.

We can see from Emela's explanations about whether and why *foundation* would fit in each of the two contexts that she has already acquired a good deal of knowledge about the word. Even when she (erroneously) determines that memories cannot serve as a *foundation,* Emela demonstrates her understanding of one of the word's key meaning elements: the idea that a *foundation* usually supports something else. Still, her explanation reveals an important misconception—that is, the "support" provided by *foundation* is constrained to a physical support. It appears from this excerpt and from other interactions with Emela about the word that she does not yet understand that its meaning can be extended to a mental state.

This excerpt provides a glimpse into the kinds of observations that my colleagues and I have made during classroom discussions, reflecting on vocabulary lessons, and from scores of interviews with language-minority middle school students enrolled in ESL classes. Developing deep, flexible understanding of new vocabulary is hard work—and this is particularly true when the words students are working to learn are *general academic vocabulary words* that convey abstract meanings and carry "multiple senses." By *multiple senses,* I refer to words that carry multiple meanings and the meanings are related. For example, *foundation,* as seen above, carries a mental sense (the base for a memory) as well as a physical sense (the base of a structure). Many general academic words carry multiple senses, such as *acquire* (take possession through a purchase or gain knowledge of something by studying it) or *reside* (people can live in house or thoughts can live in the imagination).

In this chapter, I address the challenge of supporting ELs to develop knowledge of general academic words that is both deep and flexible. I begin by explaining why deep, flexible word knowledge is critical, and how this knowledge is embedded in the expectations of the CCSS. I then define *general academic words* and argue that these words merit a healthy dose of instructional time. Next, I turn to the issue of why acquiring new word meanings of general academic words can be so tricky—paying particular attention to this issue of multiple senses—and I explain how and why these challenges might be accentuated for ELs. Finally, I provide examples of instruction from my work with researchers and expert teachers that show promise for supporting ELs to develop deep, flexible representations of academic words.

Why Is Deep, Flexible Knowledge about Words Important?

Many factors influence how well we understand what we read, and certainly among the most important are how many words we know and how much we know about them (Perfetti & Stafura, 2014; Stahl & Fairbanks, 1986). Simply put, when reading materials are loaded with unfamiliar words, it is very difficult to comprehend them. Unfortunately, typical practices in vocabulary instruction are unlikely to have an impact on comprehension. For example, giving students lists of definitions to memorize is notoriously common yet ineffective for improving comprehension (Beck, McKeown, & Omanson, 1987; Ford-Connors & Paratore, 2015; Hedrick, Harmon, & Linerode, 2004; Scott, Jamieson-Noel, & Asselin, 2003).

Recent understandings about word knowledge are reflected in the CCSS, which call for students to develop knowledge about words that goes far beyond definitional associations (see Table 5.1). For example, the standards for "Vocabulary Acquisition and Use" call for sixth graders to understand nuances in word meanings and relationships between words; they call for students to attune to the meaning of words in particular contexts and to use word meanings to support comprehension. Why do the CCSS emphasize so many different forms of word knowledge and word learning skills?

The CCSS emphasize development of rich word knowledge, such as understanding how a word fits within a semantic network (e.g., how the meaning of *controversy* relates to *argument, contest, fight, issue, debate,* and *dispute*).[2] The CCSS also highlight the importance of word learning skills that are generative—that is, students are expected not only to learn

---

[2] Two helpful web-based sources for determining words in a semantic network are the Visual Thesaurus (*www.google.com/webhp?sourceid=chrome-instant&ion=1&espv=2&ie= UTF-8#q=visual+thesaurus*) and WordNet's "synsets" (*https://wordnet.princeton. edu/wordnet/citing-wordnet*; Princeton University, 2010).

TABLE 5.1. CCSS in English Language Arts for Vocabulary Acquisition and Use (Sixth Grade)

CCSS.ELA-LITERACY.L.6.4: Determine or clarify the meaning of unknown and multiple-meaning words and phrases based on grade 6 reading and content, choosing flexibly from a range of strategies.

CCSS.ELA-LITERACY.L.6.4.A: Use context (e.g., the overall meaning of a sentence or paragraph; a word's position or function in a sentence) as a clue to the meaning of a word or phrase.

CCSS.ELA-LITERACY.L.6.4.D: Verify the preliminary determination of the meaning of a word or phrase (e.g., by checking the inferred meaning in context or in a dictionary).

CCSS.ELA-LITERACY.L.6.5: Demonstrate understanding of figurative language, word relationships, and nuances in word meanings.

CCSS.ELA-LITERACY.L.6.5.B: Use the relationship between particular words (e.g., cause/effect, part/whole, item/category) to better understand each of the words.

CCSS.ELA-LITERACY.L.6.6: Acquire and use accurately grade-appropriate general academic and domain-specific words and phrases; gather vocabulary knowledge when considering a word or phrase important to comprehension or expression.

Note. Copyright © 2010 National Governors Association Center for Best Practices and Council of Chief State School Officers. All rights reserved.

new word meanings through instruction, but also to become equipped with the knowledge and analytic skills to infer meanings of new words. These emphases on rich word knowledge and generative word-learning skills are paramount. The reason why they are so critically important is because of the link between word knowledge and reading comprehension. There is now a good deal of evidence that word knowledge supports comprehension—not when it is shallow—but instead when it is multifaceted, precise, and flexible (Beck et al., 1987; Ouellette, 2006; Baumann, Kame'enui, & Ash, 2003; Nation & Snowling, 2004; Pearson, Hiebert, & Kamil, 2007; Perfetti & Stafura, 2014; Stahl & Fairbanks, 1986). *Multifaceted knowledge* includes familiarity with a word's synonyms, antonyms, and hyponyms; understanding its grammatical role; and having a sense of its register (i.e., the social situations in which the word would likely be used and what level of formality it would convey). *Precision* refers to accuracy of meaning and an understanding of the nuances of meaning. When I refer to *deep* word knowledge, this is knowledge that is both multifaceted and precise. *Flexibility* refers to the understanding of which meaning elements of a particular word apply to a particular context, as I address extensively in the upcoming section on multiple meanings.

The kind of deep, flexible word knowledge that helps us read with understanding does not result from a single exposure or from memorizing a definition. Instead, depth of word knowledge develops over time, incrementally, from an accumulation of varied experiences with words that lead to flexible, nuanced representations of words' core meaning elements (Beck et al., 1987; Bolger, Balass, Landen, & Perfetti, 2008; Frishkoff, Perfetti, & Collins-Thompson, 2011; Nagy & Scott, 2000; Reichle & Perfetti, 2003). When we have rich, flexible knowledge about a word, we are in a good position to bring relevant connections to bear to make sense of the word when we encounter it in a new context (Perfetti, 2007; Perfetti & Hart, 2002; Nagy & Scott, 2000), such as understanding that *foundation* can be not only the base or support of a brick and mortar structure, but also the base or support on which ideas or memories are established.

What Are General Academic Words?

General academic words are words that are not frequently heard in conversation, but are frequently encountered when reading academic texts. These words (e.g., *erode, bias, analogous*) tend to be abstract and frequently carry meanings that are fundamental for understanding the message or information in a text. They are not content-specific words or specialized terms, but instead appear in many content areas. They are words that are important for conveying abstract ideas, arguing positions, and communicating complex ideas.

The resource that was used to identify the targeted academic words in this chapter is the Academic Word List (AWL), developed by Averil Coxhead (2000; see *www.victoria.ac.nz/lals/resources/academicwordlist*). The list is based on an analysis of a large corpus of university-level reading materials (including books, journal articles, etc.), drawn from diverse content areas. The list is far from exhaustive, but it does identify 570 word families that appear frequently in academic texts across disciplines. There are 570 "headwords" on the list, with one headword per word family (e.g., for the headword *principle*, there are three words in the family: *principled, principles, unprincipled*). The AWL is a useful resource because it serves as a good starting point for identifying academic words that ELs will likely encounter in their reading for all subjects. It is well worth instructional time to support ELs to develop deep, flexible knowledge of these words, as these words are likely to have an impact on comprehension in reading in various subject areas.

Academic words distinguish themselves from other types of vocabulary in notable ways. First, they tend to be abstract—*mutual* and *inherent* are two great examples of this—so understanding their meaning is rarely a question of knowing a word's synonym or labeling an image, but is situated in how the word is used in context. For example, consider words such as *inherent, ambiguous,* or *deviate*. Second, they often have multiple senses, depending upon the context or discipline in which they appear.

What Are Multiple Meanings? Why Are Multiple Meanings Important for Learning Academic Words?

In English, many words carry multiple meanings. For example, we have a *key* to a door, the *key* to a beloved's heart, a test's answer *key*; and we type on the *key*board, among others.

It is important to keep in mind that there are notable and important differences between types of multiple-meaning words. Many psycholinguists characterize multiple meaning words into two major categories (for a review, see Eddington & Tokowicz, 2015):

- *Multiple-sense words.* These are closely related, polysemous words (also called *polysemes*). Multiple-sense words have different *but related* meanings or senses (e.g., *foundation* of a building, *foundation* of a friendship).
- *Homonyms.* These are words that share a label (same spelling and perhaps pronunciation) but are virtually unrelated in meaning (e.g., a piece of buttered *toast* versus a champagne *toast*).

In reality, many multiple-meaning words fall on a continuum somewhere in-between, but the categories are helpful for drawing attention to the degree of *relatedness* between the meanings (Hoffman & Woollams, 2015). As mentioned previously, this chapter is concerned with the former—multiple senses—because many general academic words have multiple senses.

Sometimes it is not difficult to grasp how the meaning of a multiple-sense word extends to a new context in which its related meaning applies. In these cases, the relationship is quite transparent or predictable (e.g., when we can use *wheels* to refer to a whole car rather than just part of a car). However, relations are sometimes less predictable. Frequently, one form is more literal (concrete, physical) and the other is more figurative, as we saw when Emela puzzled over the meaning of *foundation*.

Words that have multiple meanings offer some processing advantages in comprehension, at least for monolinguals. Several studies have shown a "polysemy advantage" for speed of lexical access and semantic relatedness judgments for adults when they are reading in their native language (for a review, see Eddington & Tokowicz, 2015). Although still an area of active research, there is evidence from neuroscience (Beretta, Fiorentino, & Poeppel, 2005) that the related senses have a single underlying representation in the lexicon, which would help explain why activating one sense might more efficiently activate other senses. Interestingly, this line of research has revealed that multiple-sense words are processed differently from homonyms, because multiple-sense words are connected in meaning whereas homonyms are not.

The question is, what kind of instruction will support ELs to see these connections and capitalize on them? What is the most productive way for these students to learn about the relationships? How successfully will they flexibly apply the appropriate sense to its corresponding context?

Why Do Multiple-Meaning Words Seem to Be Especially Hard for ELs?

Learning to manage a word's multiple senses may be particularly challenging for ELs, who often hold narrow understandings of word meanings, as we saw in Emela's understanding of *foundation*, and as has been shown in other studies (Jiménez, García, & Pearson, 1996). There is evidence that ELs tend to know fewer senses of words in a target language (i.e., English) compared with words in their source language (Finkbeiner, Forster, Nicol, & Nakamura, 2004). Recent research suggests that whether a given word has multiple senses in the learner's source language (L1) or in the target language (L2)—so called *translation-ambiguous words*—might affect how the words are represented in memory (Tokowitz & Kroll, 2007). For example, the word *corner* in English translates to *rincón* (outside corner) or *esquina* (inside corner) in Spanish, affecting how the word is learned in English by Spanish speakers, and vice versa. Some research evidence with adults suggests that multiple-sense words may be especially difficult for ELs because of their "translation-ambiguous" status. But there is some evidence that learning a word's multiple senses from the outset, rather than teaching just one sense and delaying instruction about other senses, might alleviate the difficulty that these words present (Degani, Tseng, & Tokowicz, 2014).

In my research with my colleague Margaret McKeown, the challenges that multiple-meaning words pose to linguistically diverse ELs have been readily apparent. In one study (Crosson, 2014) with students enrolled in an ESL program, we taught several general academic words that hold multiple senses in English, such as *foundation, extract, acquire,* and *sustain.* We worked with 32 students representing 11 different home languages in three middle school ESL classes. The majority of these students spoke Nepali as their home language with one or two students speaking the following home languages: Albanian, Arabic, Bosnian, Burmese, French, Hindi, Jamaican Creole, Karen (within the Sino-Tibetan languages), Russian, and Uzbek. These students were designated "intermediate" or "advanced" ESL by their district, where classification decisions were made based on the Assessing Comprehension and Communication in English State-to-State (ACCESS) exam. We anticipated that the instruction to develop deep, flexible knowledge of academic words would be most appropriate for ELs who had developed a relatively high level of proficiency, which is why we worked with students at the intermediate and advanced levels.

In the instructional program Robust Academic Vocabulary Encounters (RAVE; Crosson & McKeown, 2016; McKeown, Crosson, Beck, Sandora, & Artz, 2013, 2014; McKeown, Crosson, Sandora, Artz, & Beck, 2013), ELs were given "friendly definitions" and participated in multiple interactions in which they were guided to analyze the meaning of several academic words across a variety of contexts (Beck, McKeown, & Kucan, 2002). Each instructional cycle comprised eight 20-minute lessons and focused on eight target academic words. Instruction was "robust," such that it was designed to engage students in analyzing word meanings, generating examples, and justifying word usage (Beck et al., 2002). Of the three classes, one teacher implemented six RAVE instructional cycles and two teachers taught two RAVE cycles. Students were guided to apply word meanings to a variety of contexts over the course of several lessons, for approximately 12 encounters with each word in an instructional cycle. Contexts were deliberately designed to illustrate multiple senses, and instruction was designed to get students to manage senses with flexibility, as is explained in the next section. For example, for the word *extract,* students were exposed to contexts in which red dye was extracted from a cochineal bug, a splinter was extracted from a foot, a confession was extracted from a criminal, and the truth was extracted from a little sister.

During the study, we conducted interviews about multiple-sense words with 30 of the 32 participating students. In these interviews, we talked with students about their understanding of general academic words that they were learning in the program, and we presented them with sample sentences asking whether the word fit and was intelligible in that context (about half of sentences were plausible uses of the target words). These sentences were selected from a depth-of-academic-word-knowledge measure (Crosson, McKeown, Beck, & Ward, 2012, 2013). For example, for the word *sustain,* we presented students with the following sentences:

- An exciting story will *sustain* children's interest. (mental sense)
- You should run slowly during the long race to *sustain* your energy. (physical sense)
- The child was rushed to the hospital to *sustain* his injury. (implausible)
- We wondered where our *sustain* had gone. (implausible)

When students answered that the target word would or would not fit in the context, we would probe their understanding, asking what it would mean, or why they thought it didn't fit.

We found that, overall, ELs in our study had more difficulty understanding words with multiple senses than academic words that did not convey more than one sense (e.g., *ambiguous, notion*). However, there was quite a bit of variability in students' understanding of multiple-sense words. That is, understanding varied from student to student, and we also noted trends in how understanding varied from word to word. For example, Figure 5.1 contrasts students' understanding of *foundation* with that of *sustain*. Students clearly found managing the multiple senses of *sustain* easier than managing the senses of *foundation*. For *foundation*, we found that students tended to learn one sense or the other. Although the physical sense was understood slightly more frequently than the mental sense, it seemed that the real difficulty was for ELs to manage *both senses simultaneously.* In other words, it was difficult for them to hold in mind the two related senses, as they tended to focus on and apply only the physical sense or only the mental sense.

See, for example, in the following excerpt how, unlike Emela's understanding of *foundation*'s physical sense only, another student understood the mental—but not the physical—sense of *foundation*. In this excerpt, Krishna, a Hindi-speaking seventh grader, explains his reasoning about why *foundation* could fit in one context but not the other:

INTERVIEWER: (*Reading the context*) "We planted flowers around the *foundation* of the building." So does that word make sense in there?

KRISHNA: Nope.

INTERVIEWER: Nope. Okay. Can you tell me why?

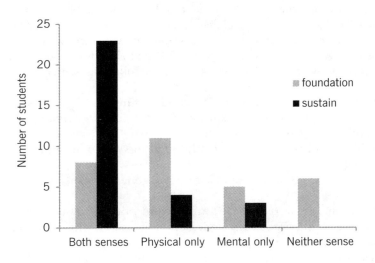

FIGURE 5.1. ELs' knowledge of multiple senses of the academic words *foundation* and *sustain* (*n* = 30).

KRISHNA: Because . . . flower . . . order to put a flower . . . you need to put a seed first, so that it can . . .

INTERVIEWER: Oh . . . so it could grow. How about, "His childhood vacations at the beach were the foundation of his love for the ocean." Does that make sense?

KRISHNA: Um . . . Yes, it does.

INTERVIEWER: And can you tell me why?

KRISHNA: Because it's starting like . . . he went like . . . for example, I went to the beach yesterday, right? So I started to love it . . . love it . . . I go, go, go. So, from now . . . from today . . . I started . . .

Krisha's difficulty with the physical sense may lie in part in his idea that *foundation* indicates the very beginning of something. Although it makes sense to think of a foundation as something that is there from the beginning, he had difficulty applying this idea with flexibility to the context about the *foundation* of a building.

In contrast to both Emela and Krisha, who were among 16 students interviewed who each managed just one sense of *foundation,* only eight students were able to flexibly apply the core meaning of foundation to understand both the physical and mental senses. Here we see how Etoile's understanding of the word enabled her to access the meaning of both contexts:

INTERVIEWER: (*Reading the context*) "We planted flowers around the *foundation* of the building." Does it fit?

ETOILE: Yes. Because the foundation is the first . . . thing . . . the first block . . . to create the house . . . and the *foundation* is kind of to . . . how do you say . . . in English? (*Gestures bottom.*)

INTERVIEWER: (*Reading the context*) "His childhood vacations at the beach were the *foundation* of his love for the ocean." Can *foundation* fit there?

ETOILE: Yes it can, because you cannot see the ocean everywhere . . . so . . . if it was his first vacation at the beach . . . his . . . he can't . . . it's the foundation of his love for the ocean.

Etoile seems to be relying especially on the idea that the *foundation* of something is what comes first, or is associated with the first time, but she also has the idea that it is something that is at the base, as indicated from her gesture. She seems to have a rich enough understanding of this word to apply her ideas with flexibility to both the physical base of a building and the love of the ocean.

What Kind of Instruction Is Likely to Support ELs to Develop Knowledge of Multiple Senses?

In light of the challenges of developing deep, flexible knowledge of multiple senses of academic words, in this section I provide some examples of the kind of interactions that may support students in their efforts to do so. Three principles are discussed. The first is to teach a "core meaning" that captures the essential meaning elements of the word that apply across senses and contexts. The second is to teach multiple senses right from the outset. The third is to engage students in interactions with the word that lead them to explicitly compare and contrast the senses.

Teach a Core Meaning

As mentioned earlier, when general academic words carry multiple meanings, they are typically multiple-sense words (i.e., *polysemes*), not homonyms. This distinction is important because, as polysemous words, the senses that general academic words carry are related in meaning. Instruction should be designed to emphasize those connections to promote meaningful links between their representations in memory. This is the purpose of teaching a core meaning.

To teach a core meaning, definitions must be "friendly" (Beck et al., 2002), such that they use accessible language and convey information not only about what the word means but also how it is used. In addition, definitions that teach core meanings also capture the word's key meaning elements. Consider some examples:

- If you *sustain* something, you keep it going.
- A *foundation* gives support on which something else can be built.
- Something that *exceeds* goes beyond what is expected or allowed.

Each of these definitions was written to emphasize the core meaning of the word across its senses. The definition should convey the overlapping meaning relationships between the senses so that the core meaning can be applied to the different senses and allow the learner to derive the specific meaning in context. The goal is to promote meaningful connections between senses instead of separate representations.

Introduce Multiple Senses from the Outset

Also mentioned earlier in this chapter, there is some evidence from second-language acquisition research that teaching the multiple meanings of words from the outset might alleviate the difficulty that they present to learners (Degani et al., 2014). To do so, in the RAVE program, target words are presented with two contexts to give students an idea of the senses—right when the words are introduced. For example, the word *sustain* is presented in one context describing how mountain gorillas need to eat constantly to *sustain* their weight. The other context is about texting as a way to *sustain* friendships (see Figure 5.2). In addition to the two contexts, students are given the core meaning in a friendly definition. To prompt them to integrate the relevant meaning elements with the contexts, they are asked to explain how the meaning of *sustain* fits each context.

Explicitly Contrast Multiple Senses

In RAVE, interactions that bring to the surface the similarities and differences between senses have been effective in helping ELs manage them flexibly. For example, in one activity, called "What's the Sense of It?," students are presented with two questions that are grounded in the same or a similar context, but each uses a different sense of the target word. For example:

- If your zoo membership is *valid*, what does that mean?
- If your point about why zoos are good for animals is *valid*, what does that mean?

The goal of this activity is to surface the differences between the two senses. In another activity, called "What's the Difference?," students are asked to apply the general academic word in two different contexts. For example:

- How might you *confine* a dozen jumping beetles?
- How might parents *confine* their children's choices of what to order at a restaurant?

Sustain weight—physical sense	Sustain friendships—mental sense
Mountain gorillas are huge animals that eat mainly leaves, stems, and vines. Because they need so much food to *sustain* their enormous weight, they spend most of the day eating, from 6:00 A.M. until 6:00 P.M.	Texting is a popular way for teens to *sustain* friendships. By texting, teens are able to keep in touch with each other quickly and easily, from anywhere, many times a day.

FIGURE 5.2. Two contexts presented to ELs to introduce the physical and mental senses of the word *sustain*.

The first item targets the physical sense of confine—restricting movement or keeping someone/something in one location. The second item gets at the mental sense of *confine*. The following excerpt illustrates how this activity supported students to contrast the two senses of the word *confine*. Notice that the teacher concludes the interaction by bringing students back to the friendly definition, which sums up the core meaning.

TEACHER: A beetle's like a bug. A jumping beetle. How might you *confine* a dozen jumping beetles?

RIANTI: Dozen. Like, many.

TEACHER: Saleem, what do you think?

SALEEM: Put them in a wine jar.

TEACHER: All right, put them in a jar with a lid. Right? You're confining them to a spot so they can't jump everywhere.

STUDENTS: Yeah.

TEACHER: To be confined is to be kept in a certain area. Okay, how might parents confine their children's choices about what to order at a restaurant?

DURGA: They can tell them "You can order this much only"—like, you know, this much food.

SALEEM: And you could, like, go to another store by yourself.

TEACHER: That's not going to *confine* the children's choices. They can say, like Durga told us, "You can only order from this particular page of the menu." Or you can confine them by what?

SALEEM: Money.

TEACHER: How much it costs, right? So that's a way to confine what they order. You have to order from this page, or you have to order things that are under $5.00. That's confining their choices, right? So if something is *confined*, it must stay in just one place or be used in just one way.

One challenge to keep in mind is that it's important to balance the encounters with a word's various senses. For example, for the word *foundation*, students were exposed to multiple contexts for the both the mental and physical senses, such as:

• Patricia lost the debate because she had no *foundation* for her opinions.
• This observation became the *foundation* of Darwin's theory.

- What would make a good *foundation* for a skyscraper? Plastic or steel? Why?
- What would make a good *foundation* for a tent?

In this section, I have argued that instruction to support ELs to flexibly apply a word's appropriate sense to its corresponding context reflect three principles: Teach the word's core meaning; teach the word's multiple senses right from the outset; and contrast the meanings of the different senses. Although the examples discussed in this section are drawn from the RAVE academic vocabulary program, teachers certainly can integrate these practices into language arts instruction, whether guiding students to understand the meaning of general academic words encountered in content-area reading, in word study, or in activities to build language awareness (Scott, Skobel, & Wells, 2008). These practices can also be applied in situations when it becomes apparent that an EL's word knowledge is limited to only one sense. In this case, providing a friendly definition with a core meaning that can encompass the multiple senses should be helpful. Inviting students to contrast the senses through examples (as in the activity "What's the Sense of It?") can guide them to see the meaning elements shared in the different senses, as well as the distinctive meaning elements that allow us to extend the word to other meanings and contexts.

Conclusion

This chapter has focused squarely on developing ELs' deep, flexible knowledge of academic words. However, the longer-term, overarching goal of this approach is to support comprehension of academic texts. It is widely acknowledged that ELs face considerable challenges when they confront the complexities of academic language in their content-area reading (Bailey, 2007; Crosson & Lesaux, 2013, Scarcella, 2003; Schleppegrell, 2004; Snow & Uccelli, 2009). We know that one of the defining characteristics of academic language is the prevalence of general academic vocabulary, as a cornerstone of academic language is the use of a "prestige lexis" (Schleppegrell, 2004). ELs with limited knowledge of academic vocabulary words are likely to have difficulty making sense of the ideas and information in the texts they read, and this difficulty is likely to cut across different subject areas. When a single word, such as *foundation,* carries more than one meaning, this can complicate the picture significantly. It also opens up an opportunity to engage students in word play, teach students a metalinguistic stance toward language learning, and draw on their capacity as bilingual or multilingual individuals to analyze language.

ACKNOWLEDGMENTS

I am grateful to Margaret McKeown for providing constructive comments on this chapter and for her invaluable collaboration on this intervention research project. I would like to thank Nancy Artz, Cheryl Sandora, and Shelley Tavis for contributing to the research reported in this chapter. This work would not be possible without the partnership of administrators and educators in the Pittsburgh Public Schools, especially Mark McMahon, Christine Tapu, Jon Covel, and Deb Friss, as well as the students enrolled in the English as a Second Language Program.

REFERENCES

Bailey, A. L. (2007). *The language demands of school: Putting academic English to the test*. New Haven, CT: Yale University Press.

Baumann, J. F., Kame'enui, E. J., & Ash, G. E. (2003). Research on vocabulary instruction: Voltaire redux. In J. Flood, D. Lapp, J. R. Squire, & J. M. Jensen (Eds.), *Handbook of research on teaching the English language arts* (pp. 752–785). Mahwah, NJ: Erlbaum.

Beck, I. L., McKeown, M. G., & Kucan, L. (2002). *Bringing words to life: Robust vocabulary instruction*. New York: Guilford Press.

Beck, I. L., McKeown, M. G., & Omanson, R. C. (1987). The effects and uses of diverse vocabulary techniques. In M. G. McKeown & M. E. Curtis (Eds.), *The nature of vocabulary acquisition* (pp. 147–163). Hillsdale, NJ: Erlbaum.

Beretta, A., Fiorentino, R., & Poeppel, D. (2005). The effects of homonymy and polysemy on lexical access: An MEG study. *Cognitive Brain Research, 24*, 57–65.

Bolger, D. J., Balass, M., Landen, E., & Perfetti, C. A. (2008). Contextual variation and definitions in learning the meaning of words. *Discourse Processes, 45*(2), 122–159.

Coxhead, A. (2000). A new academic word list. *TESOL Quarterly, 34*(2), 213–238.

Crosson, A. C. (2014, May). *Supporting linguistically diverse students to develop deep, flexible knowledge of words*. Paper presented at the 2014 International Reading Association Annual Conference, New Orleans, LA.

Crosson, A. C., & Lesaux, N. K. (2013). Pinpointing the challenging aspects of academic language: Does knowledge of connectives play a special role in the reading comprehension of English language learners and English-only students? *Journal of Research in Reading, 36*, 241–260.

Crosson, A. C., & McKeown, M. G. (2015, July). *English as a second language (ESL) students' multifaceted knowledge of academic words*. Paper presented at the 22nd annual meeting of the Scientific Studies of Reading, Kona Beach, Hawaii.

Crosson, A. C., & McKeown, M. G. (2016). How effectively do middle school learners use roots to infer the meaning of unfamiliar words? *Cognition and Instruction, 34*, 1–24.

Crosson, A. C., McKeown, M. G., Beck, I. B., & Ward, A. (2012, July). *Developing an assessment to measure depth of knowledge of academic vocabulary.* Paper presented at the 19th annual meeting of the Society for the Scientific Studies of Reading, Montreal, Quebec, Canada.

Crosson, A. C., McKeown, M. G., Beck, I. B., & Ward, A. (2013, April). *An innovative approach to assessing depth of knowledge of academic words.* Paper presented at the annual meeting of the American Educational Research Association, Philadelphia, PA.

Degani, T., Tseng, A. M., & Tokowicz, N. (2014). Together or apart?: Learning of ambiguous words. *Bilingualism: Language and Cognition, 17*(4), 749–765.

Eddington, C. M., & Tokowicz, N. (2015). How meaning similarity influences ambiguous word processing: The current state of the literature. *Psychonomic Bulletin and Review, 22*(1), 13–37.

Finkbeiner, M., Forster, K., Nicol, J., & Nakamura, K. (2004). The role of polysemy in masked semantic and translation priming. *Journal of Memory and Language, 51,* 1–22.

Ford-Connors, E., & Paratore, J. R. (2015). Vocabulary instruction in fifth grade and beyond: Sources of word learning and productive contexts for development. *Review of Educational Research, 85*(1), 50–91.

Frishkoff, G. A., Perfetti, C. A., & Collins-Thompson, K. (2011). Predicting robust vocabulary growth from measures of incremental learning. *Scientific Studies of Reading, 15*(1), 71–91.

Hedrick, W. B., Harmon, J. M., & Linerode, P. M. (2004). Teachers' beliefs and practices of vocabulary instruction with social studies textbooks in grades 4–8. *Reading Horizons, 45*(2), 103–125.

Hoffman, P., & Woollams, A. M. (2015). Opposing effects on semantic diversity in lexical and semantic relatedness decisions. *Journal of Experimental Psychology: Human Perception and Performance, 41*(2), 385–402.

Jiménez, R. T., García, G. E., & Pearson, P. D. (1996). The reading strategies of bilingual Latina/o students who are successful English readers: Opportunities and obstacles. *Reading Research Quarterly, 31,* 90–112.

McKeown, M. G., Crosson, A. C., Beck, I. B., Sandora, C., & Artz, N. (2013, April). *An academic vocabulary intervention to enhance word knowledge and comprehension for middle school students.* Paper presented at the 2013 annual meeting of the American Educational Research Association, San Francisco, CA.

McKeown, M. G., Crosson, A. C., Beck, I. B., Sandora, C., & Artz, N. (2014, April). *Word knowledge and comprehension outcomes for the second year of implementation of an academic vocabulary intervention.* Paper presented at the 2014 annual meeting of the American Educational Research Association, Philadelphia, PA.

McKeown, M. G., Crosson, A. C., Sandora, C., Artz, N., & Beck, I. B. (2013). In the media: Expanding students' experience with academic vocabulary. *The Reading Teacher, 67,* 45–53.

Nagy, W. E., & Scott, J. A. (2000). Vocabulary processes. In M. L. Kamil, P. B. Mosenthal, P. D. Pearson, & R. Barr (Eds.), *Handbook of reading research* (Vol. 3, pp. 69–284). Mahwah, NJ: Erlbaum.

Nation, K., & Snowling, M. (2004). Beyond phonological skills: Broader language skills contribute to the development of reading. *Journal of Research in Reading, 27,* 342–356.

Ouellette, G. P. (2006). What's meaning got to do with it?: The role of vocabulary in word reading and reading comprehension. *Journal of Educational Psychology, 98*(3), 554–566.

Pearson, P. D., Hiebert, E. H., & Kamil, M. L. (2007). Vocabulary assessment: What we know and what we need to learn. *Reading Research Quarterly, 42*(2), 282–296.

Perfetti, C. A. (2007). Reading ability: Lexical quality to comprehension. *Scientific Studies of Reading, 11*(4), 357–383.

Perfetti, C. A., & Hart, L. (2002). The lexical quality hypothesis. In L. Verhoeven, C. Elbro, & P. Reitsma (Eds.), *Precursors of functional literacy* (pp. 189–213). Amsterdam/Philadelphia: Benjamins.

Perfetti, C. A., & Stafura, J. (2014). Word knowledge in a theory of reading comprehension. *Scientific Studies of Reading, 18*(1), 22–37.

Reichle, E. D., & Perfetti, C. A. (2003). Morphology in word identification: A word-experience model that accounts for morpheme frequency effects. *Scientific Studies of Reading, 7*(1), 219–238.

Scarcella, R. (2003). Academic English: A conceptual framework. *Linguistic Minority Research Institute Newsletter.* Santa Barbara: University of California at Santa Barbara.

Schleppegrell, M. J. (2004). *The language of schooling: A functional linguistics perspective.* Mahwah, NJ: Erlbaum.

Scott, J. A., Jamieson-Noel, D., & Asselin, M. (2003). Vocabulary instruction throughout the day in twenty-three Canadian upper-elementary classrooms. *Elementary School Journal, 103*(3), 269–286.

Scott, J. A., Skobel, B. J., & Wells, J. (2008). *The word-conscious classroom.* New York: Scholastic.

Snow, C. E., & Uccelli, P. (2009). The challenge of academic language. In D. R. Olson & N. Torrance (Eds.), *The Cambridge handbook of literacy* (pp. 112–133). Cambridge, UK: Cambridge University Press.

Stahl, S. A., & Fairbanks, M. M. (1986). The effects of vocabulary instruction: A model-based meta-analysis. *Review of Educational Research, 56,* 72–110.

Tokowicz, N., & Kroll, J. F. (2007). Number of meanings and concreteness: Consequences of ambiguity within and across languages. *Language and Cognitive Processes, 22,* 727–779.

WordNet (n.d.). In "WordNet" online resource, Princeton University. Retrieved from *https://wordnet.princeton.edu.*

CHAPTER 6

Using Strategy Instruction to Promote Reading Comprehension and Content Learning

Alison Boardman and Cristin Jensen Lasser

Reading is a complex process for all of us, a task that is becoming increasingly more challenging with the demands and opportunities of the digital age. Reading for understanding can be complicated for emergent bilingual learners when they are able to read phonetically but may struggle to comprehend. The issues only become more pronounced when emergent bilingual youth are in middle school or high school, when language learning intersects with fluctuating motivation, personal interest, familiarity with text topics, and difficult content. Even adults who are competent speakers and readers of English are likely to leaf through the newspaper or a website, choosing to read one article and not another, based on their goals for reading.

In classrooms, students often do not have much choice about what they read. Think about the typical content of a school day through the perspectives of emergent bilingual learners. The day begins with a science class where the topic is, for example, the earth's structure and the content includes *seismic waves, lithosphere, core,* and *crust.* The next class is English language arts (ELA), where the focus is on a story of a young boy, a refugee from Nazi Germany, who goes to work in a logging camp in the northwest of the United States. This text brings in terms related to the boy's Jewish heritage (*kosher*) as well as a host of words related to a logging camp (e.g., *jacks* for loggers). ELA is followed by social studies, where the focus is on the U.S. Constitution with key concepts such as *federalism* and *separation of powers.*

All students need to be exposed to challenging content (Common Core State Standards [CCSS]; National Governors Association Center for Best

Practices & Council of Chief State School Officers [NGA & CCSSO], 2010), but for many emergent bilingual learners, the challenge may be intense, especially in contexts where little support is provided in either their native language or in navigating vocabulary and unfamiliar topics while reading. When we consider how difficult it is to learn rigorous academic content while simultaneously developing the language skills needed to take in this new information and to process and represent understanding (Coleman & Goldenberg, 2012), it should not be surprising when emergent bilingual learners lag behind their grade-level peers in reading performance.

Strategy-based reading models offer promise for increasing metacognition, reading comprehension, and equitable participation. We first provide research on reading strategy instruction to promote comprehension and content learning for adolescent emergent bilingual learners. We then use Collaborative Strategic Reading to illustrate how teachers across content areas can teach before, during, and after reading strategies with scaffolds that allow students of various learning and language backgrounds to work together to learn from challenging texts. Finally, we present recommendations for practice.

Reading Strategy Instruction and Emergent Bilingual Learners

An important shift in instructional expectations resulting in part from the CCSS and the Next Generation Science Standards (NGSS) is the way reading is approached in secondary science, social studies, mathematics, and even language arts classrooms. Teachers are now being asked to approach reading differently, not just as a means to gather content-specific information, but also as an opportunity to teach students the discipline-specific reading skills that are particular to a designated content area. For example, students in social studies need to know how to read texts that represent multiple perspectives, a task requiring much more than "understanding" what the text is about: "Analyze the relationship between a primary and secondary source on the same topic" (CCSS.ELA.RH.6-8.9). And in high school science, NGSS expect students to use texts to evaluate claims: "Evaluate the hypotheses, data, analysis, and conclusions in a science or technical text, verifying the data when possible and corroborating or challenging conclusions with other sources of information" (RST.11–12.8).

Yet, if students are to use texts to think like historians and scientists, they also need foundational reading comprehension skills to help them understand what they read. Often referred to as *general reading strategies,* instruction in this area "seeks to uncover and teach strategies, routines, skills, language, and practices that can be applied universally to content area learning and are by definition generalizable to other domains" (Fagella-Luby, Graner, Deshler, & Drew, 2012, p. 69). *Discipline-specific strategies* build on general reading strategies. One is not more important than the other, but rather, for our adolescent emergent bilingual learners and other students who require support to access grade-level text, the teaching of general reading strategies continues to be important in secondary settings. Armed with the ability to apply general reading strategies in content classrooms, students are ready to combine their understanding of text with the higher-order applications that are required in the examples described above.

The National Reading Panel (2000; August & Shanahan, 2006) and RAND Reading Study Group (2002) have identified several instructional strategies associated with improved outcomes in reading comprehension, especially for emergent bilingual learners: (1) teach students to monitor their comprehension and the procedures for adjusting when difficulties in understanding arise; (2) use cooperative learning practices while implementing comprehension strategies in the context of reading; (3) provide graphic and semantic organizers that assist students in writing or drawing relationships; (4) provide support for questioning strategies that assist students in answering critical questions about the passage, feedback to students regarding their answers to questions about the text, and opportunities for students to ask and answer questions about the text; (5) teach students to write important ideas about what they've read and to summarize these ideas after reading longer passages; (6) combine multiple strategies; (7) embed comprehension instruction within subject-matter learning, such as history or science; (8) provide explicit strategy instruction, particularly for low-achieving students; and (9) build vocabulary knowledge. These are all reading strategies that support understanding, but may not be automatically deployed by students who have difficulty with comprehension. For those students who are reading below grade level and for emergent bilingual learners, teachers can provide explicit instruction in reading strategies, including what the strategy is, how to perform it, when it is used, and why it is important in the reading process. When students are taught the strategies used by strong readers and apply them over time, comprehension improves.

From the expansive National Reading Panel list above, we highlight several recommendations that have been well established to support reading comprehension. Although these are not the only high-yield strategies, we have chosen them because they are accessible to emergent bilingual learners, are widely used in reading strategy interventions, and can be combined in various ways to support comprehension.

Visual Images

One of the most effective ways to tap into emergent bilingual students' background knowledge and experiences related to the content, concepts, and academic vocabulary of a lesson is through the use of visual images (Harvey & Goudvis, 2000; Herrera, 2010; Herrera, Perez, Kavimandan, & Wessels, 2013; Tompkins, 2007; Wormeli, 2005). Visual images provide emergent bilingual learners with comprehensible input that may help them access and articulate prior knowledge of a topic. Teachers can then use students' interpretation of a visual image (provided as a supplement by the teacher or contained within a text) as a way to enhance students' memory and understanding of new concepts, identify misconceptions, and fill in gaps when students are building knowledge about a specific topic.

Explicit Vocabulary Instruction

Another strategy that facilitates reading comprehension and content learning for emergent bilingual students is explicit and interactive vocabulary instruction (Marzano, 2004; Baker et al., 2014) that occurs throughout the week. Keys to vocabulary learning are the selection of target words and the practice opportunities that are provided to students. (See Crosson, Chapter 5, this volume, for a detailed discussion of selecting and teaching vocabulary.) As students develop their understanding of essential vocabulary, they can expand upon and use this knowledge of individual words to comprehend key concepts and ideas.

Student-Generated Questions

Students can ask questions at any phase of the reading process, but teaching and prompting student-driven questions is essential. Many teachers tell us that they have important questions to ask students as a way to scaffold their learning or to check for understanding. Although teachers can certainly ask questions of students, valuing and creating opportunities for students to ask and answer each others' questions is associated with improved reading comprehension. For example, Berkeley, Marshak, Mastropieri, and Scruggs (2011) taught seventh graders, 23% of whom were emergent bilingual learners, a prereading self-questioning strategy they used during reading. Using grade-level social studies materials, emergent bilingual learners improved their comprehension and content learning. Taboada and Buehl (2012) reported similar results when teaching a postreading questioning strategy to students in middle school science classrooms. Both emergent bilingual learners' questioning skills and their comprehension improved after the intervention. Further, in a study of student text-based discussions in collaborative learning groups, Eppolito, Boardman, Lasser, and Wang (2016) found that when students were discussing each others' questions, they reached the highest levels of thinking, as measured by Bloom's Taxonomy (i.e., analyze, evaluate, create)—a level of thinking that is important for language development.

Oral Language Development

Recent reviews of best practices emphasize the importance of incorporating discussions into content teaching as a means to improve reading comprehension (Lawrence, Crosson, Paré-Blagoev, & Snow, 2015; Murphy, Wilkinson, Soter, Hennessey, & Alexander, 2009) and content learning (Baker et al., 2014). Teachers are encouraged to provide daily opportunities for students to talk with one another about the content they are learning.

Cooperative learning is one way to increase the amount and quality of discussion for all learners. Though definitions vary (e.g., Johnson & Johnson, 2008; Kagan & Kagan, 2009; Cooper, 1999), in general, *cooperative learning* refers to using small, student-led, heterogeneous groups to accomplish both group and individual learning goals through negotiated, discussion-based participation. When all students are active and participating members of the learning community, the contribution of each individual is valued by the group and benefits the collective learning. Many models for teaching comprehension strategies utilize some form of cooperative grouping (e.g., Klingner, Vaughn, Boardman, & Swanson, 2012; Pressley et al., 1992; Vaughn et al., 2013).

When done well, cooperative learning supports a variety of learners (Cohen, Lotan, Scarloss, & Arellano, 1999; Cohen & Lotan, 2014; Klingner & Vaughn, 2000; Slavin, 1991; Vaughn et al., 2009) and can enhance student engagement and learning, especially for students whose native language is different from that of their peers and the curriculum. For example, in a study of 37 fifth-grade emergent bilingual learners, Klingner and Vaughn (2000) found that up to 25% of student discourse included students helping one another. Similarly, Antil, Jenkins, Wayne, and Vadasy (1998) reported enhanced academic achievement with cooperative learning. The authors noted the benefit of "kid talk," that is, the use of familiar, modified language to discuss academic concepts. Calderon and colleagues have also identified the benefits of cooperative learning on reading and language development (Calderón, Hertz-Lazarowitz, & Slavin, 1998; Calderón et al., 2005). For emergent bilingual learners, these researchers and others have emphasized the importance of (1) using heterogeneous groups; (2) explicitly teaching social and group work skills; and (3) actively monitoring, facilitating collaboration, and providing feedback on both group work and student learning (Baker et al., 2014; Calderón et al., 1998; Eppolito et al., 2016; Herrell & Jordan, 2015). Further, encouraging students to discuss ideas about text in their primary language (or a combination of English and the primary language) allows them to activate all available resources for comprehension (Ballenger, 1997; Hampton & Rodgriguez, 2001; Kearsey & Turner, 1999).

Connecting Reading and Writing

Integrating reading and writing also supports reading comprehension and content learning (Baker et al., 2014). For example, students can write questions about what they read, respond in writing, or extend their learning with longer writing assignments. Key here is that students combine skills that simultaneously develop language use and support content understanding. By reading, sharing ideas, listening to others, offering feedback, and documenting their emerging understanding and questions in writing, students greatly increase their learning potential (e.g., Saunders & Goldenberg, 1999). Blackorby and colleagues (2014) found that middle school students who received reading strategies instruction that included a writing component made significant gains on the state assessment in writing when compared with students who did not receive the same instruction.

Multicomponent Models

Multicomponent approaches to teaching reading strategies typically include a set of strategies to be applied in a routine before, during, and after reading. These models are recommended in elementary (Shanahan et al., 2010) and upper grades (Edmonds et al., 2009) and are often used with expository text in content-area classrooms. Both teachers and students become familiar with these reading routines, which can incorporate a host of evidence-based practices for teaching and learning.

A recent study provides an example of how reading strategies can be incorporated into content learning. Including 239 teachers from 41 schools in the same state, Herrera, Perez, Kavimandan, Holmes, and Miller (2011) found that teachers in classrooms with emergent bilingual students demonstrated higher-quality instruction when intentional strategy instruction was incorporated into their lessons. These same authors proposed the use of biography-driven instruction (BDI) when working with emergent bilingual learners. "BDI strategies assist teachers in providing all learners with the tools, skills, and knowledge necessary to support their own learning within a grade-level, standards-based, and standards-driven curriculum" (Herrera et al., 2013, p. 2). These BDI strategies include:

- Incorporating students' background knowledge and experiences regarding literacy and language development into subsequent instruction.
- Fostering a learning community in which students are encouraged to share personal connections to the content being taught.
- Being explicit about standards and expectations for cognitively demanding activities while simultaneously monitoring students' progress through these activities with feedback.
- Allowing opportunities for students to articulate thinking and promoting elaboration by "revoicing" student connections (Herrera et al., 2013).

Other multicomponent models that have been used with emergent bilingual learners and native English speakers in heterogeneous general education classrooms include reciprocal teaching (Palincsar & Brown, 1984), Collaborative Strategic Reading (Klingner et al., 2012), transactional strategies instruction (Pressley et al., 1992), and Promoting Acceleration of Comprehension and Content through Text (PACT; Vaughn et al., 2013). Interestingly, recommendations do not lead to using one particular set of strategies over another, and each may be useful in different contexts. In the remainder of this chapter, we focus on Collaborative Strategic Reading (CSR), a representative example of a multicomponent strategic reading approach that incorporates the recommended practices in a comprehensive manner that is appropriately applied in multiple content areas.

Collaborative Strategic Reading

CSR combines cooperative learning (e.g., Johnson & Johnson, 1989) and explicit reading comprehension strategy instruction (e.g., Palinscar & Brown, 1984) to promote content learning, language acquisition, and reading comprehension in diverse classrooms that include emergent bilingual learners (Klingner et al., 2012; Klingner, Vaughn, & Schumm, 1998). Originally designed as an extension to models of reciprocal teaching (Palinscar & Brown, 1984), CSR provides access for emergent bilingual learners in inclusive general education classrooms comprised of students from a wide range of learning and language backgrounds (see Klingner & Vaughn, 1996). From the start, components were incorporated to support emergent bilingual learners, such as activating background knowledge and encouraging students to draw on their native language along with English during text-based discussions. Research on CSR has yielded positive effects for struggling readers, emergent bilingual learners, students with disabilities, as well as average and high-achieving students in upper elementary and middle school classrooms (e.g., Boardman, Klingner, Buckley, Annamma, & Lasser, 2015; Boardman, Buckley, Vaughn, Reutebuch, Roberts, & Klinger, 2016; Klingner, Vaughn, Argüelles, Hughes, & Ahwee, 2004; Klingner & Vaughn, 1999; Vaughn et al., 2011). Over the years, we have worked with practitioners to support the integration of CSR into content classrooms, most frequently at the upper elementary and middle school levels. In the following sections, we use examples drawn from more than 400 classrooms participating in two large-scale studies of CSR across several school districts to explore the components of the model and implications for practice.[1]

CSR is comprised of five reading strategies that are used together while students read content-specific text in student-led cooperative learning groups. Strategy use is supported by a number of classroom resources, including a *learning log* (see Figure 6.1), on which students record their ideas throughout the reading process; *cue cards* (see Figure 6.2) that guide role experts (i.e., Leader, Clunk Expert, Gist Expert, Question Expert) to facilitate the process for each strategy; and student resources that include lists of affixes, fix-up strategies, discussion stems, and question starters. Teachers begin by introducing the strategies one at a time to students, using modeling and guided practice, and then by having students apply strategies in cooperative learning groups. Teachers also provide explicit instruction on cooperative learning practices so students learn to both use strategies and to work together (see *toolkit.csrcolorado.org* for classroom resources and online professional learning modules). In the following sections, we explain the CSR process, emphasizing supports for emergent bilingual learners.

Preview

The Preview portion of CSR, designed to engage students and have them attend to lesson objectives, provides a brief introduction to the content of the text. The teacher first introduces the topic. Next, students brainstorm individually what they already know and then share ideas with a partner or their small group. Teachers might offer students more than one brainstorm prompt as a scaffold. For example, when students in eighth-grade science are learning about the merging of technology and human resources, the following two brainstorm prompts could be provided. *What do you know about the increasing ability of technology?* (requires students to make a

---

[1]The examples described here were drawn from research supported by Grant No. R305A080608 from the Institute of Education Sciences, U.S. Department of Education, and by Grant No. U396B100143 from Investing in Innovation, U.S. Department of Education.

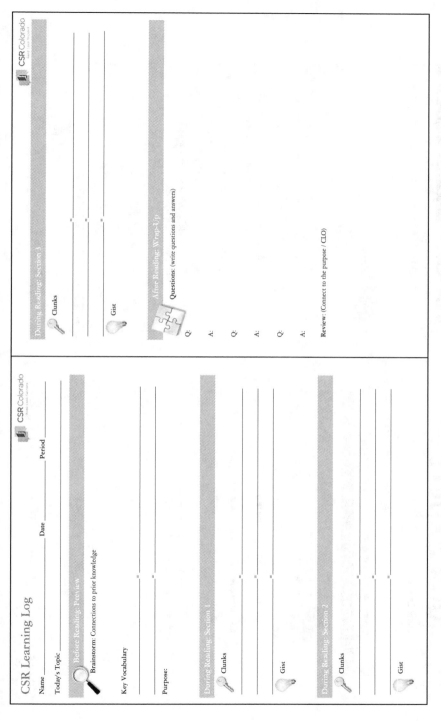

FIGURE 6.1. CSR learning log. From Klingner, Vaughn, Boardman, and Swanson (2012). Reprinted with permission from John Wiley & Sons, Inc.

Clunk Expert

The Clunk Expert will:
- make sure that students write their clunks in their learning logs.
- help students use fix-up strategies to figure out the meaning of unknown words or ideas.
- prompt group to justify their answers using textual evidence.

DURING READING

- Who has a clunk?
- Does anyone know the meaning of the clunk?

IF NO: (no one knows the meaning of the clunk)
- Turn over this card. →

IF YES: (someone knows the meaning of the clunk)
- (Name), please explain what the clunk means.

 Use textual evidence: reread the sentence and make sure the definition makes sense.

 Write the definition in your learning log.

DURING READING

IF NO: *(no one knows the meaning of the clunk) Support your group to use the fix-up strategies to figure out the meaning of your clunks.*

Discussion
[use fix-up strategies]
1. Reread the sentence with the clunk, looking for key ideas.
2. Reread the sentences before and after the clunk, looking for clues.
3. Break the word apart. Identify a prefix, suffix, root word, or smaller word you know.
4. Look for a cognate that makes sense.

 Let's reread the sentence and make sure the definition makes sense.

 Write the definition in your learning log.

[Repeat steps for additional clunks]

FIGURE 6.2. CSR Clunk Expert cue card. From Klingner, Vaughn, Boardman, and Swanson (2012). Reprinted with permission from John Wiley & Sons, Inc.

content connection) or *How can technology make your life easier?* (allows students to make a personal connection to the content). Sharing brainstorming ideas is a low-stakes practice that demonstrates early in the reading process that everyone has something to contribute and that everyone participates. After brainstorming, the teacher might also choose to introduce a few key concepts or vocabulary terms using visual aids, demonstrations, or a short video clip to contextualize meaning. Finally, the teacher sets the purpose for reading. This purpose is closely aligned with the content and/or language objective of the lesson. Overall, these CSR Preview practices should take about 10 minutes to complete.

Click and Clunk

After reading a short section of text (usually ranging from a few paragraphs to about a page in length), students stop to individually identify confusing words or ideas (clunks) and then use fix-up strategies to figure them out (click). Click and Clunk is a metacognitive strategy that cues students to notice when understanding breaks down and to take action to repair the misunderstanding. Students use one or more of the following fix-up strategies: (1) reread the sentence with the clunk and look for key ideas to help you figure out the word; (2) reread the sentences before and after the sentence with the clunk; (3) break the word apart and look for word parts or smaller words you know; and (4) look for a cognate that makes sense.

Consider the following section of text:

> Life history strategies of virtually all taxa vary along a slow–fast gradient. Slow strategies are characterized by slow growth, low total parental effort for fewer offspring but high effort per offspring. Fast strategies are characterized by the opposite. (Martin, 2015, p. 659)

After the first sentence, you might wonder what the author means by a "slow–fast gradient." Rereading the sentences around the clunk might help, because the slow–fast aspect of life history strategies are explained (fix-up strategy #2), as will making connections to the word *grade* as it is used in relation to roads (e.g., the grade on a road varies). This usage must refer to variation that occurs along a continuum from slow to fast (fix-up strategy #3). In Spanish, some people might make a connection to the term *gradiente* (fix-up strategy #4). As one of the sixth-grade science teachers from our study noted regarding the use of fix-up strategies among students in mixed-language groups:

> "Just allowing them to use different types of language support brings that in too for language learners. But then also students who aren't

language learners, they can be in a group with someone who is a language learner and knows those cognates, and a native-English speaker could learn more from that bilingual student as well" (interview, November 2013).

Fix-up strategies, along with the support of group members, help students unpack difficult words and ideas, as well as create a routine in which engaged readers use resources when they are confused by something they read.

Get the Gist

After students complete the Click and Clunk strategy, they move on to generating the main idea or *gist* of the section. They do so by first identifying the most important "who" or "what" that the section discusses. Then students identify the most important information, or key ideas, about the "who" or "what." Students next write their own gist statement in a complete sentence of about 10 words. Finally, students share their gist sentence with group-mates and provide each other with feedback. The Gist Expert uses his or her cue card (see Figure 6.1 for a sample cue card) to guide students through the steps of writing and discussing gist statements (an important aspect of this strategy because the cue card scaffolds the process by breaking down the steps), reminding students when to work individually and when to work together, and providing discussion frames that support high-quality dialogue (e.g., "How are our gists similar and different?"; "My gist is similar to _____'s because. . . . "). Students then read the next section of text and repeat the Click and Clunk and Get the Gist processes.

General Questions

In CSR, students generate questions at different levels after reading the entire text. They write questions that are factual (i.e., the question and the answer are found in one place in the text) and questions that require synthesis, inferencing, or making connections. There is an emphasis on writing important questions that help them understand and remember the text— the types of questions a teacher might put on a quiz. Some teachers use Raphael's (1986) Question–Answer Relationships as a question generation guide, whereas others apply different questioning models or encourage students to ask questions using a range of question words (*who, what, when, where,* and *why*). Question starters support emergent bilingual learners by providing the form for the question writing in English as well as other languages (e.g., "What are some of the reasons for _____?"; "*¿Cuáles* *son algunas de las razones por las cual* _____?"). We have often observed students referring to the Spanish (or other language) question starters before writing questions in English. Students ask and answer each others' questions in their small groups or may move to other groups to ask, answer, and discuss questions.

Review

The final step in CSR is Review. Students first write a few sentences summarizing the most important information from the passage. They then share their writing with their small group, providing evidence for why their review statement includes the most important information. Once students have reviewed their key ideas, the teacher brings students back together for a whole-class review that might include focusing on discipline-specific literacy strategies (e.g., evaluating the author's claims in science), making connections to big ideas or learning objectives, or extending learning with additional activities such as a lab in science or an essay comparing and contrasting viewpoints in ELA.

Once students have learned the CSR strategies, they typically apply them with a content-focused text during one or more class periods weekly. If implementation is schoolwide, students might use CSR once a week in their social studies, science, and language arts classrooms. Regardless, teachers are integral to the successful application of CSR strategies because they facilitate individual and group learning and collaboration in small groups. In addition, teachers decide when to fine-tune strategy use with mini lessons for the whole class or small groups of students who may need additional support. Above all, teachers are encouraged to *use* CSR to teach their content rather than *doing* CSR simply to practice reading. Although the distinction may seem nuanced, research supports a focus on comprehension of important content that begins with selecting high-quality texts that are aligned with the curriculum, and promoting use of strategies and peers as a means to learn new and essential grade-level material.

Recommendations for Teachers and Schools

Over the years, we have worked closely with teachers, coaches, administrators, and school district personnel to implement CSR in ways that are beneficial to students and feasible for teachers. Although the following recommendations are not exhaustive, they do represent some key lessons learned. Please also see Chapter 7 (this volume) in which Ossa Parra and her colleagues offer important recommendations related to facilitating discussions in student-led groups; the facilitation of high-quality discussions is an essential component of CSR instruction.

Maintain a Focus on Reading Specific to the Content Area

Content-area teachers are responsible for teaching content that addresses their curriculum standards. For this reason, there can be tension when there is a perception that reading and language development take priority over the essence of the course material. For example, consider the NGSS for middle school around engaging in argument based on evidence: "Standard MS-ESS3-4: Construct an argument supported by evidence for how increases in human population and per-capita consumption of natural resources impact Earth's systems." CSR can be a useful model to support students in reaching this standard. Teachers might involve students in a series of CSR lessons to help them gather evidence from texts that focus on human consumption of natural resources that will be used to construct an argument. (For more information on teaching students to write arguments, see Brisk, Kaveh, Scialoia, & Timothy, Chapter 8, this volume.) Through CSR, they will apply reading strategies, check their understanding with peers, and begin to draw conclusions—a process that supports improved reading outcomes and increased content learning.

Content-area teachers can support students in their efforts to attain these standards and develop reading comprehension using CSR in several ways. In a study analyzing student discussions that included emergent bilingual learners and nonemergent bilingual learners in heterogeneous middle school science and social studies classrooms, Eppolito and colleagues (2016) found that student participation was more equitable (i.e., emergent bilingual learners participated similarly to nonemergent bilingual learners) and that the quality of discussion in student-led groups was higher (e.g., more discussion of higher-level content-related ideas) when teachers focused on the content of the text and used discipline-specific academic language coupled with modeling on how to talk about academic content. We caution against providing feedback that focuses solely on the process of CSR at the expense of attending to content learning. Additionally, we encourage practitioners to promote collaboration among students rather than positioning themselves as the authority that knows all of the correct answers. For example, if a student says, "We don't know what this section is about," join the conversation with the small group of students, using the CSR strategies as an entry point, rather than telling students what they need to know. A teacher might respond by saying, "Gist Expert, where is the group stuck?" and then proceed by working through the gist strategy alongside students to see where understanding is breaking down and to facilitate a resolution.

Integrate Reading Strategies into the Curriculum

Although many studies have examined the impact of reading comprehension models on student outcomes, these practices are often tested by inserting reading comprehension instruction into a teacher's weekly curriculum (e.g., Thames et al., 2008; Vaughn et al., 2011). Yet even models like CSR that are known to support comprehension and content learning as part of content-area instruction are often treated as a supplement or add-on (e.g., using a reading on how mountains are formed during a unit on the Bill of Rights), which may hinder the transfer of skills and the sustainability of a practice. If teachers feel that reading is not related to content understanding, they are unlikely to promote the practice or to continue it over time. It is also difficult for students to find relevance from a text that is disconnected from the content.

We recently observed 15 middle school science, social studies, and language arts teachers throughout a week of instruction to understand the extent to which they integrated CSR into their instruction (Boardman, Moore, Scmidt, & Scornavacco, 2016). Findings indicated that high-integration teachers embedded CSR lessons into their curriculum and reinforced CSR strategy use throughout the week. These teachers discussed student growth as a result of CSR and the ways that CSR fit into their teaching. For example, one teacher began each week with a CSR lesson to "set the tone" for the week of instruction (interview, May 2015). The reading she selected for her CSR lesson launched the topic for the week (e.g., analyzing the role of formal vs. informal education) and was referenced throughout each lesson we observed. Another common theme among high-integration teachers was the use of portions of CSR daily to reinforce students' reading, writing, and speaking skills. For instance, one teacher had students working in collaborative groups daily, writing main-idea statements and generating questions and answers from their readings at the end of each lesson. The importance of CSR for student learning and for teaching their curriculum was evident for all of these teachers who had found ways to seamlessly integrate CSR and reading strategies into their content-area classes.

Use Cross-Content School Models to Increase Teacher Collaboration

When teachers in different content areas use a common instructional model, they are able to collaborate and plan in new and different ways. In one urban district whose students were comprised of 35% emergent bilingual learners, social studies, science, and language arts teachers implemented CSR weekly with students, focusing on using the same reading strategies to access discipline-specific texts. Collaboration occurred in various ways, from more standard team planning (e.g., science teachers working together to select appropriate texts and thoughtfully integrate CSR into the curriculum) to larger professional learning communities and data teams. For example, in one school, teachers selected main-idea writing as a schoolwide student learning goal. Teachers across content areas met monthly to discuss student progress in main-idea generation. They brought student CSR work samples and discussed key areas of instruction, such as how to provide feedback to students during small-group work and on their written products. As one teacher noted:

"CSR gave an entry point for science and social studies teachers, especially into data teams because our data teams are based on literacy, so by having teachers trained in CSR, we were more able to think about integrating more literacy strategies into our classroom and to be mindful of that data" (interview, March 2015).

Another teacher in the same school commented:

"One of the goals that we set at the beginning of the year for CSR for us at [school name] is common language and common strategies. It's something that has become very important to us over the last couple of years, making sure that as kids go from classroom to classroom, no matter what the content is, that they are hearing the same language, especially around Gists and Clunks" (interview, March 2015).

And as noted by a teacher in another school, "CSR supports everything in the building . . . and because it moves [from] content area [to] content area and grade to grade. . . . There's just this thread that strengthens the culture of the building" (interview, May 2015). In addition to the benefits of using a schoolwide model for reading comprehension, teachers have also learned that planning is important. For example, because it is an intensive reading model that uses a predictable structure and requires students to maintain a high level of engagement and focus, it can be demanding to use CSR in its entirety in different subject areas on the same days. For this reason, teachers in some schools have chosen to designate a "CSR day" (e.g., science on Tuesdays, social studies on Thursdays).

For emergent bilingual learners in particular, common routines such as these can decrease the cognitive load of figuring out what is happening in each individual class and allow students to devote resources to the learning of the day. Further, practicing similar reading strategies across classes provides important rehearsal time for developing listening, speaking, reading, and writing skills that can increase learning outcomes.

Conclusion

Emergent bilingual learners have always needed access to rigorous content and learning activities that develop their age-appropriate thinking and learning capacity and increase their language learning. Given that the new standards emphasize the importance of providing students with rigorous reading opportunities, the demands are raised for teachers and students alike. Models such as CSR hold promise for teaching students reading strategies that can transfer across content areas and become available to them in daily life. When teachers in different disciplines work together to integrate CSR meaningfully into their curricula, they share a common language that goes beyond lesson planning to focus on improving the achievement and opportunities for all students, regardless of where they are in their language or learning trajectories.

REFERENCES

Antil, L. R., Jenkins, J. R., Wayne, S. K., & Vadasy, P. F. (1998). Cooperative learning: Prevalence, conceptualizations, and the relation between research and practice. *American Educational Research Journal, 35*(3), 419–454.

August, D., & Shanahan, T. (2006). *Executive summary: Developing literacy in second-language learners: Report of the National Literacy Panel on language-minority children and youth.* Mahwah, NJ: Erlbaum.

Baker, S., Lesaux, N., Jayanthi, M., Dimino, J., Proctor, C. P., Morris, J., et al. (2014). *Teaching academic content and literacy to English learners in elementary and middle school* (NCEE 2014-4012). Washington, DC: National Center for Education Evaluation and Regional Assistance.

Ballenger, C. (1997). Social identities, moral narratives, scientific argumentation: Science talk in a bilingual classroom. *Language and Education, 11*(1), 1–14.

Berkeley, S., Marshak, L., Mastropieri, M. A., & Scruggs, T. E. (2011). Improving student comprehension of social studies text: A self-questioning strategy for inclusive middle school classes. *Remedial and Special Education, 32*(2), 105–113.

Blackorby, J., Lenz, K., Campbell, A., Wei, X., Greene, S., Padilla, C., et al. (2014). *Denver Public Schools CSR Colorado: Evaluation of the 2012–13 school year.* Menlo Park, CA: SRI.

Boardman, A. G., Buckley, P., Vaughn, S., Reutebuch, C. K., Roberts, G., & Klingner, J. K. (2016). Collaborative strategic reading for students with learning disabilities in upper elementary classrooms. *Exceptional Children,* 1–19.

Boardman, A. G., Klingner, J. K., Buckley, P., Annamma, S., & Lasser, C. J. (2015). The efficacy of Collaborative Strategic Reading in middle school science and social studies classes. *Reading and Writing: An Interdisciplinary Journal, 28*(9), 1257–1283.

Boardman, A. G., Moore, B., Schmidt, K., & Scornavacco, K. (2016, April).

Sustainable practice: Integrating reading comprehension instruction into middle school content teaching. Presented at the American Educational Research Association annual meeting, Washington, DC.

Calderón, M., August, D., Slavin, R., Duran, D., Madden, N., & Cheung, A. (2005). Bringing words to life in classrooms with English-language learners. In E. H. Hiebert & M. L. Kamil (Eds.), *Teaching and learning vocabulary: Bringing research to practice* (pp. 115–136). Mahwah, NJ: Erlbaum.

Calderón, M., Hertz-Lazarowitz, R., & Slavin, R. (1998). Effects of bilingual cooperative integrated reading and composition on students making the transition from Spanish to English reading. *Elementary School Journal, 99*(2), 153–165.

Cohen, E. G., & Lotan, R. A. (2014). *Designing groupwork: Strategies for the heterogeneous classroom* (3rd ed.). New York: Teachers College Press.

Cohen, E. G., Lotan, R. A., Scarloss, B. A., & Arellano, A. R. (1999). Complex instruction: Equity in cooperative learning classrooms. *Theory Into Practice, 38*(2), 80–86.

Coleman, R., & Goldenberg, C. (2012, February). The Common Core challenge for English language learners. *Principal Leadership*, pp. 46–51.

Cooper, R. (1999). Improving intergroup relations: Lessons learned from cooperative learning programs. *Journal of Social Issues, 55*(4), 647–663.

Edmonds, M. S., Vaughn, S., Wexler, J., Reutebuech, C., Cable, A., Tackett, K. K., et al. (2009). A synthesis of reading interventions and effects on reading comprehension outcomes for older struggling readers. *Review of Educational Research, 79*(1), 262–300.

Eppolito, A., Boardman, A. G., Lasser, C. J., & Wang, C. (2016). *Let's give them something to talk about: English learners' participation and academic language use in science and social studies.* Manuscript submitted for review.

Faggella-Luby, M. N., Graner, P. S., Deshler, D. D., & Drew, S. V. (2012). Building a house on sand: Why disciplinary literacy is not sufficient to replace general strategies for adolescent learners who struggle. *Topics in Language Disorders, 32*(1), 69–84.

Hampton, E., & Rodriguez, R. (2001). Inquiry science in bilingual classrooms. *Bilingual Research Journal, 25*(4), 461–478.

Harvey, S., & Goudvis, A. (2000). *Strategies that work: Teaching comprehension to enhance learning.* York, ME: Stenhouse.

Herrell, A. L., & Jordan, M. L. (2015). *50 strategies for teaching English language learners.* New York: Pearson.

Herrera, S. G. (2010). *Biography-driven culturally responsive teaching.* New York: Teachers College Press.

Herrera, S. G., Perez, D., Kavimandan, S., Holmes, M., & Miller, S. (2011, April). *Beyond reductionism and quick fixes: Quantitatively measuring effective pedagogy in the instruction of culturally and linguistically diverse students.* Paper presented at the annual conference of the American Educational Research Association, New Orleans, LA.

Herrera, S. G., Perez, D. R., Kavimandan, S. K., & Wessels, S. (2013). *Accelerating literacy for diverse learners: Strategies for the Common Core classroom, K–8.* New York: Teachers College Press.

Johnson, D. W., & Johnson, R. T. (1989). Cooperative learning: What special educators need to know. *The Pointer, 33*, 5–10.

Johnson, D. W., & Johnson, R. T. (2008). *Cooperation in the classroom* (8th ed.). Edina, MN: Interaction Book.

Kagan, S., & Kagan, M. (2009). *Kagan cooperative learning.* San Clemente, CA: Kagan.

Klingner, J. K., & Vaughn, S. (1996). Reciprocal teaching of reading comprehension strategies for students with learning disabilities who use English as a second language. *Elementary School Journal, 96*(3), 275–293.

Klingner, J. K., & Vaughn, S. (1999). Promoting reading comprehension, content learning, and English acquisition though Collaborative Strategic Reading (CSR). *The Reading Teacher, 52*, 738–747.

Klingner, J. K., & Vaughn, S. (2000). The helping behaviors of fifth graders while using Collaborative Strategic Reading during ESL content classes. *TESOL Quarterly, 34*, 69–98.

Klingner, J. K., Vaughn, S., Argüelles, M. E., Hughes, M. T., & Ahwee, S. (2004). Collaborative Strategic Reading: "Real world" lessons from classroom teachers. *Remedial and Special Education, 25*, 291–302.

Klingner, J. K., Vaughn, S., Boardman, A., & Swanson, E. (2012). *Now we get it!: Boosting comprehension with Collaborative Strategic Reading.* New York: Wiley.

Klingner, J. K., Vaughn, S., & Schumm, J. S. (1998). Collaborative Strategic Reading during social studies in heterogeneous fourth-grade classrooms. *Elementary School Journal, 99*, 3–22.

Lawrence, J. F., Crosson, A. C., Paré-Blagoev, E. J., & Snow, C. E. (2015). Word generation randomized trial discussion mediates the impact of program treatment on academic word learning. *American Educational Research Journal.*

Martin, T. E. (2015). Age-related mortality explains life history strategies of tropical and temperate songbirds. *Science, 349*, 966–970.

Marzano, R. J. (2004). The developing vision of vocabulary instruction. In J. F. Baumann & E. J. Kame'enui (Eds.), *Vocabulary instruction: Research to Practice* (pp. 100–117). New York: Guilford Press.

Murphy, P. K., Wilkinson, I. A., Soter, A. O., Hennessey, M. N., & Alexander, J. F. (2009). Examining the effects of classroom discussion on students' comprehension of text: A meta-analysis. *Journal of Educational Psychology, 101*(3), 740–764.

National Governors Association Center for Best Practices & Council of Chief State School Officers. (2010). *Common Core State Standards for English language arts and literacy in history/social studies, science, and technical subjects.* Washington, DC: Authors.

National Reading Panel. (2000). *Report of the National Reading Panel: Teaching children to read.* Reports of the subgroups (NIH Publication No. 00-4754). Washington, DC: U.S. Government Printing Office.

Palinscar, A. S., & Brown, A. L. (1984). Reciprocal teaching of comprehension-fostering and comprehension-monitoring activities. *Cognition and Instruction, 1*(2), 117–175.

Pressley, M., El-Dinary, P. B., Gaskins, I., Schuder, T., Bergman, J. L., Almasi, J., et al. (1992). Beyond direct explanation: Transactional instruction of reading comprehension strategies. *Elementary School Journal, 92*(5), 513–555.

RAND Reading Study Group. (2002). Reading for understanding: Towards an R&D program in reading comprehension. Retrieved October 1, 2012, from *www.rand.org/multi/achievementforall/reading/readreport.html*.

Raphael, T. E. (1986). Teaching question answer relationships, revisited. *The Reading Teacher, 39*(6), 516–522.

Saunders, W. M., & Goldenberg, C. (1999). The effects of instructional conversations and literature logs on limited- and fluent-English-proficient students' story comprehension and thematic understanding. *Elementary School Journal, 99*, 277–301.

Shanahan, T., Callison, K., Carriere, C., Duke, N. K., Pearson, P. D., Schatschneider, C., et al. (2010). *Improving reading comprehension in kindergarten through 3rd grade: A practice guide* (NCEE 2010-4038). Washington, DC: National Center for Education Evaluation and Regional Assistance.

Slavin, R. E. (1991). Synthesis of research of cooperative learning. *Educational Leadership, 48*(5), 71–82.

Taboada, A., & Buehl, M. M. (2012). Teachers' conceptions of reading comprehension and motivation to read. *Teachers and Teaching, 18*(1), 101–122.

Thames, D. G., Reeves, C., Kazelskis, R., York, K., Boling, C., Newell, K., et al. (2008). Reading comprehension: Effects of individualized, integrated language arts as a reading approach with struggling readers. *Reading Psychology, 29*(1), 86–115.

Tompkins, G. E. (2007). *Teaching writing: Balancing process and product* (5th ed.). Columbus, OH: Merrill.

Vaughn, S., Klingner, J., Swanson, E. A., Boardman, A. G., Roberts, G., Mohammed, S., et al. (2011). Efficacy of Collaborative Strategic Reading with middle school students. *American Educational Research Journal, 48*, 938–964.

Vaughn, S., Martinez, L. R., Linan-Thompson, S., Reutebuech, C. K., Carlson, C. D., & Francis, D. J. (2009). Enhancing social studies vocabulary and comprehension for seventh-grade English language learners: Findings from two experimental studies. *Journal of Research on Educational Effectiveness, 2*(4), 297–324.

Vaughn, S., Swanson, E. A., Roberts, G., Wanzek, J., Stillman-Spisak, S. J., Solis, M., et al. (2013). Improving reading comprehension and social studies knowledge in middle school. *Reading Research Quarterly, 48*(1), 77–93.

Wormeli, R. (2005). *Summarization in any subject: 50 techniques to improve student learning*. Alexandria, VA: Association for Supervision and Curriculum Development.

Worthy, J., Moorman, M., & Turner, M. (1999). What Johnny likes to read is hard to find in school. *Reading Research Quarterly, 34*(1), 12–27.

CHAPTER 7

Dialogic Reasoning

Supporting Emergent Bilingual Students' Language and Literacy Development

Marcela Ossa Parra, Christopher J. Wagner, C. Patrick Proctor, Christine M. Leighton, Dana A. Robertson, Jeanne R. Paratore, and Evelyn Ford-Connors

A small group of students in Ms. Grant's third-grade classroom is reading the book *Old Cricket* by Lisa Wheeler and illustrated by Ponder Goembel (2003). The book tells the story of a cricket that avoids doing work by pretending to have a number of all-too-convenient injuries. He explains that he has pains in his neck, back, and head to excuse himself from almost any work. When he meets a hungry crow, he does everything he can to avoid getting eaten, and, in the process, incurs the very injuries he had pretended to have. After the class reads and develops a common understanding of the text, Ms. Grant creates small groups of four to six students and asks them to discuss the following question: "Do you think Old Cricket was clever or foolish?" The following is an excerpt from one of these discussion groups.

CARLOS: I think he's clever, because he tricked all the animals and outsmarted the crow.

JENNY: Well, I disagree with Carlos. I think he's foolish, because he tricked his cousin that he had a cramp and a cough and his back hurt to not work.

CARLOS: So, that's why he's clever, because he tricked them by saying that he had a cramp and a cough.

SHAWN: I agree with Carlos that he is clever, 'cause he tricked some of the animals to give him food, and at the end of the story he made the crow choke.

119

LISA: I think he's foolish, because if he had worked and built his house, the crow would not have chased him.

ALMA: I think he was foolish, because he pretended to be hurt.

CARLOS: Alma, I disagree with you, because if he were foolish, he would have gotten eaten up by the crow right off the bat. He was not foolish, he was clever—that's why he ran away from the crow, and that's when he really broke his back. And that's when he was smart and clever and went to the doctor. If he were foolish, he wouldn't have gotten all the food, like Shawn said, and he wouldn't have tricked all the animals, he wouldn't have gotten away from the bird. It's all these stuff that makes him clever.

MS. GRANT: You know what, though? I'm just going to go against your view for a second. He ended up getting hurt. Don't you find that ironic? You know, he pretended he was hurt all along, and then he ended up really hurting himself. That's not that clever, is it? I don't know. What do you think?

JENNY: Yeah, I agree with Carlos now. He's clever because he threw food at the crow to make him choke, and not come after him and kill him.

In this example, the students took charge of the conversation, spoke freely to one another, and built on each others' ideas. They shared their positions on the question and supported their ideas with specific details from the text. Altogether, the students spoke meaningfully about the text, listened to each other talk, and managed a complex social activity with little adult support.

This is the essence of a small-group discussion framework we call Dialogic Reasoning (DR). The DR framework presented here emerges from our ongoing work with PreK–5 teachers in multilingual classrooms comprised of English monolingual and emergent bilingual students from a variety of home language backgrounds. Over the course of our 4-plus years of work, we are finding that DR, when done well, provides an instructional context for emergent bilingual students to (1) develop and deepen their understandings of text; (2) engage in thoughtful, argumentative, and productive dialogue with one another; and (3) develop oral and written language proficiency. We offer this chapter as an initial implementation guide for teachers who want to get started with small-group discussions in their classrooms.

The Role of Talk in Language and Literacy Learning

It is important for students to talk about academic topics with each other and their teachers. Too often, we see vertical discourse patterns in classrooms in which the teacher dominates classroom talk, with popcorn-like instances of individual students making single, one- to three-word contributions to a whole-group discussion (Silverman et al., 2014). Instruction needs to include more horizontal discourse patterns, where classroom talk is better distributed across teachers and students. The Common Core State Standards (CCSS) provide a good rationale for such a move. As Hakuta and Santos (2013) concluded, the CCSS "raise the bar for learning, call for increased language capacities in combination with increased content sophistication, and call for a high level of discourse in classrooms across subject areas" (p. 451).

This focus on language and text in the CCSS is what drove us toward small-group instructional approaches in our professional development work. The DR framework enables teachers to shift from traditional participation structures in which their talk and ideas predominate, to these more horizontal structures where students have opportunities to build knowledge with their peers. In this sense, DR promotes engagement in meaningful talk in which students with varying levels of English language proficiency are able to practice and use language in authentic contexts with complex texts. Below we present three interrelated factors that support the need to focus on talk in multilingual classrooms: (1) using talk to support reasoning; (2) promoting second-language acquisition through authentic communication; and (3) forging links between language development and literacy outcomes.

Using Talk to Support Reasoning

Because literacy practices involve not only ways of reading and writing, but ways of speaking, thinking, and interacting with texts and other individuals, the contexts in which literacy is used and learned lead to particular ways of thinking and doing (Gee, 2012; Vygotsky, 1978). Talk is a key social and cognitive tool that shapes reasoning and meaning making during different literacy practices, such as small-group, text-based discussions (Mercer, Wegerif, & Dawes, 1999; Resnick, Salmon, Zeitz, Wathen, & Holowchak, 1993; Wells, 2007; Wilkinson, Soter, & Murphy, 2010). It is through talk that teachers and their students are able to engage in what Mercer (2000) called "interthinking," in which they combine their cognitive resources to achieve particular purposes. *Interthinking* during DR is a reciprocal process in which positions are advanced and critically assessed by other students. Students' individual thought processes are enhanced as they participate in social practices in which their arguments are examined and contested (Kuhn, 2015). For example, during the DR discussion that opened this chapter, students considered different evidence from the text to determine if Old Cricket was clever or lazy, and this led Jenny to reconsider her original stance.

During DR discussions students are exposed to, and practice, the norms underlying critical reasoning (Kuhn, Zillmer, Crowell, & Zabala, 2013; Reznitskaya, Kuo, Clark, Miller, Jadallah, et al., 2009). Students are positioned as valuable conversational partners, whose interpretations and judgments about texts are encouraged and carefully considered. Participation in these social practices supports engagement in complex thinking about texts, and also socializes students as appreciated members of a learning community with important knowledge and perspectives.

Second-Language Acquisition through Purposeful and Authentic Communication

As articulated above, collaborative discussions are typically grounded in sociocultural perspectives on thought and social practice. For emergent bilingual learners, this perspective links with much second-language acquisition research in which language is viewed as a complex communicative system designed to achieve meaningful interaction. In a sociocultural view, language acquisition occurs through participation in activities in which learners have opportunities to use language meaningfully to build understanding (Valdés, 2012). Small-group discussions that are thoughtfully facilitated emphasize second-language acquisition as situated in authentic communication and pragmatic competence, rather than on pronunciation and grammatical competence (Valdés, Capitelli, & Alvarez, 2011).

This perspective is consistent with Krashen's (1984) observations that emergent bilingual learners must have exposure to *comprehensible input* that stretches them beyond their current levels of proficiency. Done well, small-group discussions that include both monolingual and bilingual peers provide emergent bilingual learners with exposure to English monolingual models within a well-specified dialogic space. Relatedly, well-facilitated discussions provide emergent bilingual learners not just with the opportunity to hear input that is comprehensible, but also the opportunity to produce output that is comprehensible (Swain & Lapkin, 1995). In other words, small-group discussions are a valuable context in which to promote second-language acquisition because they provide emergent bilingual learners with opportunities to participate in authentic conversations in which they listen to different language models and express their own ideas in a context where they have the support to make themselves understood.

Some have argued that comprehensible output does not serve as an adequate driver of language acquisition due to the *scarcity hypothesis* (Krashen, 1994), which states that student output is simply too minimal to achieve critical linguistic mass to drive acquisition. However, this hypothesis operates under a traditional, teacher-driven notion of instruction. If we can devise ways in which small-group discussions can become integral and consistent instructional routines, we remove the scarcity of student language output and combine comprehensible input and output as symbiotic drivers of language acquisition.

Oral Language Proficiency Supports Reading Comprehension

Second-language acquisition applies to emergent bilingual learners, but DR, construed as a driver of language proficiency generally, becomes an effective tool for native English speakers as well. And, if we accept the potential of collaborative discussions to promote language proficiency, we might then extend the relevance of the approach to its potential effects on reading outcomes. It has been clearly documented, over decades now, that reading comprehension is strongly associated with oral language proficiency for monolingual and bilingual populations alike (Hoover & Gough, 1990; Proctor, August, Carlo, & Snow, 2006). Indeed, more recent research has also begun to articulate the possibility that language proficiency is even more important for emergent bilingual learners than for their monolingual counterparts (Limbird, Maluch, Rjosk, Stanat, & Merkens, 2014), and that the importance of language for reading emerges earlier in reading development than was previously believed (Kieffer & Vukovic, 2013).

The type of oral language promoted by small-group discussions is important here. We are not talking about identifying a doorknob or asking how to get to the cafeteria. These are important dimensions of learning English, and should be part of any solid English-as-a-second-language curriculum. For the purposes of this chapter and this approach, however, we are talking about meaningful, text-based interactions that support exposure to, and practice with, language use in engaging contexts (Cheung & Slavin, 2012; Zhang, Anderson, & Nguyen-Janiel, 2013).

Given the above, the argument for small-group discussions, designed with emergent bilingual learners' participation at the forefront, is as follows. If we leverage small-group, social thinking in the service of second-language acquisition and development, we are also developing students' language proficiency to promote reading comprehension. We came to this realization through our ongoing work on DR with a team of PreK–5 elementary teachers in a multilingual school in Boston, Massachusetts. Although other models of text-based talk for elementary classrooms do exist (see Table 7.1 for an overview), few if any models have been specifically designed to support the learning needs of emergent bilingual learners. In the following section, we explain the DR model as it has evolved in this school-based setting by briefly describing the nature of our school–university partnership—Enhancing Literacy Instruction through Collaboration and Interactive Technology (ELICIT)—followed by a DR implementation primer.

TABLE 7.1. Models of Small-Group Discussion

Type	Stance	Control	Purpose
Book Club (Raphael & McMahon, 1994)	Aesthetic	Students	Give students time to share thoughts, ask each other questions, and make personal connections with texts and peers.
Collaborative Reasoning (Chinn, Anderson, & Waggoner, 2001)	Critical–analytic	Students	Promote critical reading and thinking and engage students in text by taking and defending a position about a text.
Grand Conversations (Eeds & Wells, 1989)	Aesthetic	Teacher	Help students construct meaning from shared readings by showing students how to build off of the thinking of others.
Instructional Conversations (Tharp & Gallimore, 1988)	Efferent and aesthetic	Teacher	Foster comprehension by asking questions that prompt students to analyze text, make inferences and predictions, and think critically.
Junior Great Books (Junior Great Books, 1992)	Efferent	Teacher	Foster comprehension and interpretation of text.
Literature Circles (Short & Pierce, 1998)	Aesthetic and critical–analytic	Students	Encourage students to support their own ideas, listen to others, and consider different perspectives.
Quality Talk (Wilkinson, Soter, & Murphy, 2010)	Critical–analytic	Shared	Foster high-level comprehension of literary text using authentic questions and prompt students to uptake, elaborate, and link each others' ideas.
Questioning the Author (Beck, McKeown, Sandora, Kucan, & Worthy, 1996)	Critical–analytic	Teacher	Promote improved understanding and a critical disposition toward texts through engaging students in asking questions about the author's choices.

Note. An aesthetic stance draws on personal experiences to inform discussions; a critical–analytic stance draws on interpretation of evidence from the text to inform discussions; an efferent stance draws factual details from text to inform text discussion.

The ELICIT Collaborative

ELICIT is an ongoing exploration of teachers' literacy practices with a specific focus on articulating and expanding classroom applications of DR. These explorations are design-based and iterative (Reinking & Bradley, 2008; see also O'Hara, Pritchard, & Zwiers, Chapter 11, this volume) in which monthly face-to-face meetings lead to decisions about instructional practices, which are then video-recorded by teachers for group reflection. Recorded instructional practices are uploaded to a secure website and are co-viewed by researchers and teachers, and reflection on these videos forms the basis for subsequent face-to-face meetings. This repeated cycle of reflection and revision of instructional practices is the basis of our ongoing work and practice with DR. See Figure 7.1.

During the first year of this process, we identified Collaborative Reasoning (Chinn, Anderson, & Waggoner, 2001; see Table 7.1) as a starting point for implementing small-group discussions. At the time, the approach was novel to our group, and as such, the initial work with this model involved learning to design and implement lessons. As our design-based work continued, it became clear that teachers needed to modify the model to meet various classroom realities, including unique instructional contexts, teaching styles, grade levels, and the language and learning needs of the high number of emergent bilingual students in these classrooms. These real-world demands resulted in our shifting away from some traditional approaches linked with Collaborative Reasoning in the service of creating a more flexible, teacher-adapted model for classroom talk.

Changes were made to integrate discussions into both narrative and informational genres and across longer instructional units. The Collaborative Reasoning model was also adapted to meet the developmental needs of children across the elementary grades from PreK through grade

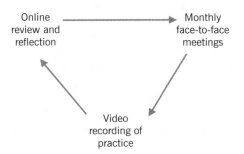

FIGURE 7.1. Design-based ELICIT model.

5 (Collaborative Reasoning is typically undertaken with upper elementary school-age children). Finally, our work was structured around understanding not only the developmental nuances of participating in text-based talk, but also the linguistic demands and affordances the approach provided for emergent bilinguals. We specifically focused on the participation practices of emergent bilingual children and considered how text and question selection, group structures, and teacher facilitation affected the Collaborative Reasoning approach. In light of these shifts in how the model was adapted over time, we renamed the approach *Dialogic Reasoning* to avoid confusion with the more structured components of Collaborative Reasoning.

An Overview of DR

Figure 7.2 illustrates the goals and core competencies of the DR model. DR begins by asking students to take a critical stance when engaging with texts. Students are expected to take a position on a major question or problem, develop reasons to support their positions, and locate and use appropriate evidence from the text to support their positions. In their influential piece, Chinn et al. (2001) describe this combination of (1) focusing on a dilemma or problem, (2) considering different viewpoints, and (3) appealing to the text for evidence as a *critical–analytic stance*. These components also undergird the DR approach. Taking a critical–analytic stance requires students to consider their own arguments, the text, and the talk of other peers. During DR students engage in meaningful talk that supports the development of their text-based reasoning skills, the acquisition of second-language skills, and the development of the language proficiency crucial for reading and writing.

All of this work takes place in unique developmental, linguistic, and instructional contexts that affect the ways in which DR is implemented. Thus, the DR model is designed to be flexible, and expectations and goals for discussions can be adjusted for diverse learning environments. Rather than serving as a stand-alone instructional event, these discussions are both strengthened by, and strengthen, existing curricula through close integration with other literacy instruction. Language supports, vocabulary instruction, and the building of background knowledge are all part of the instruction that accompanies the use of DR in the classroom (e.g., see Beaulieu-Jones & Proctor, in press). Teachers in the ELICT Collaborative adapted DR to their curriculum by, for example, engaging their students in extensive online or library research before a discussion. In these cases the text base for the discussion was not a single text, but instead encompassed multimodal texts from the Internet, news articles, and books.

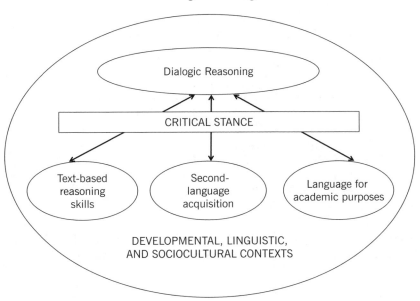

FIGURE 7.2. ELICIT conceptual model.

Implementing DR

In this section, we provide an implementation primer for DR, which is summarized in Table 7.2. Although not meant to be exhaustive, the topics addressed here outline the major planning and instructional elements that ought to be addressed before beginning the process of DR.

Planning DR Discussions

Craft a "Big Question"

DR discussions are based on a "big question." This is often a yes/no question to which there is no correct answer and that requires students to (1) take a position and (2) use evidence from a text or set of texts to defend their chosen stance. Students are encouraged to speak without raising their hands or waiting to be nominated to speak by the teacher, using classroom norms that support respectful talk. The goal is to promote genuine human conversations, in which ideas are presented, wrestled with, rearticulated, and negotiated. Simple yes/no questions can take on profound meaning as when, for example, a fifth-grade ELICIT teacher asked her students, in

TABLE 7.2. DR Implementation Primer:
Foster Classroom Habits That Encourage Student Talk

Planning DR discussions

1. Craft a "big question."
2. Select an appropriate text/text set.
3. Support comprehension of text and discussion of issue.
4. Support students in preparing their arguments.
5. Organize students in flexible groups.

Enacting DR discussions

1. Facilitate student talk.
2. Gradually release responsibility.
3. Connect to writing.

the context of having read a set of biographies including Nelson Mandela, Cesar Chávez, and Rosa Parks, whether it is okay to ever break an unjust law

Select an Appropriate Text

Though DR can be used with a single text, discussions can be extended across multiple texts or text sets, or a single big question can even be used to drive an entire unit. For example, two PreK teachers in the ELICIT Collaborative structured a monthlong unit on penguins around the DR question "Should penguins be kept in an aquarium or should they live in the wild?" Texts focused on habitats, migratory patterns, and animal life in aquariums. The unit included a trip to the local aquarium to view penguins and ask questions of the aquarium staff. In this example, the DR question drove the children's investigations and observations, and provided a reason for collecting evidence, reading, and further explorations about penguins.

Texts can be either narrative or informational, and can be drawn from language arts or other disciplines. Content areas, such as science and social studies, often provide rich topics and big questions that allow students to take a stance and use text-based evidence to support a position.

A text is appropriate for DR when it lends itself to a good discussion—and not all texts do that. Topics such as lying, cheating, stealing, and other moral or ethical ambiguities are often the best candidates for DR discussions. Folktales are typically filled with moral dilemmas. There are many controversial topics in science that could be addressed in DR discussions, such as humans' decisions regarding the environment and the use of technology. Furthermore, students could be engaged in DR discussions to consider their hypotheses about the different scientific phenomena that they are studying.

Fictional narratives and social studies biographies, in which the protagonist must make a hard decision that carries multiple consequences, are also good for DR discussions. In other work, we developed a text set comprised of *One Green Apple* (Bunting, 2006), *The Name Jar* (Choi, 2001), and the story "My Name Is José Miguel—not Joe, not Mike" from the anthology *Yes! We Are Latinos* (Ada & Campoy, 2013). All of these texts present quasi-biographical accounts of immigrant children struggling with their recent arrivals to the United States, particularly as they engage the institution of school. The overarching DR discussion question for this text set was "Should people try to blend in so they can make friends?" This seemingly simple question engaged students in the larger and more complex themes of assimilation and acculturation and allowed for connections to be made within and across texts, and with children's personal experiences in school.

These two components—question development and text selection—interact with each other to lay the groundwork for student participation and engagement. For example, the DR question ("Was Old Cricket clever or foolish?") at the outset of this chapter required students to consider whether what might be considered a character flaw (i.e., Old Cricket's penchant for lying to avoid work) might also be construed a strength. Whereas the story does provide ample character development, it does not provide a final answer to this question, allowing students to develop their own ideas based on the text. Table 7.3 contains other texts and questions that ELICIT teachers found effective for engaging their students in DR discussions. (For more information on text selection, see Hiebert, Chapter 4, this volume.)

Support Comprehension of Text and Discussion Issue

It is impossible to have a truly successful DR discussion if the text in question has not been comprehended in the first place. It has been established that language proficiency is often a key dimension of reading that drives comprehension difficulties among emergent bilingual learners (Kieffer & Vukovic, 2013). Although not the focus of this chapter, here we take the time to simply remind the reader that all good principles of reading instruction apply in a DR instructional setting, particularly as those principles apply to the reading process of emergent bilingual learners (see Boardman & Jensen Lasser, Chapter 6, this volume, for more on reading comprehension). At the same time, DR discussions may reveal gaps or misunderstandings in students' comprehension of the text, and can provide opportunities for students to return to the text to correct misunderstandings or glean missed information.

Given the pronounced linguistic challenges emergent bilingual learners often face when reading for comprehension, we suggest developmentally appropriate reading instructional approaches that target language to drive comprehension. That is not to say that emergent bilingual children in the early elementary years (or even later) do not need decoding instruction. Just like most children learning to read, they do. However, we know that bilingual children tend to look similar to their monolingual counterparts when it comes to cracking the alphabetic code, but are too often markedly different from their monolingual peers with respect to language proficiency. Providing instruction around challenging vocabulary, thoughtful guided reading practices, close readings of text, and the application of tried-and-true reading comprehension strategy instruction are all examples of effective instructional approaches that help build emergent bilingual readers' comprehension of text.

TABLE 7.3. Sample Texts and Questions for Dialogic Reasoning

PreK to second grade	
Leola and the Honeybears: An African-American Retelling of Goldilocks and the Three Bears by Melodye Rosales	"Did Leola make a good decision when she went in the Honeybears' Inn?"
Anansi Goes Fishing retold by Janet Stevens	"Do you think Warthog is fair to Anansi?"
The Ant and the Grasshopper: An Aesop's Fable retold by Tom Paxton and illustrated by Phillip Webb	"Should the ants share their food with Grasshopper?"
Click, Clack, Moo: Cows That Type by Doreen Cronin and illustrated by Betsy Lewin	"Was it okay for the cows to go on strike?"
Matthew & Tilly by Rebecca C. Jones and illustrated by Beth Peck	"Are Matthew and Tilly good friends?"

Third–fifth grade	
Old Cricket by Lisa Wheeler and illustrated by Ponder Goembel	"Was Cricket clever or foolish?"
A Day's Work by Eve Bunting and illustrated by Ronald Himler	"Was Francisco's decision to lie for work the right decision?"
American Slave, American Hero: York of the Lewis and Clark Expedition by Laurence Pringle, Cornelius Van Wright, and Ying-Hwa Hu	"Was Clark fair to York?"
Shiloh by Phyllis Reynolds Naylor	"Should Marty have hidden Shiloh?"

Support Students in Preparing Their Arguments

When preparing for discussions, emergent bilinguals (indeed, all students new to DR) benefit from scaffolds such as graphic organizers that make content and the relationships between concepts visually explicit (Baker et al., 2014; Goldenberg, 2008). For example, building a semantic map is an effective strategy for activating students' prior knowledge, and it provides a visual representation of necessary vocabulary and conceptual relationships that prepares students for DR discussions. T-charts are also an effective strategy for helping emergent bilingual (and monolingual) students prepare arguments for discussion. These provide a scaffold to help students select relevant textual evidence in favor of their positions with reasons why they selected this evidence.

A note of caution, however, is to be careful with discussion scaffolds. Although such idea-generation activities support students' participation, we have found that an overreliance on graphic organizers during DR can lead to students' reading of prepared statements rather than engaging in authentic talk. Students should be aware that graphic organizers are starting points, but genuine interactions are the goal for DR discussions.

Organize Students in Flexible Groups

ELICIT teachers usually organize students in groups of five to eight. Flexible grouping is recommended to ensure that emergent bilingual learners have opportunities to engage with students with different reading levels and language proficiencies (Brisk & Harrington, 2007; Paratore, 2000). All students benefit from participating in heterogeneous DR groups where they have opportunities to engage in conversation with peers who have different English language proficiencies. Native English speakers are valuable language models, and bilingual peers who speak a common home language may provide translation support and enable "translanguaging," whereby English and the common home language complement one another to enhance comprehensibility of input and output. To provide students with a range of ideas and discussion contexts, we recommend changing groups over time and using different grouping criteria, such as interests, linguistic background, and/or reading level.

Enacting DR Discussions

Facilitate Student Talk

It takes time to get to the point where the teacher can simply step back and allow students to manage a constructive DR conversation. During that time, the teacher still plays a key role in supporting students' dialogic reasoning. As facilitator, the teacher functions as a more sophisticated thinker who supports students' participation in novel discourse practices (Maloch, 2002). This is a context for teachers to follow students' reasoning and to guide them in becoming more expert participants in these discussions. It is also a context in which students can voice and refine their understandings (Applebee, Langer, Nystrand, & Gamoran, 2003).

Different talk moves can help teachers to support students' participation in discussions (Jadallah et al., 2011; Waggoner, Chinn, Yi, & Anderson, 1995; Wilkinson et al., 2010). Table 7.4 presents some of these teacher facilitation moves. Talk moves that promote more equitable participation

TABLE 7.4. Teacher Facilitation Moves

Move	Description	Example
Prompt	Ask students to be more explicit in their argumentation by asking them to state their position or reason, provide evidence, or respond to a challenge.	"Is there evidence in the story that supports what you are saying? Can anyone think of another reason or example?"
Ask for clarification	Ask students to clarify what they mean, particularly when they use vague or imprecise language.	"Do you mean [X] or [Y]? Do you mean to say [paraphrase] . . . ?"
Challenge	Present countering ideas or ideas that students haven't thought about yet.	"Some people might say [give a reason from the opposing view point]. If you were [name of character], would you . . . ?"
Encourage participation	Ask more quiet students to contribute to the discussion.	"Carlos, would you like jump in here?"
Summarize	Sum up positions presented by students or describe the discussion process.	"You seem to be pretty much split on whether it was bad luck or a bad case of nerves. Some of you believe it was bad luck, 'cause sometimes things just happen, and some of you thought it was nerves."
Foster independence	Encourage students to talk to each other, rather than to and through the teacher.	"Hands are down. Let's talk to each other."
Redirect	Ask students to consider discussion question or present a follow-up question.	"So if we take what you're saying, and bring it back to the question at hand, should she speak up to the teacher or should she let it ride?"

in discussions are oriented toward encouraging quieter students to participate and supporting more talkative students to self-regulate their own talk. Although the goal is student talk, there also may be moments when students are silent. Wait time is important during DR to give students space to take charge of their talk (a notably effective practice with emergent bilinguals). At the end of a DR discussion, take time to recap the main points discussed and to poll students to see where they stand in their thinking and whether opinions have changed as a result of the discussion.

Talk moves that support productive discussions raise students' awareness about the discourse of argumentation (Maloch, 2002). For example, prompting students to explicitly state their positions and reasons when their arguments are not clear, or to provide evidence when they fail to do so, shows students what type of discourse is valued in DR discussions. Summaries based on the discussion process, rather than on its content, also help students become aware of how to think productively with others (Maloch, 2002). Teachers can influence students' collaboration and productive thought during peer-led discussions by providing effective models, given that students often appropriate their teachers' talk moves (Jadallah et al., 2011).

Gradually Release Responsibility

As may be obvious by this point, the gradual release of responsibility is a necessary characteristic of DR implementation. Although students are encouraged to manage all aspects of discussion as independently as possible, starting out, this is never the case. In true Vygotskian tradition, DR discussions get better over time, with the teacher initially assuming a good deal of responsibility for how the discussion progresses and flows. Over time, however, students assume greater responsibility for their own judgments about which positions and arguments are stronger than others, and for the pacing and direction of the discussion generally. Good discussions result in students' willingness and capacity to respond to one another's arguments, challenging each other respectfully when they disagree, and engaging in authentic dialogue. This takes time and skillful release of responsibility over the course of a school year.

Connect to Writing

Finally, emergent bilingual learners benefit from writing opportunities that enable them to extend their understanding of new content (Lesaux, Kieffer, Kelley, & Harris, 2014). Writing before DR discussions can help students to brainstorm, organize their thinking, and consider evidence from the text that may be relevant to the discussion. For example, students might use a graphic organizer to identify key arguments and supporting evidence from the text. After the discussion, students may write to incorporate new ideas from the discussion with their existing ideas, reflect on alternate views that were presented, or account for new evidence from the text.

DR discussions can play a particularly powerful role in helping students generate new ideas for their writing. For example, Ms. Brennan had her fourth-grade students read *Sadako and the Thousand Paper Cranes* (Coerr, 1977). Prior to the DR discussion, she asked her students to write a response to the following prompt: "Would it be understandable for Sadako's family to blame the U.S. for Sadako's death? Why or why not? Give reasons and examples to support your answer." After the discussion students wrote again about the same question. Their responses after the discussion were longer and included more ideas than in their initial responses (Wagner, Ossa Parra, & Proctor, 2016). (For more strategies on writing, see Brisk, Kaveh, Scialoia, & Timothy, Chapter 8, this volume.)

Conclusion

DR is an instructional framework that supports meaningful engagement in text-based talk that is consistent with the renewed emphasis placed by the CCSS on the role of language, speaking, and listening in the elementary classroom. Done with diligence and persistence, a DR approach in the classroom stands to promote horizontal discourse patterns that decenter teacher talk, privilege social thinking, push on second-language acquisition, and promote oral language proficiency, all with the needs of emergent bilingual children front and center. These attributes of DR function symbiotically in the service of improved literacy outcomes that extend beyond the language arts classroom and into content areas.

REFERENCES

Ada, A. F., & Campoy, F. I. (2013). My name is José Miguel—not Joe, not Mike. In *Yes! We are Latinos* (pp. 24–28). Watertown, MA: Charlesbridge.

Applebee, A. N., Langer, J. A., Nystrand, M., & Gamoran, A. (2003). Discussion-based approaches to developing understanding: Classroom instruction and student performance in middle and high school English. *American Educational Research Journal, 40*(3), 685–730.

Baker, S., Lesaux, N., Jayanthi, M., Dimino, J., Proctor, C. P., Morris, J., et al. (2014). *Teaching Academic content and literacy to English learners in elementary and middle school.* Washington, DC: U.S. Department of Education.

Beaulieu-Jones, L., & Proctor, C. P. (in press). A blueprint for implementing small-group collaborative discussions. *The Reading Teacher.*

Beck, I. L., McKeown, M. G., Sandora, C., Kucan, L., & Worthy, J. (1996). Questioning the author: A yearlong classroom implementation to engage students with text. *Elementary School Journal, 96*(4), 385–414.

Brisk, M., & Harrington, M. M. (2007). Working effectively with bilingual students. In M. E. Brisk & M. M. Harrington (Eds.), *Literacy and bilingualism: A handbook for ALL teachers* (pp. 15–47). Mahwah, NJ: Erlbaum.

Bunting, E. (2006). *One green apple.* New York: Clarion Books.

Cheung, A. C. K., & Slavin, R. E. (2012). Effective reading programs for Spanish-dominant English language learners (ELLs) in the elementary grades: A synthesis of research. *Review of Educational Research, 82*(4), 351–395.

Chinn, C. A., Anderson, R. C., & Waggoner, M. A. (2001). Patterns of discourse in two kinds of literature discussion. *Reading Research Quarterly, 36*(4), 378–411.

Choi, Y. (2003). *The name jar.* New York: Dragonfly.

Coerr, E. (1977). *Sadako and the thousand paper cranes.* New York: Puffin.

Eeds, M., & Wells, D. (1989). Grand conversations: An exploration of meaning construction in literature study groups. *Research in the Teaching of English, 23*(1), 4–29.

Gee, J. P. (2012). *Social linguistics and literacies: Ideology in discourses* (4th ed.). London: Routledge.

Goldenberg, C. (2008). Teaching English language learners: What the research does—and does not say. *American Educator, 32*(2), 8–23, 42–44.

Hoover, W. A., & Gough, P. B. (1990). The simple view of reading. *Reading and Writing, 2*(2), 127–160.

Jadallah, M., Anderson, R. C., Nguyen-Jahiel, K., Miller, B. W., Kim, I., Wu, X. (2011). Influence of a teacher's scaffolding moves during child-led small group discussions. *American Educational Research Journal, 48*(1), 194–230.

Junior Great Books. (1992). *The Junior Great Books curriculum of interpretive reading, writing, and discussion.* Chicago: Great Books Foundation.

Kieffer, M. J., & Vukovic, R. K. (2013). Growth in reading-related skills of language minority learners and their classmates: More evidence for early identification and intervention. *Reading and Writing, 26*, 1159–1194.

Krashen, S. D. (1984). *Writing, research, theory, and applications.* Oxford, UK: Pergamon.

Krashen, S. D. (1994). The input hypothesis and its rivals. In N. Ellis (Ed.), *Implicit and explicit learning of languages* (pp. 45–77). London: Academic.

Kuhn, D. (2015). Thinking together and alone. *Educational Researcher, 44*(1), 46–53.

Kuhn, D., Zillmer, N., Crowell, A., & Zabala, J. (2013). Developing norms of argumentation: Metacognitive, epistemological, and social dimensions of developing argument competence. *Cognition and Instruction, 31*(4), 456–496.

Lesaux, N. K., Kieffer, M. J., Kelley, J. G., & Harris, J. R. (2014). Effects of academic vocabulary instruction for linguistically diverse adolescents evidence from a randomized field trial. *American Educational Research Journal, 51*(6), 1159–1194.

Limbird, C. K., Maluch, J. T., Rjosk, C., Stanat, P., & Merkens, H. (2014).

Differential growth patterns in emerging reading skills of Turkish-German bilingual and German monolingual primary school students. *Reading and Writing, 27*(5), 945–968.

Maloch, B. (2002). Scaffolding student talk: One teacher's role in literature discussion groups. *Reading Research Quarterly, 37*(1), 94–112.

Mercer, N. (2000). *Words and minds: How we use language to think together.* London: Routledge.

Mercer, N., Wegerif, R., & Dawes, L. (1999). Children's talk and the development of reasoning in the classroom. *British Educational Research Journal, 25*(1), 95–111.

Paratore, J. R. (2000). Grouping for instruction in literacy: What we've learned about what works and what doesn't. *The California Reader, 33*(4), 2–10.

Proctor, C. P., August, D., Carlo, M. S., & Snow, C. (2006). The intriguing role of Spanish language vocabulary knowledge in predicting English reading comprehension. *Journal of Educational Psychology, 98*(1), 159–169.

Raphael, T. E., & McMahon, S. I. (1994). Book club: An alternative framework for reading instruction. *The Reading Teacher, 48*(2), 102–116.

Reinking, D., & Bradley, B. A. (2008). *On formative and design experiments: Approaches to language and literacy research.* New York: Teachers College Press.

Resnick, L. B., Salmon, M., Zeitz, C. M., Wathen, S. H., & Holowchak, M. (1993). Reasoning in conversation. *Cognition and Instruction, 11*(3/4), 347–364.

Reznitskaya, A., Kuo, L., Clark, A., Miller, B., Jadallah, M., Anderson, R. C, et al. (2009). Collaborative reasoning: A dialogic approach to group discussions. *Cambridge Journal of Education, 39*(1), 29–48

Short, K. G., & Pierce, K. M. (Eds.). (1998). *Talking about books: Literature discussion groups in K–8 classrooms.* New York: Heinemann.

Silverman, R. D., Proctor, C. P., Harring, J. R., Doyle, B., Mitchell, M. A., & Meyer, A. G. (2014). Teachers' instruction and students' vocabulary and comprehension: An exploratory study with English monolingual and Spanish–English bilingual students in grades 3–5. *Reading Research Quarterly, 49,* 31–60.

Swain, M., & Lapkin, S. (1995). Problems in output and the cognitive processes they generate: A step towards second language learning. *Applied Linguistics, 16*(3), 371–391.

Tharp, R. G., & Gallimore, R. (1988). *Rousing minds to life.* Cambridge, UK: Cambridge University Press.

Valdés, G. (2012, January). *Summary comments.* Notes presented at the Understanding Language Conference, Stanford, CA.

Valdés, G., Capitelli, S., & Alvarez, L. (2011). *Latino children learning English.* New York: Teachers College Press.

Vygotsky, L. S. (1978). *Mind in society: The development of higher psychological processes.* Cambridge, MA: Harvard University Press.

Waggoner, M., Chinn, C., Yi, H., & Anderson, R. C. (1995). Collaborative reasoning about stories. *Language Arts, 72*(8), 582–589.

Wagner, C. J., Ossa Parra, M., & Proctor, C. P. (2016). Student reasoning in oral and written discourse: A study of teacherdesigned Collaborative Reasoning in a linguistically diverse classroom. Manuscript submitted for publication.

Wells, G. (2007). Semiotic mediation, dialogue, and the construction of knowledge. *Human Development, 50*(5), 244–274.

Wheeler, L. (2003). *Old cricket.* New York: Atheneum.

Wilkinson, I. A., Soter, A. O., & Murphy, K. (2010). Developing a model of quality talk about literary text. In M. McKeown & L. Kucan (Eds.), *Bringing reading research to life* (pp. 142–168). New York: Guilford Press.

Zhang, X., Anderson, R. C. & Nguyen-Janiel, K. (2013). Language-rich discussions for English language learners. *International Journal of Educational Research, 58,* 44–60.

CHAPTER 8

Writing Arguments

The Experience of Two Mainstream Teachers Working with Multilingual Students

María Estela Brisk, Yalda M. Kaveh, Pat Scialoia,
and Beverly Timothy

The ability to argue is helpful in many real-life situations and essential in a democratic society. The purpose of arguments is to persuade the audience to a position or point of view, or to persuade the audience to do something. Other types of arguments explore both sides of an issue in order to reach an informed recommendation or judgment (Butt, Fahey, Feez, & Spinks, 2012; Derewianka, 1990). Argument writing is simultaneously a demanding task while also, together with narratives, a natural or universal one, "rooted in the human psyche" (Wilkinson, 1986, p. 137).

National surveys on writing at the elementary level showed that writing has not been a curricular priority. In the early grades, narrative writing assignments predominate (Cutler & Graham, 2008), whereas in the later elementary years students are mostly assigned short pieces related to content learning, such as answering content questions, writing summaries, and taking notes. The type of writing that students will need later in education and life, such as generating arguments and writing research reports, are assigned very infrequently (Gilbert & Graham, 2010).

Currently, many school districts feel the pressure to teach argumentation because the Common Core State Standards (CCSS; National Governors Association Center for Best Practices & Council of Child State School Officers [NGA & CCSSO], 2010) not only identify it as one of the three written text types, together with narrative and informational/explanatory types, but also consider it a priority, noting that "an argument is a reasoned, logical way of demonstrating that the writer's position, belief, or conclusion is valid" (NGA & CCSSO, 2010, Appendix A, p. 23). The purpose of arguments, according to the CCSS, is to "to change the reader's point of view, to bring about some action on the reader's part, or to ask the reader to accept the writer's explanation or evaluation of a concept, issue, or problem" (NGA & CCSSO, 2010, Appendix A, p. 23). Argument writing is appropriate in the context of English language arts, history/social studies, and science. Although argumentative writing is promoted in the CCSS, little guidance is provided as to the specific features of argument writing, especially language demands.

The purpose of this chapter is to recommend content and strategies for teaching argument writing in upper elementary grades toward a goal of enabling students to present a reasoned perspective of one point of view. The arguments that present both points of view are appropriate for older students (Brisk, 2015; Christie, 2012). The sources informing the recommendations in this chapter are a review of the literature and the experiences of two fifth-grade teachers. These teachers have participated in a 7-year schoolwide project to develop a genre-based writing pedagogy informed by systemic functional linguistics (SFL; Brisk, 2015). The focus on language is paramount in this approach and is thus especially helpful for emergent bilingual learners.

Development and Instruction of Argument Writing

This section (1) explores the findings in the literature with respect to how elementary students develop the ability to present a cogent position in writing, and (2) provides suggestions proposed by researchers on ways to support this development.

Young Learners and Argument Writing

Argument writing can be a challenging task due to children's insufficient developmental and rhetorical maturity as writers, the complex features of the genre, and children's low level of exposure to it. Producing an argumentative piece of writing that is logical, clear, and convincing requires a high level of linguistic and cognitive complexity and can be challenging for developing writers (McCann, 1989; Nippold, Ward-Lonergan, & Fanning, 2005). Children first learn textual structures that directly transfer from speech to writing, such as those of narratives. However, they acquire the structure of argument, which relies more heavily on an abstract interaction with an imaginary audience, at a later point (Crowhurst, 1990). Several studies have investigated the structure of written arguments across different grade levels. The findings unanimously show an increasing complexity of argumentative writings with the increase in age and grade level. In early grades, students' argument writings are generally short, lack concluding statements, and show less use of reason and evidence (McCann, 1989). Young writers use less cohesive devices and limited vocabulary and demonstrate a far less mature use of conjunctions in their arguments (Crowhurst, 1978).

Young writers' performance on argument-writing tasks is usually not as adept as their performance on narrative writing due to the higher structural complexity of argumentation. Whereas the structure of narratives resembles the chronological structure of external reality, arguments have a nonchronological organization. They usually include longer clauses and more complex constructions (Crowhurst, 1980, 1990). Generating content is also more complicated in argument writing. Whereas children can draw from their experiential knowledge to write a story, they need to rely on less extensive and more scattered sources of information in their memory to come up with the relevant content to make an argument. In addition, writing persuasively is a more abstract task because it requires generalization and often an imaginary audience (Brisk, 2015).

Writing arguments is also difficult for young writers because of the infrequency of their exposure to this genre of writing (Knudson, 1991, 1992; Cutler & Graham, 2008; Gilbert & Graham, 2010). Young learners are rarely encouraged to compose a written argument in elementary school, "either because it is judged too difficult, or because expressive writing is more highly valued" (Crowhurst, 1990, p. 357). A lack of sufficient exposure contributes to the limited development of the organizational structures and linguistic forms needed to acquire formal arguments (Crowhurst, 1990).

Instruction to Support Argument Development

Despite the controversies around children's ability to write arguments and the lack of emphasis on this genre in elementary school instruction, argument writing has been in increasingly high demand for successful performance on high-stakes testing, as well success in college, work, and social life (Anderson, 2008; NGA & CCSSO, 2010; Ferretti & Lewis, 2013; Gilbert & Graham, 2010). Argument writing is a developmental skill that can be improved as a result of classroom instruction, increased exposure through reading, frequent opportunities for practice, and constructive feedback from teachers and other knowledgeable adults as children move to higher grade levels in school (Nippold et al., 2005). Without receiving instruction on argument writing, elementary school students tend to lose their focus on the purpose of the genre and gradually "drift" into narrative writing, with which they have greater familiarity (Crowhurst, 1990). However, when receiving adequate instruction, young writers, including those who normally struggle with writing, show evidence of effective argument writing (Anderson, 2008; Gilbert & Graham, 2010).

The literature on teaching argument writing suggests several ways to teach this genre in the early grades. These strategies include, but are not limited to, scaffolding argumentative writing through oral discussion, choosing audience and topics that are real and have authentic purpose for students, exposing students to argumentative texts through reading, and modeling the language of argumentation. These strategies are described in more depth in the following sections.

Scaffold Argumentation through Oral Discussion

A practical way to initiate the scaffolding of children's argumentative writing skills is to foster children's natural ability to argue orally. As Ferretti and Lewis (2013) assert, "dialogic support is essential for the development of reflective argumentative writing" (p. 114). When teachers scaffold argumentative writing through talk, explicit modeling, and engaging discussions, young students' writings exhibit additional characteristics of persuasive thinking and writing (Anderson, 2008; Ossa Parra et al., Chapter 7, this volume).

Engaging in large- and small-group discussions prior to writing helps students clarify their thoughts and form a logical structure for their argument before they start to write (Crowhurst, 1990). Teachers can model appropriate ways of agreeing and disagreeing in an argument. They can also provide visual representations, such as a picture of a two-sided scale with one side of the argument on each side, as a way to facilitate the discussion and to remind the students to "weigh" each side of the argument attentively before taking a stance (Nippold et al., 2005). (See Ossa Parra, Chapter 7, this volume, for additional ideas on ways to incorporate student-led discussion into classroom activities.)

Choose Audience and Topics That Are Real and Have Authentic Purpose for Students

An effective way to teach argument writing is to assign topics that are "contextually relevant" for students and have real-life purposes (Crowhurst, 1990, p. 357). Giving students the authority to address arguments to people in their school or neighborhood helps them engage with their audience in unique ways. In addition, giving children the choice to write about issues they feel strongly about helps them take advantage of their background knowledge in their writing (Anderson, 2008).

Expose Students to Argumentative Texts through Reading

Reading books and texts written in the argumentative style exposes students to the structure and linguistic features of this genre and provides them with a model before they start their writing. More specifically, students benefit from reading argumentative texts and deconstructing them in terms of purpose, text structure, and language (Brisk, 2015). Furthermore, teachers can use the topics in literature to pose questions that can lead to arguments.

Strategies for Teaching the Language of Written Arguments

Teachers' explicit instruction on the linguistic features of persuasive writing significantly improves students' argumentative writing quality (Crowhurst, 1991). Teachers can provide printed "prompt cards" that contain keywords and phrases to make an argument in order to help young writers substitute conversational words with more sophisticated ones (Nippold et al., 2005). Rothery (1989) suggests including activities that give students opportunities to understand and use the technical vocabulary relevant to the topic (e.g., together with students, underlining everyday vocabulary used by the students in their writing and replacing with technical terms, as in the sentence "Rocks are made."). This approach helps students not only to produce more linguistically advanced writings, but also to consolidate their knowledge about the text and the language structures of the target genre (Khote, 2014). In addition, activities that teach students about making appropriate language choices when writing to different audiences can help students develop a sense of audience awareness and of the voice used for writing arguments (e.g., making a T chart with a thesis statement on top and a different audience on each side and brainstorming reasons appropriate for each audience, given the thesis) (Brisk, 2015).

Teaching Argument Writing: The Story of Two Classrooms

Beverly and Pat (chapter coauthors) are fifth-grade teachers who have been participating for 5 and 7 years, respectively, in a large research project to implement writing instruction in their PreK–5 school informed by SFL, a theory of language that has analyzed the patterns of text structure and language used in various writing genres. All grades have been implementing writing instruction in a variety of genres with positive impact on students' writing development. The whole school has seen improvement in English language arts (ELA) state tests. In addition, emergent bilingual students have shown steady English proficiency development as assessed by the

Assessing Comprehension and Communication in English State-to-State (ACCESS) test (Brisk & Kaveh, 2016; Brisk & Ossa-Parra, 2016).

Teachers for each grade level planned genre units together in connection with their reading and content-area curricula. For each class, the writing of two students who were English language learners and represented different levels of proficiency was analyzed every year to help guide instruction and gain an understanding of overall student development and challenges (Brisk, 2015). To start the unit, teachers gave students a cold prompt or "uncoached" piece to gauge their ability to write in the genre of the unit. This piece informed the content of the unit and also served as baseline against which to compare the writing produced at the end of the unit.

In the argument unit described in this chapter, Pat's and Beverly's classes explored issues of interest to the students as well as topics from their new reading curriculum. Two emergent bilingual students were chosen as focus students for each class. Angel and Bernardo,[1] in Pat's class, were both Spanish speakers with intermediate to advanced English proficiency. Eugenia and Lucas, in Beverly's class, were also Spanish speakers. Eugenia had intermediate English proficiency level; Lucas was a recent arrival from the Dominican Republic with a beginning level of proficiency in English (he was proficient in oral and written Spanish). The rest of the students in both classes included additional Spanish-speaking emergent bilinguals; fluent English-speaking bilinguals from a variety of language backgrounds, including Vietnamese, Cape Verdean, and Haitian; and two or three monolingual English speakers.

Pat and Beverly started the year with the unit on argument, which took 6 weeks to complete. They each had their own fifth-grade classroom, but they shared common planning time where they planned together and traded resources. They spent between 45 minutes to 1 hour on writing instruction every day. Activities during reading time supported the argument unit as well.

Pat's Classroom

Pat started the unit by giving students a cold prompt to gauge their argument writing skills. Then he spent time reading a variety of mentor texts with his students in different content areas, including ELA, science, and social studies. Pat prompted his students to take a stance in relation to the readings and have oral debates with him and each other. Pat started the argument unit with the question of whether kids should play video games. The class read and discussed a series of texts on the advantages and disadvantages of video games. The class then deconstructed each piece with a

---

[1] All students names used are pseudonums.

focus on text structure and language. The deconstruction of text structure included finding the thesis statement or claim, the reasons provided, and the evidence. The class then identified features of the language in the texts with regard to the intended audience and evaluative vocabulary or language that showed the author's point of view. Students also learned how to increase the "volume" of this vocabulary. For example, Angel wrote "*tremendously* educational" instead of just "*very*."

During this process, Pat gradually released responsibility to his students. The deconstruction started as a whole-class activity with direct instruction from Pat, but was later conducted by groups, pairs, and individual students. Pat continued to provide support to the students during independent work. Eventually, the whole class would come back together to discuss the results of the deconstruction process. Pat explained his approach as follows: "We do everything as a whole class to start the process, so I can ensure that the children understand the process and the purpose of *how* we are writing, not *what* we are writing. The HOW is important at this point. As I model and we co-construct, I hand it over to them and become a spectator."

The deconstruction was followed by construction of argumentative paragraphs by individual students. Pat presented his students with the prompt, "Video games are definitely good for kids to play," and tasked them to come up with three supporting reasons for this statement, and later, to support those reasons with evidence. Pat finds that assigning the same prompt to all students allows for collaboration among them. He allows his students to borrow ideas and language, persuasive as well as content specific, from their peers as they move the writing process forward. Pat believes the initial consistency makes the instruction more productive, because it gives him the opportunity to provide a wide variety of examples to his students to take the class writing skills to the next level.

Although Pat's students wrote their paragraphs individually, the revision process was done in a highly iterative and interactive way. First, he demonstrated the revision process with the whole class by deconstructing a former student's argumentative piece and discussing possible revisions. Subsequently, Pat asked his students to reread their own writing and join a partner to highlight the elements of argumentative text structure and language with multicolored markers (which he provided). Later, students gathered on the carpet for a whole-class discussion, led by Pat, on the purpose, text structure (claim, reason, and evidence), and language (audience, evaluative vocabulary, grading, and technical vocabulary) of the students' argumentative pieces. As the final step in the revision process, Pat asked his students to follow the approach used in the classroom to deconstruct and critique their argumentative pieces on video games as homework. They shared their results with Pat and their peers and received further feedback on the aspects of language, including voice, modality, audience, and use of technical vocabulary. The students received feedback from their peers and Pat throughout the writing and revision process, rather than waiting until the end. Pat believes that peer feedback is essential in raising the confidence and the comfort level of all his students, especially emergent bilingual learners.

In order to direct the students' attention to the language of argument, Pat created his own metalanguage by defining two perspectives: positive and negative. During the whole-class discussion, he asked students to identify the words that revealed the stance of the author, either as positive or negative, and discuss them with their classmates. Pat modeled this by deconstructing the language of *Should There Be Zoos?: A Persuasive Text,* by Stead and Ballester (2000): "In this example, he's telling you how bad something is, so she's going to use words such as *abusive* and *beating*—this is a negative piece of writing" (p. 18).

Focus Students' Access to Argumentative Writing

Pat considers the emergent bilingual students as full members of his classroom community and does not single them out. In this example, he supported them by designing groups in strategic ways. During the argument unit, the two focus students, Angel and Bernardo, worked together in a pair or as parts of a larger group and provided support for each other. After giving instructions, he often checked to make sure that they understood the assignment. He also used their good work to illustrate how students were supposed to do an assignment, establishing their status as capable learners.

Beverly's Classroom

Similar to Pat, Beverly started the augment unit with the reading and deconstruction of mentor texts. Beverly's class deconstructed the same mentor texts on video games that were used in Pat's class. The deconstruction started in a whole-class format, with Beverly modeling and guiding the process, and then transitioned to group work as the students got enough practice with it. The deconstruction was focused on purpose, text structure, and language. For deconstructing the purpose and structure of the texts, Beverly helped her students identify thesis statements, reasons, and evidence in the argumentative pieces. She focused the deconstruction of language mainly on identification of the intended audience.

Beverly took a different approach in the next stage of the argument unit. Rather than asking students to write individual arguments, she and her students jointly constructed a whole-class argumentative piece. She used the existing controversy around the principal's decision to convert the cafeteria into a movement space as an opportunity to write an argument. Beverly wrote two opposing thesis statements on a chart paper with the help of her students: "Bring back the cafeteria" and "Keep the movement space." The class decided the audience would be adults as well as children in the school.

The class jointly brainstormed reasons for each thesis statement while Beverly wrote them on the chart paper. The students were divided into two groups, based on the claim they wanted to support. Then Beverly divided the students on each side into smaller groups and assigned each group one of the reasons under its claim of choice. Members of the groups first brainstormed supporting evidence for their reasoning and then wrote their paragraphs.

Beverly constantly reinforced the purpose of the genre and helped the students be mindful of the language of argumentation by reminding them of the intended audience. She encouraged them to insert additional evaluative vocabulary (e.g., "No one wants *disease-carrying* mice and flies *invading* our space") and to increase the volume in their writings (e.g., *tremendously, fabulous*). Once the groups felt satisfied with their paragraph, they dictated them to Beverly, who wrote exactly what they read to her. Once all the paragraphs were completed, Beverly and her students jointly revised them. Beverly modeled making revisions to the students before asking them to get back to their groups and edit the language of their paragraphs. The students revised their paragraphs with attention to elements of language for argumentative writing (i.e., audience awareness and voice) as well as general grammar. One of the most salient language issues in these students' writing was the use of appropriate person. In this case, because of the general nature of the claim, consistent use of third person was deemed most appropriate. The students spent a lot of time eliminating the pronoun *you* when it was used inappropriately or inconsistently. Students posted the final versions of the two arguments outside their classroom for the whole school to see.

Beverly's class worked on another whole-class argument titled "Should college athletes be paid, yes or no?," following the same process. However, in contrast to the piece on the cafeteria that allowed students to draw evidence from their personal experience, the argument on college athletes' payment required students to conduct research for background information and supporting evidence. Consequently, group writing began by conducting research on the Internet using tablets and laptops provided by the teacher. The groups took notes in a graphic organizer designed for collecting reasons and evidence during this process (Brisk, 2015). After the class revised and finalized their jointly constructed piece, Beverly asked them to write an individual piece on the same topic arguing for their stance of choice.

Having noticed that the uncoached pieces did not include a conclusion, for the most part, and the one that did just repeated the thesis statement,

Beverly taught students how to wrap up their arguments. She wrote on chart paper the thesis and two conclusions, one that repeated the thesis and one that reinforced the thesis by expanding, rather than merely repeating, the idea. Students first identified which one was a repetition and which one was not and then discussed the merits of the one that reinforced rather than repeated the claim. The students then worked on the conclusion of their own arguments.

Focus Students' Access to Argumentative Writing

Beverly's minimal knowledge of Spanish at first made her feel highly challenged by having Lucas, the recent arrival, in her class. However, soon she found ways to support Lucas in ways that allowed him to be fully functional in the classroom. Beverly encouraged him to write in Spanish and assigned him to groups with at least one bilingual Spanish–English speaker so that they could work in two languages, allowing Lucas to fully participate in tasks.

In addition, Beverley provided Spanish translations to Lucas through assistance from the visiting Spanish-speaking researcher, the bilingual students in the class, and the translation software on her computer. Lucas was also given a tablet for translating English sentences to Spanish, or vice versa, in order to understand the content and to communicate with the teacher and the monolingual English-speaking classmates. Lucas used the tablet to access the Spanish version of the English materials. Most importantly, Beverly always attempted to make Lucas proud of his first language by motivating him to use Spanish. She often checked on Lucas's work, asking him and the other bilingual students to help her read what he had written in Spanish. When the students shared their work with the whole class, Beverley asked Lucas to share his Spanish writings, followed by a bilingual discussion of his work.

Eugenia, the intermediate-level student, needed some support with grammar and spelling, but she seemed to have no major problems understanding the content and communicating with her classmates. However, Beverly still provided emotional and linguistic support to her in class by putting her in charge of group work in order to position her as a leader in the class.

Student Work: Improvement and Challenges

Students' writing was analyzed at the beginning and end of the unit using a rubric that includes the purpose of the genre, structural elements, and important language features (Brisk, 2015, pp. 293–94). The uncoached piece written at the beginning of the unit to gauge what the students were capable of doing and to highlight their difficulties showed that students understood the purpose of arguments, wrote a thesis statement, and used some reasons. Evidence and a concluding statement were missing. In addition, the language did not reflect the author's point of view. The final individual arguments showed improvement in a number of areas, whereas some remained a challenge, either for the whole group or for particular individuals.

Most students wrote final arguments with a clear thesis followed by different and well-stated reasons supported by evidence. Only Lucas added some background to the thesis with his first sentence: "*En Estados Unidos hay estudiantes universitarios que tanbien son atletas. El problema es si deben pagarles si o no.*" [In the United States there are college students who are also athletes. The issues is whether they should be paid, yes or no.]

The most noticeable improvement in students' arguments was the inclusion of evidence using technical language, awareness of audience, and the use of language resources to express point of view in the effort to persuade the reader. For example, Angel wrote:

> Video games are tremendesly educational. Such as FIRST in Math because it helps you in your math skills like mutiplication division and Adition. Another fabulous website is RazKids it helps you in your reading skills. Kids can choose any kind of book at any level. This skill will help you at school and you will become more independent.

The evidence includes specific names of programs and the skills they improve. The reasons and evidence were tactically chosen to persuade an adult audience. Writing all sentences as statements made for an authoritative stance, and use of evaluative vocabulary and grading (increasing or decreasing the volume of the evaluative vocabulary) (e.g., *tremendously, fabulous*) revealed the author's point of view. This piece also shows one of the most constant challenges: maintaining a consistent voice by using the third person throughout when writing a generalized essay rather than one directed to a specific reader. Thus, it would have been more appropriate to follow the first sentence in third person with "Such as FIRST in Math because it helps *kids* in *their* math skills. . . . "

Other challenges found in most students' writing included reasoning that was not completely clear. For example, Eugenia wanted to make the point that student athletes do not make it to the professional level in most cases as one of the reasons why college athletes should be paid.

> Many college athletes don't make it to the pros. Even if your kid is good at sports in high school, get a scholarship, and excels in college there's almost no way they are going to go to the pros.

However, the connection between this reason and her thesis was left up to the reader to make. Often, when reading their pieces aloud, students were capable of clarifying what they meant.

Of the four emergent bilingual focus students, Eugenia improved the most with respect to the flow of information in paragraphs. In the following paragraph, she included a topic sentence, placing what she is talking about at the beginning of the sentence, and the sentences are connected with each other:

> The NCAA basketball tournaments or "March Madnes," have become a huge business. As forbes' Chris Smith worote, CBS Turner Brcade asting make more than $1 billion of the games, "thanks in part to $100,000 ad rate for 30-seconds spot during the final four."

Research to Practice: What and How to Teach Argumentation That Supports Bilingual Learners

Writing arguments is a difficult task for elementary-age children, despite the fact that children attempt persuasion from an early age. Nevertheless, instruction in elementary years lays the foundation for writing strong arguments in middle and high school.

A set of recommendations emerged from the extant literature and our own research on teaching practices and student learning in the two classrooms described in this chapter. These suggestions/recommendations, which are supportive of emergent bilingual students as well as all other elementary students, apply to teaching how to write persuasive essays in fourth grade and above. (For additional information about the research on argument writing with all elementary grades, see Brisk, 2015, Chapter 8).

Suggestions are organized with respect to (1) how to teach; (2) what to teach (see Table 8.1); and (3) the additional supports for emergent bilingual learners provided by the two classroom teachers.

How to Teach: Apprenticing Students to Argument Writing

A unit on argumentation can take from 6 to 8 weeks, depending how many arguments students write and how much research they need to do. In addition, teachers can practice argumentation in relation to readings or current issues. A number of deliberate steps enable students to reach competency and feel confident in argument writing. Students are never asked to write without first analyzing and practicing the features and language of a genre together with the teacher.

TABLE 8.1. What to Teach: Content of Writing Instruction

Recommendation	Explanation
1. Teach the purpose of an argument.	The purpose of an argument is to persuade the audience about something or to do something.
2. Teach text structure of an argument.	An argumentative essay includes a thesis, a series of reasons supported by evidence, and the reinforcement of the thesis as a conclusion. Depending on the audience, the thesis needs to be preceded by background information.
3. Teach about audience and voice.	Focusing on audience and voice is essential in guiding students to choose effective language for their arguments. Audience also influences the content of an argument. Types of sentences, grammatical person, modality, evaluative vocabulary, and grading are aspects of language that help create specific voice.
4. Teach to write fluid paragraphs with a clear topic sentence.	Learning to create well-formed and clear paragraphs allows students to write what they really mean. Three areas are important to work on: having a topic sentence that introduces the reason they are writing about, having beginning sentences that clearly signal what they are writing about, and creating a flow of meaning from one sentence to the next by developing the topic, rather than having a string of sentences with isolated ideas.

1. *Practice oral argumentation throughout the year.* Students need experience with oral argumentation before writing to practice structural elements of an argument and to experience an audience with different points of view (Ferretti & Lewis, 2013). The teachers in this chapter orally practiced various topics brainstormed by the class before the writing started. In addition, both teachers practiced Dialogic Reasoning throughout the year. Dialogic Reasoning discussions developed by the ELICIT Collaborative (see Ossa Para et al., Chapter 7, this volume) are derived from Collaborative Reasoning (Zhang & Dougherty Stahl, 2011). This approach encourages discussions among a group of students in response to a text-based question. The texts and questions are carefully chosen so that students understand that there is no correct answer, per se. Students take a position and defend it using evidence from the text. The discussions are student-run, with teachers as members of the groups, participating only when redirection or introducing a new position is warranted. Students speak freely without prompting from the teacher. They learn to listen to their peers and respectfully respond to what the other students say. To close the discussions, students write their arguments. In preparation for these discussions, students are taught how to speak and listen and to use the language of argumentation.

Through these oral discussions, students practice taking positions in relation to a claim and facing the opposite point of view.

2. *Choose authentic topics.* The topics of the essays revolve around issues in students' lives or ideas that emerge from the curriculum content. For example, students wrote about video games, whether the cafeteria should be turned into an indoor gym, education for girls in Afghanistan, and whether the character Marty in the book *Shiloh* (Naylor, 2000) should have a rifle. In fifth grade, students also applied their knowledge of persuasion to writing science arguments connected to their experiments and inquiry activities.

3. *Read and deconstruct published texts.* Reading arguments with students familiarizes them with the genre. In addition, it is important to explicitly show students how authors achieve their purpose, structure the text, and use language by deconstructing sample texts. The deconstruction activities can focus on one element at a time or groups of elements. For example, Pat and Beverly deconstructed multiple texts focusing first on purpose, then on the structure of the text, and finally on language. It is important that the focus of this activity is not reading comprehension, but language and structural choices authors make to successfully construct an argument (i.e., reading as a writer). In addition to using mentor texts written as an argument, teachers can use fictional narratives where the characters in them argue. These are good examples of the language of argumentation, but not of the structure of the genre—for example, *Dear Mrs. La Rue* (Teague, 2002) and *I Wanna Iguana* (Orloof, 2009).

4. *Jointly construct arguments.* Teachers together with students co-construct the different stages of the argument, moving from the thesis to the conclusion as a way to explicitly teach the students how to write arguments. This joint construction is done with the whole class working on various sections (Rothery, 1989) or, as Beverly chose to do, in a combination of whole-class and group construction.

5. *Individual construction of text.* Once students are confident in their knowledge of argument writing, they are encouraged to write on their own. Some teachers let students choose their topic from their own experience or from topics related to a content area. Pat and Beverly found that having students initially write individual arguments on the same topic led to productive collaboration drafting and revising their texts.

6. *Plan using graphic organizers.* Before students write their own arguments, they should engage in planning by using a graphic organizer with a space for the thesis and background information, several boxes for reasons with boxes for evidence, and final a place for the reinforcement of the position (e.g., see Brisk, 2015, p. 295, for a sample graphic organizer).

At this point it is advisable to conference with the students to check that there is coherence between the thesis and the reasons, that reasons are different, and that the evidence supporting the reasons makes sense. It is easier to revise at this stage than to do it after the students have drafted their pieces.

7. *Teach through contrasting choices.* One approach to teaching students aspects of the structure or the language is to show them both appropriate and less appropriate choices while discussing the function of the more appropriate choice. Beverly used this strategy to help students write their conclusion by reinforcing, but not just repeating, the thesis statement. Similar activities can be carried out with language features. For example, discuss the difference in the effect of these sentences: (a) "Daily, we walked into a room filled with wrappers and milk spills"; and (b) "Daily, we walked into a *disgusting* room filled with wrappers and *giant* milk spills." The second sentence includes evaluative vocabulary that reflects the author's point of view.

8. *Teach the language of argumentation throughout the unit.* Concurrent with teaching structure, teachers familiarize the students with the topic-specific language and demonstrate how the audience demands attention on the language choices they make. For example, Pat and Beverly decided that the audience was going to be the school community, which includes both adults and children. They pointed out to their students that for adults, their language needs to be not only understandable but also formal or professional, whereas for children, it needs to be understandable, first and foremost. Pat addressed evaluative vocabulary by making lists with the students of words that reveal a positive (e.g., *amazing, healthy*) and negative (e.g., *decay, unhealthy, boring*) stance. Students added to this list throughout the unit. Beverly discussed how the use of *you* when writing an essay takes away the authoritative voice of their argument. The use of third person is much stronger. The use of second person is appropriate when writing letters or advertisements wherein the writer directly addresses the audience.

Other grammatical aspects of language that change the voice are modality and sentence types. With modals, students need to strike the balance between being assertive and yet respectful. "You should allow us to go on the field trip" is both assertive and respectful when writing to their principal, where "You must allow us . . ." is not respectful. Although children like to include questions and exclamations in their writing, declarative sentences are more assertive and formal. Exclamations, commands, or questions work better in a brochure than in an essay. Another feature of students' writing that weakens the strength of their voice is the use of phrases that foreground the position of the writer, such as "*I* think that . . ." or "*I* believe that. . . ."

9. *Encourage collaboration among students.* Because the relationship between author and audience is paramount in arguments, students working in collaboration are constantly aware of what others think about the points they are making in their writing. In addition, students support and learn from each other when researching, drafting, and revising together. Pat and Beverly constantly move from whole-class to group activities, creating an atmosphere in which all students feel that they are learning together.

10. *Teach students how to revise.* Students need to be explicitly taught how to revise to do both peer and individual revisions of their papers. For example, Pat projected an example of an argument from the previous year. Using the argument graphic organizer, he had the whole class analyze the text structure of the piece as well as features of language. Students are better prepared to revise and help each other improve their piece if they have collaborated together with the teacher on an example. This practice helps them be specific in their revisions or suggestions rather than just express their approval or disapproval.

Specific Supports for Emergent Bilingual Students: Creating a Bilingual Classroom Context

The recommendations listed above are supportive of emergent bilingual students, given the explicit instruction about the intricacies of English discourse and the language features of arguments. There is much literature recommending what teachers should do to create classroom contexts appropriate for emergent bilinguals (Brisk, 2006; De Jong, 2011). This research is beyond the scope of this paper about writing argumentation. However, it is important to point out what Pat and Beverly used to enhance bilingual students' participation in their unit on argumentation, such as allowing the free use of native languages, positioning bilingual learners as experts, and encouraging mutual support among students. They used the following strategies supportive of all students in the process of acquiring English proficiency:

- Positioned students as experts; for example, by placing emergent bilingual students in charge of a group, reading and explaining the Spanish sections of a book, and using their work as exemplars.
- Encouraged students to work collaboratively to support each other; for example, by sharing tasks in carrying out research, commenting on each other's drafts, and "borrowing" technical language from each other.
- Ensured that the emergent bilingual students understood the task when the class broke into groups.

Beverly, who does not speak Spanish, carried out additional strategies to support a Spanish-speaking newcomer:

- Placed the student in a pair or group with other fluent bilinguals who could use both languages to carry out the activities of the group to integrate the newcomer.
- Used translation to enhance comprehension with the support of other students, an iPad translator program, and a bilingual researcher who came weekly to her class.
- Used translation to allow the newcomer whole-class participation. When the newcomer expressed his opinion or shared his work, the other bilingual students engaged in the discussion and facilitated comprehension for English speakers.
- Used materials in Spanish included in the publisher's webpage.

All these strategies supported emergent bilingual students, making it possible for them both to learn how to write arguments and to feel like full-fledged members of the classroom community, contributing with their knowledge as well as developing themselves.

Conclusion

The systematic and language-rich approach to teaching argumentation described in this chapter has been applied and improved over time with successful results in an urban school. The work the teachers described in this chapter demonstrates that teaching argument to elementary-age children is possible and desirable, if difficult. Explicit and collaborative instruction helps young students begin to grasp the logic, structure, and language of arguments. This SFL approach helps implement the demands of CCSS and specially benefits emergent bilingual learners, given the explicit focus on the language of argumentation that is lacking in the CCSS. Students progress at different paces, but they all enjoy the power that the ability to argue gives them. This is a desirable skill for members of a democratic society, where the ability to argue is essential to accomplish goals in a variety of everyday, professional, and academic settings.

REFERENCES

Anderson, D. D. (2008). The elementary persuasive letter: Two cases of situated competence, strategy, and agency. *Research in the Teaching of English, 42*(3), 270–314.

Brisk, M. E. (2006). *Bilingual education: From compensatory to quality schooling* (2nd ed.). Mahwah, NJ: Erlbaum Associates.

Brisk, M. E. (2015). *Engaging students in academic literacies: Genre-based pedagogy for K–5 classrooms.* New York: Routledge.

Brisk, M. E., & Kaveh, M. Y. (2016). Mainstream teachers for successful multilingual classrooms: The case of a school that embraced a genre-based pedagogy to teach writing. In S. Hammer & K. M. Viesca (Eds.), *Multilingual learners: What teachers should do and will know—An international comparison.* New York: Routledge.

Brisk, M. E., & Ossa-Parra, M. (2016). Mainstream classrooms as engaging spaces for emergent bilinguals: SFL theory, catalyst for change. In R. Harman (Ed.), *Critical systemic functional linguistics: Promoting language awareness and social action among K–12 students and teachers.* New York: Springer.

Butt, D., Fahey, R., Feez, S., & Spinks, S. (2012). *Using functional grammar: An explorer's guide* (3rd ed.). South Yarra, UK: Palgrave Macmillan.

Christie, F. (2012). *Language education throughout the school years: A functional perspective.* Chichester, UK: Wiley-Blackwell.

Crowhurst, M. (1978). *The effect of audience and mode of discourse on the syntactic complexity of the writing of sixth and tenth graders* (doctoral dissertation). Available from *http://www.proquest.com/products-services/dissertations/Find-a-Dissertation.html.*

Crowhurst, M. (1980). Syntactic complexity in narration and argument at three grade levels. *Canadian Journal of Education/Revue canadienne de l'éducation, 5*(1), 6–13.

Crowhurst, M. (1990). Teaching and learning the writing of persuasive/argumentative discourse. *Journal of Education, 15*(4), 348–360.

Crowhurst, M. (1991). Interrelationships between reading and writing persuasive discourse. *Research in the Teaching of English, 25*(3), 314–338.

Cutler, L., & Graham, S. (2008). Primary grade writing instruction: A national survey. *Journal of Educational Psychology, 100*(4), 907–919.

De Jong, E. J. (2011). *Foundations of multilingualism in education: From principles to practice.* Philadelphia: Caslon.

Derewianka, B. (1990). *Exploring how texts work.* Rozelle, Australia: Primary English Teaching Association. *Language, Speech, and Hearing Services in Schools, 36*(2), 125–138.

Ferretti, R. P., & Lewis, W. E. (2013). Best practices in teaching argumentative writing. In S. Graham, C. A. MacArthur, & J. Fitzgerald (Eds.), *Best practices in writing instruction* (2nd ed., pp. 113–140). New York: Guilford Press.

Gilbert, J., & Graham, S. (2010). Teaching writing to elementary students in grades 4–6: A national survey. *Elementary School Journal, 110*(4), 494–518.

Khote, N. V. (2014). *Engaging emergent bilinguals in the social dialogue of writing persuasively.* Unpublished doctoral dissertation, University of Georgia, Athens, GA.

Knudson, R. E. (1991). Effects of instructional strategies, grade, and sex on students' persuasive writing. *Journal of Experimental Education, 59*(2), 141–153.

Knudson, R. E. (1992). Analysis of argumentative writing at two grade levels. *Journal of Educational Research, 85*(3), 169–179.

McCann, T. M. (1989). Student argumentative writing knowledge and ability at three grade levels. *Research in the Teaching of English, 23*(1), 62–76.

National Governors Association & Council of Chief State School Officers. (2010). *Common Core State Standards for English language arts and literacy in history/social studies, science, and technical subjects.* Washington, DC: Authors.

Naylor, P. R. (2000). *Shiloh.* New York: Aladdin.

Nippold, M. A., Ward-Lonergan, J. M., & Fanning, J. L. (2005). Persuasive writing in children, adolescents, and adults: Study of syntactic, semantic, and pragmatic development. *Language, Speech, and Hearing Services in Schools, 36*, 125–138.

Orloof, K. (2009). *I wanna iguana.* New York: Putnam Juvenile.

Rothery, J. (1989). *The discussion genre: Language and social power.* Erskineville, NSW: Metropolitan East Disadvantaged School Program, NSW Department of School Education.

Stead, T., & Ballester, J. (2000). *Should there be zoos?: A persuasive text.* New York: Mondo Publishing.

Teague, M. (2002). *Dear Mrs. LaRue: Letters from obedience school.* New York: Scholastic.

Wilkinson, A. M. (1986). Argument as a primary act of mind. *Educational Review, 38*(2), 127–138.

Zhang, J., & Dougherty Stahl, K. A. (2011). Collaborative reasoning: Language rich discussions for English learners. *The Reading Teacher, 65*(4), 257–260.

CHAPTER 9

Energizing Reading

Engagement in Teaching and Learning

Ana Taboada Barber and Peet Smith

When we describe our disengaged students, we tend to use words that describe traits that are inherent to them, as children not putting enough effort or attention into their academic work. We often use language that describes the student's behaviors as independent of our attitudes and responsibilities as teachers. With many English learners (ELs), this characterization is often compounded by their limitations with oral and written English. That is, many ELs may seem particularly disengaged from learning and reading because they do not often have the words in English to convey their interests or elaborate on them. They may also have a hard time participating in class, thus passing as indifferent to the topics being discussed. Think of the times teachers have asked a question about a topic during class and students' eyes glazed over. Although many teachers understand that this vacant look may reflect limited understanding of the language, others may perceive it as a lack of interest and disengagement from school learning. The challenge for us as teachers is to overcome our own perceptions and create the classroom context that invites ELs to participate, to want to learn, and to become engaged readers and learners.

In this chapter we first delve into the concept of academic engagement and differentiate it from the similar but distinct construct of motivation. We then focus on the relationship between reading engagement and achievement, and the importance of reading engagement for all students, but especially for ELs, given their struggles with reading as they move through the upper elementary and middle grades. The remainder of the chapter focuses on four practices that have been identified to support reading and academic engagement for EL and non-EL students alike. These engagement-fostering practices include teacher support and three forms of support for student autonomy: avoiding coercion, providing choice, and facilitating the formation and realization of authentic and direction-giving values. This group of practices is not exhaustive, and we emphasize them in addition to others that have been previously identified as supporting reading engagement for all learners (e.g., see Wigfield, Mason-Singh, Ho, & Guthrie, 2014). We selected these engagement-supporting practices based on two criteria. First, some of them (e.g., meaningful academic choices) have been repeatedly found to foster engagement with various types of learners, yet they have not often been considered in relation to ELs. Second, other practices (e.g., avoiding coercion) have been less explored in relation to reading engagement and hold promise for nurturing the reading and academic engagement of all students, but especially of ELs. Thus, in this chapter we aim to explore how practices that have been described to support academic engagement in all students can be specifically beneficial for facilitating ELs' engagement in reading.

Engagement and Motivation

Although engagement and motivation are interrelated terms, they can be differentiated from each other. *Engagement* is an umbrella term or meta-construct (Fredricks, Blumenfeld, & Paris, 2004) that refers to students' actual participation or involvement in learning or reading. As such, engagement includes behavioral, cognitive, and emotional attributes associated with being deeply involved in an activity such as reading. Engaged readers can display some or all three dimensions of academic engagement. They display behavioral engagement through actions such as effort, persistence, concentration, attention, asking questions, and contributing to class discussions (Birch & Ladd, 1997; Finn, Pannozzo, & Voelkl, 1995; Skinner & Belmont, 1993). They display emotional engagement through their affective reactions to reading, such as interest, curiosity, or enjoyment (Connell & Wellborn, 1991; Skinner & Belmont, 1993). Engaged readers also display characteristics of cognitive engagement through the desire to go beyond the basic requirements and through their preference for challenge (Connell & Wellborn, 1991; Newmann, Wehlage, & Lamborn, 1992; Wehlage, Rutter, Smith, Lesko, & Fernandez, 1989) as well as their use of sophisticated reading strategies (e.g., monitoring) and their desire for conceptual learning (Guthrie, Wigfield, & You, 2012).

   Motivation, on the other hand, is a more specific construct that refers to a willingness or desire to invest time in learning (Gettinger & Walter, 2012) as well as to the beliefs, values, and goals individuals have for different activities (Eccles & Wigfield, 2002). As such, motivation relates to engagement, but it is not the same. "Motivation is what energizes and directs behavior" (Guthrie et al., 2012, p. 62), whereas engagement includes or reflects motivated action and beliefs, such that when students are motivated to read, they will be more engaged (Skinner, Kindermann, Connell, & Wellborn, 2009a; Skinner, Kindermann, & Furrer, 2009b; Guthrie et al., 2012).

Reading researchers have defined *reading engagement* as interacting with texts in ways that are both strategic and motivated (Guthrie & Wigfield, 2000). That is, engaged readers are strategic in their approaches to text, such that they know what reading strategies can help them construct meaning, are knowledgeable about how to build meaning from text, and are socially interactive while reading (Guthrie, McGough, Bennett, & Rice, 1996; Guthrie & Wigfield, 2000; Guthrie, Wigfield, & Perencevich, 2004; see also Baker, Dreher, & Guthrie, 2000). Engaged readers also express the desire to learn. Simply put, engaged readers are motivated readers.

The Close Link between Reading Achievement and Reading Engagement

Although it has been established that the relationship between motivation and reading achievement is likely to be reciprocal (e.g., Morgan & Fuchs, 2007), there is less certainty about the reciprocity of the relationship between reading engagement and achievement because this interaction is confounded by many variables (Guthrie et al., 2012). For example, third- and fifth- grade students' amount of time spent reading in school—an indicator of behavioral engagement—was associated with reading comprehension, even when controlling for background knowledge, previous grades, self-efficacy, and intrinsic motivation (Guthrie et al., 1999). Similar relationships were found for a national sample of tenth graders when controlling for socioeconomic status (SES) and past achievement (Guthrie, Anderson, Alao, & Rinehart, 1999). Yet, given the multiple dimensions of engagement (i.e., behavioral, emotional, and cognitive) as well as factors such as background knowledge, previous performance, and other cognitive dimensions of comprehension, the reciprocal relationship between engagement and achievement has not yet been fully tested. However, it stands to reason that just like high engagement leads to high reading achievement, high achievement may be conducive to higher engagement.

Despite the fact that we do not know much about the relationship between engagement and reading achievement in ELs, some researchers have explored it via mediational models. For example, it has been found that fifth-grade ELs' reading engagement partially mediates the strong relationship between academic vocabulary and reading comprehension in science. ELs' vocabulary was a key factor in their reading comprehension, but their reading engagement also had significant weight in their understanding of science texts (Taboada, Townsend, & Boynton, 2012). Reading engagement was measured by using teacher reports of students' time spent reading, self-efficacy or competence for reading, involvement in reading, student collaboration on reading-related activities, and active use of comprehension strategies. These dimensions of engagement can be approached in classroom contexts, and thus become malleable and susceptible to change if teachers are determined to support their ELs' reading engagement.

Why Should We Care about ELs' Reading Engagement?

Given the academic challenges faced by ELs, reading engagement may appear to be a facet of their school lives that can wait. Perhaps we should first cater to English proficiency, vocabulary development, or to the grammatical structures needed for effective speaking and writing? The list of priorities can become long, and attention to these students' engaged reading may seem tangential or something that is reserved for good readers. Yet, the close connection between engaged reading and reading achievement speaks to the urgency of turning our attention to ELs' engagement. Furthermore, we know that as students move through and beyond the upper elementary grades, they tend to become more disengaged from reading and learning in general. For instance, national reports have shown that 46% of fourth graders said they read for fun almost every day, whereas only 8% of eighth graders did (National Center for Education Statistics, 2011).

Not only is there a more pronounced disengagement as students move to the middle grades, but across grades students who read for fun almost every day scored highest (proficient and advanced) on the National Assessment of Educational Progress (NAEP) reading tests, while those who scored lowest (basic) reported never or hardly ever reading for fun (National Center for Education Statistics, 2011). Given that over twice as many fourth graders and three and a half times as many eighth-grade ELs score below basic reading on the NAEP in comparison to their English-speaking peers (Aud, Wilkinson-Flicker, Kristapovich, Rathbun, Wang, et al., 2013), the question of whether ELs who are weak or struggling readers would reflect patterns similar to the general population of those who hardly ever or never read for fun is an important one. There is a clear need to approach the reading challenges faced by ELs in a comprehensive manner that considers both cognitive and motivational dimensions of the act of reading. Reading engagement comprises both these dimensions.

How to Support Reading Engagement in the Classroom: Self-Determination Theory as a Framework

If the desire to learn is the ultimate expression of an engaged reader, how do we help our struggling readers, especially our ELs, become intrigued, interested, and eventually hooked into reading? As we shared earlier, our first step is not to perceive engagement as something that belongs to the student—as a trait that is not susceptible to change. Rather, we should approach student engagement as a capacity that can be enhanced and may serve to protect students against failure.

There are several instructional practices that, over the years, researchers have identified and observed to foster students' engagement. We present four of these practices in this chapter: teacher support, avoiding coercion, providing choice, and facilitating the formation and realization of authentic and direction-giving values (see Table 9.1). The latter three are all forms of autonomy support, and fall within the theoretical lenses of self-determination theory (SDT). SDT is a theory of motivation that assumes that all students, regardless of age, gender, SES, or cultural background or nationality, have inherent tendencies to grow (e.g., intrinsic motivation, curiosity, and psychological needs). These growth tendencies provide a motivational basis for engaging in learning and positive school functioning (Deci & Ryan, 1985, 2000; Reeve, Deci, & Ryan, 2004; Ryan & Deci, 2002). SDT is different from other motivational theories in that it identifies the inner motivational resources that students have and offers recommendations through which teachers can nurture and foster these resources

---

TABLE 9.1. Four Instructional Practices to Support Student Engagement

1. *Teacher support:* The extent to which teachers listen to, encourage, and respect students, and the quality of teacher–child relationships (Bingham & Okagaki, 2012).

2. *Avoiding coercion[a]:* Providing opportunities for lessening students' feelings of being controlled, such that they can develop an inner criteria for making important decisions (Assor, 2012).

3. *Providing choice[a]:* Providing opportunities for meaningful realization of the individual's desires or preferences (Katz & Assor, 2007).

4. *Facilitating the formation and realization of authentic and direction-giving values[a]:* Providing opportunities for students to form and realize authentic values, interests and goals, rather than responding to social pressures (Assor, 2012).

---

[a]Forms of autonomy support within SDT. *Autonomy support* in classroom or school contexts refers to educators' efforts to support and nurture the intrinsic need of all individuals for autonomy. The *need for autonomy* refers to individuals' desire to recognize and develop personal goals, values, and interests (Assor, 2012).

during instruction to facilitate student engagement (Niemiec & Ryan, 2009; Reeve, 2012).

In identifying these practices, we cast a wide net: We explored the reading engagement literature and the motivation literature within an SDT approach (Ryan & Deci, 2000). In our work we especially rely on SDT to promote student engagement because of its emphasis on autonomy support—a practice that, as former reading teachers, we both embrace and value. SDT proposes that students' inner resources (e.g., intrinsic motivation, need for autonomy) interact with classroom conditions that either nurture or diminish those inner tendencies to result in various levels of student engagement (Reeve, 2012). Among these inner resources, SDT identifies the three psychological needs of autonomy, competence, and relatedness. *Autonomy* refers to the need to experience behavior as emanating from the self (Deci & Ryan, 1985). Students experience autonomy when their classroom activities afford them opportunities to engage in learning that is at least somewhat endorsed and controlled by them, such that they have a sense of psychological freedom and perceived choice over their actions (Reeve, Nix & Hamm, 2003). *Competence* refers to the inherent desire to feel effective in exercising one's capacities—to seek out and master challenges (Deci, 1975). *Relatedness* is the need to establish close connections with others, such that one feels emotionally connected with others in warm and responsive relationships (Deci & Ryan, 1991). Whereas the needs for competence and relatedness have received considerable attention from other theorists (e.g., Baumeister & Leary, 1995; Elliot & Dweck, 2005; White, 1959), SDT is unique in its emphasis on the need for autonomy (Assor, 2012). In turn, autonomy support has been determined to be a key practice in fostering reading engagement for English monolingual students (e.g., Guthrie et al., 2004) as well as for ELs (e.g., Taboada, Kidd, & Tonks, 2010).

Each of the engagement-supporting practices in this chapter are theoretically rooted and empirically validated. In addition, they have been shown to work with a variety of students. We suggest specific ways in which these practices can promote reading engagement for ELs, especially those in the upper elementary and middle grades.

Teacher Support

All dedicated teachers know how much of an impact their attitudes and support can have on their students' lives. A genuine smile, a positive comment, helpful feedback, honest praise, and listening carefully all make a difference in a student's day. Yet sometimes in the rush towards academic goals and testing requirements, we may forget how especially prone to the need of teacher support ELs can be. The amount of teacher support, often defined as the extent to which teachers listen to, encourage, and respect students, and the quality of teacher–child relationships, may be especially important to racial and ethnic-minority students' engagement in school (Bingham & Okagaki, 2012). We extend the importance of teacher support to ELs, given the vulnerability that having to perform academically in a language that is being learned concurrently with academic content can create. Several researchers have argued that the amount of teacher support can help students navigate differences between home and school environments (Gay, 2000; Heath, 1983); cope with experiences of discrimination, failure, and environmental risk (Faircloth & Hamm, 2005; Garcia-Reid, 2007; Garcia-Reid, Reid, & Peterson, 2005; Gay, 2000; Roeser, Strobel, & Quihuis, 2002); and facilitate positive beliefs about learning and the importance of education (Skinner, Furrer, Marchand, & Kindermann, 2008; Strambler & Weinstein, 2010; Urdan & Schoenfelder, 2006).

A positive teacher–student relationship may be particularly beneficial for ELs who need support from teachers to navigate the classroom culture, language, and mores, which may differ from their families' cultures (Au, 1998; Heath, 1983). The uncertainties that come from having to communicate in a language that is different from the home language can bring significant anxiety to many ELs, especially those who are newcomers and are learning a new language and a new culture while having to perform academically. For these students, teacher support can be a pivotal factor in their academic engagement. For example, low-income Latino middle and high school students' perceived support from teachers was negatively associated with students' problem school behavior, such as showing up late for school and skipping class, and positively associated with students' emotional engagement, such as positive feelings about school (Brewster & Bowen, 2004). Similarly, Latino middle school students' ratings of teacher closeness and trust were positively related to students' behavioral engagement (e.g., "Trying hard is the best way for me to do well in school"; "I can work really hard in school"), after controlling for student achievement on reading and math and the quality of the parent–child relationship (Murray, 2009).

What are some basic practices we can have in place to convey our support for ELs' reading development and success? Teacher support can take multiple forms. In fact, many would argue that teacher support is more a set of attitudes and behaviors than a specific set of practices that can be learned and adopted. Although we would partly agree with that view, we also strongly believe that teachers' behaviors can change in response to learned practices. Thus, we share a few teacher-support practices from the field, in which upper elementary and middle school teachers made their support explicit and part of their instructional literacy routines for ELs. Please note that these practices refer to reading-related activities in a broad manner. That is, with the renewed emphasis brought by the Common Core State Standards (CCSS) on integrating literacy with content areas and the call for increased use of informational texts, we need to consider fostering reading engagement through teacher support across the curriculum. Also note that teacher support can take a variety of forms, so as long as these show instances of teacher willingness and efforts to listen to, encourage, and respect students.

- Have high expectations for ELs. To help ELs succeed in literacy, we need to see their cultures and languages as assets to the classroom culture. If we see their language proficiencies as obstacles to their learning, we are likely to be setting low expectations for their reading in English.

- Provide opportunities to explore students' interests and have reading materials that cater to those interests within curricular boundaries.

- Encourage one-on-one conferences focused on individual students' reading skills and content. Structure conferences to be centered on topics of interest, as well as areas of challenge within reading (e.g., "How do you think you learn most from books: by reading silently or in small groups? Why? Tell me more."). Open the floor to discuss reading styles, strengths, and weaknesses. The more ELs and all struggling readers learn about their strengths and weaknesses, the more they can focus, with teacher scaffolding, on how to improve the weaknesses. Self-monitoring is a good first step toward developing increased competence in reading.

- Encourage various forms of student pairings for reading activities, such that ELs are paired up with English-speaking peers and benefit from exposure to English, but are also paired with other ELs and share progress on reading skills and content-knowledge development with each other. Provide pairs with sustained teacher scaffolding and corrective feedback of students' conversations and interactions in relation to the reading activities.

- Teach ELs comprehension strategies so they can access a variety of texts, both with teacher assistance and on their own. If properly taught, comprehension strategies can lead to increasingly independent reading and comprehension. Providing opportunities for growing reading independence is another form of teacher care.

- Show ELs how to determine text difficulty (e.g., readability levels based on sentence length and number of unknown words in a text as well as student–text match based on topic background knowledge) so that they can make appropriate choices about texts. Provide opportunities for class discussions on cultural and language diversity so that ELs feel that their cultures and language backgrounds are valued in the classroom. Having students' unique cultural and linguistic backgrounds acknowledged is an important way to show teacher care and make ELs feel like active members of a classroom community.

- Provide a clear classroom structure, such that students know what is expected from them and what the short- and long-term goals for a unit, topic, or subject are. Classroom structure and clear expectations relieve students' anxiety.

Student Autonomy as a Means to Engagement: A Multifaceted Practice

If we said that *autonomy* is important to us as individuals and as educators, what thoughts would that statement conjure? Probably thoughts of freedom, flexibility, and developing and working toward one's own goals; opportunities to explore one's own ideas, goals, and tasks; and a sense of control over one's learning and activities. Indeed, *autonomy* encompasses many dimensions, and as such, multiple practices in the classroom can support, or hinder, students' sense of autonomous learning.

According to SDT, one crucial factor that may explain why some students are disengaged or poorly motivated is that they do not feel that school-related activities support their need for autonomy (Assor, 2012). Motivational researchers have defined *autonomy* as individuals' desire to recognize and develop personal goals, values, and interests (Assor, 2012). Supporting autonomous motives in our students is much more likely to promote flexible and creative engagement in learning (Deci & Ryan, 1985; Roth, Assor, Niemiec, Ryan, & Deci, 2009). When people are pressured and coerced to behave in specific ways, they experience frustration. In turn, this frustration has been shown to undermine engagement (Assor, Kaplan, Kanat-Maymon, & Roth, 2005; Assor, Kaplan, & Roth, 2002; Reeve & Jang, 2006). Because of the multiple facets of autonomy as a psychological need and its potential to support engaged learning and reading, we follow Assor's (2012) three principles, suggested in the motivation literature, for supporting students' autonomy in school contexts: (1) avoiding coercion, (2) providing choices, and (3) facilitating the formation and realization of authentic and direction-giving values. All three practices have been linked to student engagement. We describe how teachers can enact each of these practices, particularly with ELs in literacy contexts.

Avoiding Coercion

Avoiding coercion is a form of autonomy support because it consists of individuals' freedom to choose their own actions without feeling pressured and coerced (from outside or from within) while developing an inner criteria for making important decisions (Assor, 2012). There are different ways to avoid coercion in classroom settings. One empirically validated practice is to minimize controls. A controlling style is an enduring characteristic in which the teacher prescribes what the student should think, feel, or act; it is also accompanied by the application of pressure to make sure that the student complies with the prescription (Assor, Kaplan, Kanat-Maymon, & Roth, 2005). When a teacher minimizes controls she uses less pressuring language ("you must/ought/should") and includes more explanatory rationales for activities and tasks. However, minimizing teacher or curricular controls may be a necessary condition, but it is not sufficient for supporting students' need for autonomy. That is, although the presence of too much teacher control can undermine students' autonomy, its absence may not be enough for students to feel they can make academic choices and have some sense of direction over their learning (Assor, 2012). Other teacher behaviors, such as a tendency to intrude and interfere as students work on their assignments and/or to discourage answers that diverge from teachers' own opinions, are also highly controlling and undermine academic engagement and raise anger and anxiety (Assor et al., 2005). How can teachers develop an autonomy-supportive style that avoids coercion and control in literacy contexts? One way is having time for open literacy tasks that allow for multiple answers within reading and writing tasks. Multiple answers generate less rigidity between what is right and wrong, such that factors that delimit and control possible responses/answers may be minimized. Compare, for instance, students' reactions to writing an essay in response to specific teacher or textbook prompts versus selecting topics to write about. ELs' engagement may plummet given the limited experience with many of the topics typically offered in standardized writing prompts. Similarly, picture the case where the teacher has just taught how to identify main ideas at the paragraph level for informational science texts. To check students' understanding, two activities could be considered. In one scenario, students have to select the main idea via multiple-choice questions offering both correct and incorrect answers. Alternatively, students participate in a paired reading of two paragraphs in which each student has to (1) read aloud to his or her partner; (2) read silently and identify the main idea; (3) share the main idea with the partner; (4) provide corrective feedback to each other; and (5) share their responses with the teacher and discuss. Which one of the two activities is less coercive and more autonomy-supportive? Clearly the second one has many more opportunities for students' interactions, exchange of opinions, and feeling less threatened by "right" or "wrong" answers. Now, we are not saying that more controlling activities or tasks should be avoided at all costs. In fact, as former teachers, we see their role under specific circumstances. What we are saying is that, as teachers of very diverse classrooms with increasing literacy challenges and demands, we need to become aware of practices that are more or less conducive to student reading engagement. In doing so, we are likely to foster all students', but especially ELs', reading within and outside our classroom boundaries.

Another instructional practice that can avoid coercion and foster students' sense of autonomy is the provision of rationales or explanations for specific activities, assignments, and tasks. By having opportunities to discuss and understand the reasons *why* learning about the Civil War can help middle schoolers understand their civic roles and responsibilities (e.g., understanding how the roles and authorities of the federal government differ from those of the states) today, students are given an opportunity to contextualize information in relation to their everyday lives—they see the purpose for their learning of history in a new light. As a result, the task is likely to be perceived as less controlling and coercive. Whether students find a task completely interesting or not, it has been found that when students are provided with a clear and convincing rationale, they tend to feel less coerced into completing the assignment and have a generally more positive attitude about the task (Assor, 2012; Grolnick, Deci, & Ryan, 1997).

A good context in which to shift the emphasis to a greater sense of student control and decrease coercion is that of comprehension strategy instruction. Because of their utility across content areas, comprehension strategies are excellent cognitive tools for instilling clear rationales for students. Instead of emphasizing text comprehension in relation to test or standards requirements, strategy instruction can provide clear steps for comprehending text and unpacking understandings that are under the control of the student. If comprehension strategy instruction is explicit and leads students toward independent use over time, these strategies can become tools that allow students to meet teacher goals while also setting their own goals for comprehension. That is, to the extent that students understand the usefulness of the comprehension instruction strategy (why they need it) and how to apply it to varied texts and genres, they can unpack text in a way that feels less coercive and more under their own control. (See Boardman & Jensen Lasser, Chapter 6, this volume, for more information on teaching reading comprehension strategies.) For example, a seventh-grade teacher explains:

"When we activate background knowledge, we are thinking of what we know before and during reading so that we can connect what we know—or think we know!—with what we later read. There are different ways in which we can activate our background knowledge about a topic. One way is to use text features such as a book's front and back covers, its table of contents, the glossary, some captions, and illustrations. Why do you think that activating what we know is good for our reading?"

In the ensuing discussion, the value of linking prior knowledge with new information is established. These seventh graders are much more likely to have a purpose for background knowledge activation, and as a result, feel empowered or in control of this particular tool for their reading.

In sum, teachers may come with a variety of practices that avoid or minimize coercion and supporting students' autonomous learning. Some of these include:

- Allow space for students to voice their opinions about topics and ways of approaching them.
- Consider your responses and the opportunities provided for students' *own* responses. Students are likely to become more engaged in reading and literacy-related activities when their opinions are honored and when they have opportunities to respond to open-ended tasks that allow for more than one answer.
- Provide rationales and/or explicit explanations for tasks that are explanatory and feel authentic to students. Establishing rationales or explicit explanations can be done for content (e.g., Why do we need to know about the Civil War for our lives today?) as well as for reading skills or cognitive tools such as comprehension strategies (e.g., Why is it useful to ask questions before, during, and after reading? Why do we need to activate our prior knowledge before reading?).
- React to statements such as "I'm bored" as opportunities to acknowledge and reflect on the classroom topics and proceedings. Sometimes providing students with a relevant explanation as to *why* and *how* their learning about a topic contributes to their lives beyond school may change their dispositions.
- Challenge students to reflect on their own interests in relation to various topics. Doing so will help you provide relevant reading materials that cater to interests and curiosities that may fall beyond the prescribed requirements. This may go a long way toward nurturing ELs' autonomy and engagement.

Providing Choices

The relationship between choice and engagement has been widely researched. Choosing or having choices within the motivation literature involves an opportunity for meaningful realization of the individual's desires or preferences (Katz & Assor, 2007). Even when students are provided with a task that is relatively uninteresting to them, the inclusion of choice within that task can promote autonomous motivation and positive feelings while performing the task (e.g., Assor et al., 2002; Cordova & Lepper, 1996; Deci, Eghrari, Patrick, & Leone, 1994; Katz & Assor, 2007;

Reynolds & Symons, 2001; Zuckerman, Porac, Lathin, Smith, & Deci, 1978). Also, it is well established that students prefer to have the option to choose (e.g., Patall, Cooper, & Robinson, 2008), but they do not have to be the ones to always make the choice. For example, when parents choose activities for their children that are in agreement with their interests, children willingly engage in these activities, but if the activities are inconsistent with their interests, then children feel controlled and disengaged (Katz & Assor, 2007). Within the realm of literacy instruction, research has shown that choice of partners, reading-related activity, subtopics to read about, type of book to read, and type of knowledge display (e.g., graphic organizer, debate, museum exhibit) relate to student engagement in reading (e.g., Guthrie et al., 2004, 2007). Among ELs, we have found that fourth graders can be very articulate about the reasons why different types of choices "feel good" to them and why they help them become more engaged with the topics at hand (e.g., Taboada et al., 2010), as well as the positive impact that reading-related choices have on middle school ELs' self-efficacy and engagement in reading (Taboada-Barber et al., 2015).

Providing choice promotes student engagement not only because it is "fun," but also because it allows students to examine what is important to them. In choosing, often students need to consider what they like and do not like and why. Let's take the example of the English for Speakers of Other Languages (ESOL) teacher who builds a classroom library in which he or she purposefully stocks books of various genres, topics, reading levels, and languages. By allowing ELs to explore the library and choose books on their own, this teacher is providing an opportunity for them to also explore and reflect on their own values and interests, as well as on their individual reading levels and language preferences. This context of providing choice is particularly important for ELs, whose interests may exist outside of the typical shared childhood experiences of the majority student population. Furthermore, as part of our research with upper elementary ELs, we found that when provided with choices of several trade books on science topics in Spanish (e.g., electric circuits, energy, animal and plant adaptations, Earth science topics) fourth- and fifth-grade ELs who had emerging English proficiency purposively chose the Spanish texts to build background knowledge and as preliminary reading materials to the same topics in English (Boynton & Taboada, 2010). However, when fourth-grade ELs of intermediate to advanced English proficiency were afforded choices of Spanish literature in science, they gravitated to English reading materials, with one student explaining that he "feel[s] better reading in English, as I do not know how to read well in Spanish" (José, fourth grader; Taboada & Rutherford, 2011).

Choice menus are another way in which a teacher might introduce choice in the classroom. For example, Taboada Barber observed how a sixth-grade social studies teacher offered different ways in which students could demonstrate their learning from the text at the end of the Civil War unit. She asked students to choose three mini projects from a list of six original ones that they would like to complete. Each project was given different point values, and students had to choose three projects that totaled at least 10 points (points were balanced across projects in such a way that the topic of the mini project guided the choice and not the points). Students were asked to use books from their whole-class reading and guided reading groups as references. Options for showing their learning from text included:

- *Write a letter to a government official asking for assistance.* This option provides students with an opportunity to take the perspective of an important, in-the-field figure in Civil War history, such as Clara Barton. Students can choose to write a letter to President Lincoln or another prominent political figure about their experiences working as a nurse in a field house during the battle of Antietam. Clara Barton's experiences on the battlefield can frame the request for assistance with medical supplies. Perspective taking is needed for such writing.
- *Write a newspaper article.* This option on the choice menu again encourages perspective taking, especially for those students who prefer a journalistic style of writing. Students might take on the role of a reporter who interviews various Union and Confederate generals in order to better understand their rationale for the war.
- *Write a persuasive essay.* This option might suit the more opinionated students! One possibility could be a persuasive essay about why wars should or should not be fought within one's own country. (See Brisk et al., Chapter 8, this volume, on argument writing for additional ideas.)
- *Create a "Wanted" poster.* Abraham Lincoln has just been assassinated by John Wilkes Booth! Students might create a "Wanted" poster with a description of this person, his co-conspirators, where he was last seen, and where they think he might be headed.
- *Design a book jacket.* Students who best demonstrate their knowledge through visual creativity might choose this option. Book jackets could be created for Civil War trade books that they have read in class and would include an image and caption on the front, as well as a description of the book on the back.

Offering options on how to display text-based knowledge contributes to students' engagement for various reasons. Consider that students may demonstrate their learning successfully in different ways, such that asking an entire class to write a five-paragraph essay about the disagreements between the North and the South in the United States during the Civil War may be too restrictive for some. ELs may also feel restricted in the cognitive tools they have for truly displaying their knowledge in writing on the Civil War. So, a less language-loaded option, such as creating a "Wanted" poster for John Wilkes Booth, would allow them to opt for their topic interests as well as to capitalize on stronger ways to display their knowledge. Furthermore, the teacher may want to conference with his or her EL struggling readers individually to help them come up with specific goals for their project. For example, after reading about the Civil War, the same sixth-grade teacher mentioned above conferred with three of her EL struggling readers. She found out that two girls were very interested in focusing on the female nurses who helped soldiers on the battlefield. She encouraged them to teach the rest of the students more about these nurses through their end-of-unit project. Student expertise and voices are both honored through such an opportunity. The purpose of offering meaningful choices was to help students find an option that was aligned with their individual goals. In sum, some ways of offering meaningful choices that can lead to student autonomy and engagement are:

- Use choice menus. These can include options for book titles, comprehension strategies, partners with whom to work, knowledge display formats, or subtopics within a unit.
- Offer book choices. Have a classroom or school library that is stocked with books of varying genres, topics, and reading levels.
- Offer opportunities for knowledge displays. Offer projects and assignments of varying formats and levels that take into account ELs' language and literacy skills.
- Encourage students to think *why* they opt for certain tasks, books, work stations, etc., and not for others. Have them reflect on how their reasons connect to the choices they make within and outside the classroom.

Facilitating the Formation and Realization of Authentic Values

Helping students to form and realize authentic, direction-giving values, goals, and interests is important because it helps them develop their autonomy in relation to learning in general, and ultimately to their reading engagement in particular. However, perhaps more importantly, forming and realizing goals and values provides students with an "inner compass," or a set of internal criteria, with which to evaluate themselves and make them less dependent on others' evaluations (Assor, 2012). Although the concept of promoting opportunities for students to reflect on their own goals, values, and interests is fairly new in the motivation literature, it is particularly important for ELs. ELs' opportunities to explore their own values and goals in relation to their academic lives are practically nonexistent in the research literature or in education practice. The role of the teacher within this practice consists mostly of encouraging students, especially young adolescents and beyond, to participate in activities that allow them to examine and reflect seriously and critically on their goals, values, and interests (Assor, 2012; Kanat-Maymon & Assor, 2011) in relation to learning at large, and to reading in particular. Think of how often adolescent ELs are given the opportunity to reflect on the role that reading plays in their lives—today and for the future.

How can we encourage this type of reflective stance in the classroom? When teachers encourage their students to participate in activities, experiences, and group discussions that allow them to reflect deliberately and critically on their own goals, values, and interests, they are supporting students' examination of their own values. These activities and experiences can take the form of small-group or whole-class discussions, as long as the setting provides a safe and comfortable environment for students to discuss these issues. (See Ossa Parra et al., Chapter 7, this volume, for more information about using small-group discussions.)

A gradual way of having ELs explore their values and goals is to start by having them explore their reading interests. For example, as part of the current affairs unit in social studies, a seventh-grade teacher decided to bring in literature and nonfiction books on pop culture, current events, historical issues relevant to today's events, and remarkable people in recent history. Students spent 2 weeks reading about one to two main topics of interest to them. As part of their project they had to elaborate on why the topic(s) was of interest to them, and whether they could relate it to other interests in their lives. As a way to ensure that the discussion was focused and led to explicit statements of ELs' interests, this teacher also included language objectives as part of the unit and structured students' discussion using stems (see Table 9.2). In this way, the discussions were focused, and students had the opportunity to express and explore their interests within a semistructured discussion format.

Other opportunities for examination of values can include short student surveys, open-ended essays, or conversations wherein students can explore their thinking on topics such as the following:

1. "The activities and reading materials in class sometimes cause me to think about important things I would like to do in my life."
2. "The activities and reading materials in class help me to find out what are the things I value in people."
3. "School studies and some of my readings cause me to think of traits (characteristics) I would like to have."
4. "School studies and readings help me to think about fair and desirable ways of acting in challenging situations such as. . . ."
5. "School studies and readings help me to think about what is more

TABLE 9.2. Discussion Stems for ELs

Types of discussion	Stem
Receiving what the partner says	• *Thank you.* • *Those are good ideas.* • *That was interesting.* • *You helped me understand this in a new way.*
More elaboration and extension of the idea	• *Can you tell me more?* • *What does that mean?* • *Can you think of another example?* • *What you said reminds me of. . . .*
Clarification	• *Can you explain that a little more?* • *I'm not sure what you mean; can you say it in a different way?* • *Where in the text did you find that idea?* • *Can you tell me why you think that?*
Making connections	• *That's an interesting connection. I was thinking of something else.* • *I made that connection with. . . .* • *I think this is like. . . .* • *I remember when. . . .* • *I remember reading about. . . .* • *It reminds me of. . . .*
Adding a different perspective	• *That's interesting.* • *I hadn't thought of it in that way. I was thinking something different*

important and what is less important in life." (adapted from Assor, 2012, p. 430)

Conclusion

In this chapter we discussed academic engagement, and more specifically, reading engagement, as a proximal influence that is susceptible to change in classroom settings. In doing so, we considered how ELs' engagement in general, and with reading in particular, could be influenced by teacher and classroom practices. We focused on teacher support and three student autonomy-supportive practices as possible conduits to ELs' engagement in reading and learning. Much work, both from educational practitioners and researchers, remains to be done to fine-tune these practices and tailor them to the reading instruction and the literacy development of ELs. However, it is our hope that, by offering some initial ideas on how these practices can be promoted, teachers and school administrators will consider some contextual ways in which ELs' reading engagement can be fostered. We also hope that ELs' reading engagement is both perceived as a pivotal dimension of these students' school lives, as well as one that is under the direct impact of teachers and other educators.

REFERENCES

Assor, A. (2012). Allowing choice and nurturing an inner compass: Educational practices supporting students' need for autonomy. In S. L. Christenson, A. L. Reschly, & C. Wylie (Eds.), *Handbook of research on student engagement* (pp. 421–439). New York: Springer.

Assor, A., Kaplan, H., Kanat-Maymon, Y., & Roth, G. (2005). Directly controlling teachers' behaviors as predictors of poor motivation and engagement in girls and boys: The role of anger and anxiety. *Learning and Instruction, 15,* 397–413.

Assor, A., Kaplan, H., & Roth, G. (2002). Choice is good but relevance is excellent: Autonomy affecting teacher behaviors that predict students' engagement in learning. *British Journal of Educational Psychology, 72,* 261–278.

Au, K. H. (1998). Social constructivism and the school literacy learning of students of diverse backgrounds. *Journal of Literacy Research, 30,* 297–319.

Aud, S., Wilkinson-Flicker, S., Kristapovich, P., Rathbun, A., Wang, X., & Zhang, J. (2013). The condition of education 2013 (NCES 2013-037). Washington, DC: National Center for Education Statistics. Retrieved from *http://nces. ed.gov/pubsearch.*

Baker, L., Dreher, M. J., & Guthrie, J. T. (Eds.). (2000). *Engaging young readers.* New York: Guilford Press.

Baumeister, R. F., & Leary, M. R. (1995). The need to belong: Desire for interpersonal attachments as a fundamental human motivation. *Psychological Bulletin, 117*(3), 497–529.

Bingham, G. E., & Okagaki, L. (2012). Ethnicity and student engagement. In S. L. Christenson, A. L. Reschley, & C. Wylie (Eds.), *Handbook of research on student engagement* (pp. 65–95). New York: Springer.

Birch, S., & Ladd, G. (1997). The teacher–child relationship and children's early school adjustment. *Journal of School Psychology, 35,* 61–79.

Boynton, M. J., & Taboada, A. (2010, December). *Adolescent ELL characteristics and needs.* Paper presented at the annual meeting of the National Reading Council (NRC)/Literacy Research Association (LRA), Fort Worth, TX.

Brewster, A. B., & Bowen, G. L. (2004). Teacher support and the school engagement of Latino middle and high school students at risk of school failure. *Child and Adolescent Social Work Journal, 21,* 47–67.

Connell, J., & Wellborn, J. (1991). Competence, autonomy, and relatedness: A motivational analysis of self-system processes. In M. Gunnar & L. Sroufe (Eds.), *Self processes in development: Minnesota Symposia on Child Psychology* (Vol. 43, pp. 43–77). Chicago: University of Chicago Press.

Cordova, D. I., & Lepper, M. R. (1996). Intrinsic motivation and the process of learning: Beneficial effects of contextualization, personalization, and choice. *Journal of Educational Psychology, 88,* 715–730.

Deci, E. L. (1975). *Intrinsic motivation.* New York: Plenum Press.

Deci, E. L., Eghrari, H., Patrick, B. C., & Leone, D. R. (1994). Facilitating internalization: The self-determination theory perspective. *Journal of Personality, 62,* 119–142.

Deci, E. L., & Ryan, R. M. (1985). *Intrinsic motivation and self-determination in human behavior.* New York: Plenum Press.

Deci, E. L., & Ryan, R. M. (1991). A motivational approach to self: Integration in personality. In R. Dienstbier (Ed.), *Nebraska Symposium on Motivation: Perspectives on motivation* (Vol. 38, pp. 237–288). Lincoln: University of Nebraska Press.

Deci, E. L., & Ryan, R. M. (2000). The "what" and "why" of goal pursuits: Human needs and the self-determination of behavior. *Psychological Inquiry, 11,* 227–268.

Eccles, J. S., & Wigfield, A. (2002). Motivational beliefs, values, and goals. *Annual Review of Psychology, 53,* 109–132.

Elliot, A. J., & Dweck, C. S. (Eds.). (2005). *Handbook of competence and motivation.* New York: Guilford Press.

Faircloth, B. S., & Hamm, J. V. (2005). Sense of belonging among high school students representing four ethnic groups. *Journal of Youth and Adolescence, 34,* 293–309.

Finn, J. D., Pannozzo, G. M., & Voelkl, K. E. (1995). Disruptive and inattentive-withdrawn behavior and achievement among fourth graders. *Elementary School Journal, 95,* 421–434.

Fredricks, J. A., Blumenfeld, P. C., & Paris, A. (2004). School engagement: Potential of the concept—state of the evidence. *Review of Educational Research, 74,* 59–119.

Garcia-Reid, P. (2007). Examining social capital as a mechanism for improving school engagement among low-income Hispanic girls. *Youth and Society, 39*(2), 164–181.

Garcia-Reid, P., Reid, R. J., & Peterson, N. A. (2005). School engagement among Latino youth in an urban middle school context: Valuing the role of social support. *Education and Urban Society, 37,* 257–275.

Gay, G. (2000). *Culturally responsive teaching: Theory, research, and practice.* New York: Teachers College Press.

Gettinger, M., & Walter, M. J. (2012). Classroom strategies to enhance academic engaged time. In S. L. Christenson, A. L. Reschly, & C. Wylie (Eds.), *Handbook of research on student engagement* (pp. 653–673). New York: Springer.

Grolnick, W. S., Deci, E. L., & Ryan, R. M. (1997). Internalization within the family: The self-determination theory perspective. In J. E. Grusec & L. Kuczynski (Eds.), *Parenting and children's internalization of values: A handbook of contemporary theory* (pp. 135–161). New York: Wiley.

Guthrie, J. T., Anderson, E., Alao, S., & Rinehart, J. (1999). Influences of CORI on strategy use and conceptual learning from text. *Elementary School Journal, 99,* 343–366.

Guthrie, J. T., Hoa, L. W., Wigfield, A., Tonks, S. M., Humenick, N. M., & Littles, E. (2007). Reading motivation and reading comprehension growth in the later elementary years. *Contemporary Educational Psychology, 32,* 282–313.

Guthrie, J. T., McGough, K., Bennett, L., & Rice, M. E. (1996). Concept-oriented reading instruction: An integrated curriculum to develop motivations and strategies for reading. In L. Baker, P. Afflerbach, & D. Reinking (Eds.), *Developing engaged readers in school and home communities* (pp. 165–190). Hillsdale, NJ: Erlbaum.

Guthrie, J. T., & Wigfield, A. (2000). Engagement and motivation in reading. In M. L. Kamil & P. B. Mosenthal (Eds.), *Handbook of reading research* (Vol. 3, pp. 403–422). Mahwah, NJ: Erlbaum.

Guthrie, J. T., Wigfield, A., & Perencevich, K. C. (Eds.). (2004). *Motivating reading comprehension: Concept-oriented reading instruction.* Mahwah, NJ: Erlbaum.

Guthrie, J. T., Wigfield, A., & You, W. (2012). Instructional contexts for engagement. In S. L. Christenson, A. L. Reschley, & C. Wylie (Eds.), *Handbook of research on student engagement* (pp. 601–634). New York: Springer.

Heath, S. B. (1983). *Ways with words: Language, life, and work in communities and classrooms.* New York: Cambridge University Press.

Kanat-Maymon, Y., & Assor, A. (2011). *Supporting value exploration: Another important aspect of autonomy support.* Unpublished manuscript, Ben Gurion University of the Negev, Israel.

Katz, I., & Assor, A. (2007). When choice motivates and when it does not. *Educational Psychology Review, 19,* 429–442.

Morgan, P. L. & Fuchs, D. (2007). Is there a bidirectional relationship between children's reading skills and reading motivation? *Council for Exceptional Children, 73,* 165–183.

Murray, C. (2009). Parent and teacher relationships as predictors of school engagement and functioning among low-income urban youth. *Journal of Early Adolescence, 29,* 379–404.

National Center for Education Statistics. (2011). *The Nation's Report Card: Reading 2011* (NCES 2012-457). Washington, DC: Institute of Education Sciences, U.S. Department of Education.

Newmann, F. M., Wehlage, G. G., & Lamborn, S. D. (1992). The significance and sources of student engagement. In F. M. Newmann (Ed.), *Student engagement and achievement in American secondary schools* (pp. 11–39). New York: Teachers College Press.

Niemiec, C. P., & Ryan, R. M. (2009). Autonomy, competence, and relatedness in the classroom: Applying self-determination theory to educational practice. *Theory and Research in Education, 7,* 133–144.

Patall, E. A., Cooper, H., & Robinson, J. C. (2008). The effects of choice on intrinsic motivation and related outcomes: A meta-analysis of research findings. *Psychological Bulletin, 134,* 270–300.

Reeve, J. (2012). A self-determination theory perspective on student engagement. In S. L. Christenson, A. L. Reschley, & C. Wylie (Eds.) *Handbook of research on student engagement* (pp. 149–172). New York: Springer.

Reeve, J., Deci, E. L., & Ryan, R. M. (2004). Self-determination theory: A dialectical framework for understanding socio-cultural influences on student motivation. In S. Van Etten & M. Pressley (Eds.), *Big theories revisited* (pp. 31–60). Greenwich, CT: Information Age Press.

Reeve, J., & Jang, H. (2006). What teachers say and do to support students' autonomy during learning activities. *Journal of Educational Psychology, 98*, 209–218.

Reeve, J., Nix, G., & Hamm, D. (2003). Testing models of the experience of self-determination in intrinsic motivation and the conundrum of choice. *Journal of Educational Psychology, 95*, 375–392.

Reynolds, P. L., & Symons, S. (2001). Motivational variables and children's text search. *Journal of Educational Psychology, 93*, 14–22.

Roeser, R., Strobel, K. R., & Quihuis, G. (2002). Studying early adolescents' academic motivation, social–emotional functioning, and engagement in learning: Variable- and person-centered approaches. *Anxiety, Stress, and Coping, 15*, 345–368.

Roth, G., Assor, A., Niemiec, P. C., Ryan, R. M., & Deci, E. L. (2009). The negative consequences of parental conditional regard: A comparison of positive conditional regard, negative conditional regard, and autonomy support as parenting strategies. *Developmental Psychology, 4*, 1119–1142.

Ryan, R. M., & Deci, E. L. (2000). Self-determination theory and the facilitation of intrinsic motivation, social development, and well-being. *American Psychologist, 55*(1), 68–78.

Ryan, R. M., & Deci, E. L. (2002). An overview of self-determination theory. In E. L. Deci & R. M. Ryan (Eds.), *Handbook of self-determination research* (pp. 3–33). Rochester, NY: University of Rochester Press.

Skinner, E. A., & Belmont, M. J. (1993). Motivation in the classroom: Reciprocal effect of teacher behavior and student engagement across the school year. *Journal of Educational Psychology, 85*, 571–581.

Skinner, E. A., Furrer, C., Marchand, G., & Kindermann, T. (2008). Engagement and disaffection in the classroom: Part of a larger motivational dynamic? *Journal of Educational Psychology, 100*(4), 765–781.

Skinner, E. A., Kindermann, T. A., Connell, J. P., & Wellborn, J. G. (2009a). Engagement and disaffection as organizational constructs in the dynamics of motivational development. In K. R. Wentzel & A. Wigfield (Eds.), *Handbook of motivation at school* (pp. 223–245). New York: Routledge.

Skinner, E. A., Kindermann, T. A., & Furrer, C. J. (2009b). A motivational perspective on engagement and disaffection: Conceptualization and assessment of children's behavioral and emotional participation in academic activities in the classroom. *Educational and Psychological Measurement, 69*, 493–525.

Strambler, M. J., & Weinstein, R. S. (2010). Psychological disengagement in elementary school among ethnic minority students. *Journal of Applied Developmental Psychology, 31*, 155–165.

Taboada, A., Kidd, J. K., & Tonks, S. M. (2010). A qualitative look at English language learners' perceptions of autonomy support in a literacy classroom. *Research in the Schools, 17*, 39–53.

Taboada, A., & Rutherford, V. (2011). Developing reading comprehension and academic vocabulary for English language learners through science content: A formative experiment. *Reading Psychology, 32*(2), 113–157.

Taboada, A., Townsend, D., & Boynton, M. J. (2013). Mediating effects of reading engagement on the reading comprehension of early adolescent English language learners. *Reading and Writing Quarterly: Overcoming Learning Difficulties, 29*(4), 309–332.

Taboada-Barber, A., Buehl, M. M., Kidd, J., Sturtevant, E., Richey, L. N., & Beck, J. (2015). Reading engagement in social studies: Exploring the role of a social studies literacy intervention on reading comprehension, reading self-efficacy, and engagement in middle school students with different language backgrounds. *Reading Psychology, 36*(1), 31–85.

Urdan, T., & Schoenfelder, E. (2006). Classroom effect on student motivation: Goal structures, social relationships, and competence beliefs. *Journal of School Psychology, 44*, 331–349.

Wehlage, G. G., Rutter, R. A., Smith, G. A., Lesko, N., & Fernandez, R. R. (1989). *Reducing the risk: Schools as communities of support.* Philadelphia: Falmer Press.

White, R. W. (1959). Motivation reconsidered the concept of competence. *Psychological Review, 66*, 297–333.

Wigfield, A., Mason-Singh, A., Ho, A. N., & Guthrie, J. T. (2014). Intervening to improve children's reading motivation and comprehension: Concept-oriented reading instruction. In A. S. Karabenick & T. C. Urdan (Eds.), *Motivational interventions* (pp. 37–70). Bingley, UK: Emerald Group.

Zuckerman, M., Porac, J., Lathin, D., Smith, R., & Deci, E. L. (1978). On the importance of self-determination for intrinsically motivated behavior. *Personality and Social Psychology Bulletin, 4*, 443–446.

CHAPTER 10

Situating the English Language Arts Common Core Standards in Science

Enhancing Access to Language for Emergent Bilingual Students

Marco Bravo

For several years, Carmen, a third-grade teacher, had contemplated how she could find more time in her day to teach science. She knew that her students, especially her emergent bilingual students got very excited when they got to do science and participated more often during science instruction. Carmen notes the excitement with science in part stems from her students' natural curiosity about science, but also because language is more contextualized in science, which facilitates language learning. She wanted to harness this enthusiasm. Yet she struggled with how she might do this and considered if this would come at the expense of students' reading and writing development. She also realized that she had to navigate the new Common Core State Standards in English Language Arts (CCSS-ELA) and the Next Generation Science Standards (NGSS) in preparing her instruction, and she considered the challenges her emergent bilingual students might face in a more language-intense standards movement. The task seemed daunting.

As the era of the CCSS continues to roll out, questions remain as to the impact these instructional shifts may have on emergent bilingual students. Many of the practices set forth by both NGSS and CCSS-ELA assume proficiency in English and do not take into account the fact that emergent bilingual students have "double the work" (Short & Fitzsimmons, 2007) as they attempt to sharpen their language skills and develop content knowledge.

To give access to the Standards, teachers like Carmen will need to provide both language and science learning opportunities with ample and varied scaffolds. Such support can sustain emergent bilingual students' excitement during science instruction.

One key shift that accompanies the adoption of the CCSS-ELA includes access to and practice with more complex texts and the academic language found therein (National Governors Association Center for Best Practices & Council of Chief State School Officers [NGA & CCSSO], 2010). The standards promote students' facility with both informational and literary texts. Grappling with more complex texts across these genres can be overwhelming for students, especially as they confront language used in discipline-specific ways. Familiarity with the text structure, language use, and having the proper background knowledge will mitigate the level of student comprehension difficulties. For emergent bilingual students, an additional layer of difficulty is added, as they are required to also make sense of language structures that may seem simple for native English speakers, but form comprehension barriers for students learning English as a second language. Emergent bilingual students need to decipher such figurative language as similes, metaphors, analogies, idioms, and dual-meaning words to comprehend the ideas presented in complex texts. Consider the excerpts from a science text in Figure 10.1.

Understanding the ways in which language is used in the examples in Figure 10.1 increases the cognitive load for emergent bilingual students and requires instructional adaptations to enhance their access to the information in these texts. Implications of the NGSS (NGSS Lead States, 2013) for emergent bilingual students cut across the three dimensions of the science framework. This framework includes a focus on (1) science and engineering practices (e.g., asking questions; engaging in argument based on evidence;

Simile	"The Earth is like a ball"; "The wetlands are like a sponge."
Metaphor	"The balance of nature"; "ecological footprint."
Analogy	"DNA resembles a spiral staircase"; "Electricity flows like water."
Idiom	"Running on all cylinders"; "blinded with science."
Hypothetical	"Imagine there was fog in the bay."
Dual-meaning words	model; test.

FIGURE 10.1. Figurative language in texts.

obtaining, evaluating, and communicating information); (2) crosscutting concepts (e.g., cause and effect: mechanism and explanation, systems and system models); and (3) disciplinary core ideas (e.g., matter and its inter-actions, energy). Language becomes central to understanding and getting access to key science practices and concepts. The emphasis on science and engineering practices is a particular attempt to develop students' under-standing of the nature of science by focusing on how scientists go about their work, including how scientists use language. Learning about science as a process of discovery rather than as a collection of facts increases the likelihood that students will see and develop particular habits of mind, such as how to pose a researchable question or take a perspective in evalu-ating scientific evidence being presented. These types of practices require students to communicate their understandings in both written and spoken form (Lee, Quinn, & Valdés, 2013).

Constructing scientific explanations is one of the science and engineer-ing practices that students are expected to develop per the NGSS. Scien-tific explanations differ from other forms of explanations in that they are based on evidence that may originate from investigations and observations or from the written work of other scientists. Strong scientific explanations answer the question under study and weave together the evidence that sup-ports the conclusion that was drawn through a careful consideration of sci-entific principles. Whether in written or oral form, these explanations have to conform to the discourse of science, and it is this register of language that has been elusive for emergent bilingual students.

Returning to our third-grade teacher, Carmen, we can see that her concern about having to meet the NGSS and CCSS-ELA standards may have a solution if we consider the natural convergences that exist between these two sets of standards. The CCSS-ELA, for example, give importance to the acquisition of knowledge through reading content-rich texts, writing and speaking grounded in evidence, and obtaining and reporting findings clearly and effectively in response to a task and purpose. If students are to read content-rich texts, why not address this standard by reading science texts related to the science that is being taught during the science block? This approach would address a science standard on two fronts. First, a gen-uine practice of science—that scientists read the work of other scientists—can address the science and engineering elements of the framework. Second, texts can be a source of evidence in constructing scientific explanations and/or arguments. Reading science texts during either the ELA or science block can be one approach to achieving some "curricular economy" (Cer-vetti, Pearson, Barber, Hiebert, & Bravo, 2007). In essence, Carmen would find that time she is looking for to do science, *and* she would be developing key ELA skills at the same time.

An instructional focus on the literacy needed to do science also entails an increased cognitive load for emergent bilingual students, who will now have to contend with learning the science content, science processes, and the literacy used to build that science knowledge. Notwithstanding the challenges, researchers have found that specially crafted instruction that capitalizes on the natural convergences between science and literacy can have a synergistic effect for emergent bilingual students' science understandings and literacy development. In this chapter, the potential natural convergences between literacy and science are suggested along with the research-based instructional practices that have shown promise to enhance the literacy and science learning of emergent bilingual students and promote their natural curiosity about science.

Science and Literacy Integration

Models of science and literacy integration have suggested several reasons as to why it may be pedagogically sound to embed literacy instruction in science. Arguments concerning curricular efficiency (Pearson, Moje, & Greenleaf, 2010; Stoddart, Pinal, Latzke, & Canaday, 2002) have been suggested as well as potential synergistic effects that benefit both science learning and literacy development (Guthrie, Anderson, Alao, & Rinehart, 1999; Palincsar & Magnusson, 2001). Common to the approaches to integration is careful consideration of the natural connections between science and literacy. Below I present the approach taken by the group with which I have worked to exemplify the nature of science and literacy integration.

Seeds of Science/Roots of Reading

In 2004, literacy and science educators from the Graduate School of Education and the Lawrence Hall of Science from the University of California, Berkeley, began the Seeds of Science/Roots of Reading research program (Seeds/Roots). Literacy educators were interested in putting literacy to work the facilitate students' acquisition of the knowledge, skills, and dispositions of science, and science educators saw literacy as an additional modality to give students access to science practices and ideas. The science educators were also interested in finding more time in the school day for science. They saw teaming up with literacy educators as one approach to ensure that more science was taught in primary grade classrooms. Both literacy and science educators also wanted to test the limits and the potential for integrating science and literacy for emergent bilingual students. The program materialized in curricular materials for grades 2–5 with sets of accessible books, hands-on activities, assessments, and an innovative teacher's guide that allows teachers to modify the curriculum to fit the needs of different learners, especially emergent bilingual students. The informational books are used strategically to provide context for the hands-on investigations students conduct, to model science processes, as well as to provide content that is difficult to observe through firsthand experiences (e.g., observing the surface of the moon, observing microscopic organisms) (Cervetti & Barber, 2008). Such purposes for informational reading provide students with authentic reasons for reading and align nicely with the CCSS-ELA goal of ensuring that students read more informational books.

Instruction of other literacy skills such as writing, vocabulary, listening, and speaking are also carefully crafted in ways that support, and do not eclipse, students' discovery of science practices and concepts. For example, rather than focusing on writing conventions instruction, Seeds/Roots focuses on expository writing with an emphasis on science writing genres (e.g., scientific explanations, procedures, descriptions, summaries). Instructional supports are also offered to help students build an understanding of the importance of organization and academic language as they write. Moreover, the science books they read offer examples of the type of writing students are expected to compose, further deepening writing development and reading comprehension.

Through a series of efficacy and research studies, the Seeds/Roots research group has shown promise of integrating science and literacy, illustrating the potential for science and vocabulary learning (Bravo, Cervetti, Hiebert, & Pearson, 2007; Wang & Herman, 2005) as well as science and writing (Cervetti, Barber, Dorph, Pearson, & Goldschmidt, 2012). Moreover, the approach has been found to be particularly beneficial for emergent bilingual students (Bravo & Cervetti, 2014; Goldschmidt & Jung, 2009).

The curriculum development effort centers on the premise that there are natural convergences between literacy and science (Cervetti et al., 2007). These include the notion that robust vocabulary development, as viewed by literacy educators, is similar to what science educators refer to as *conceptual development*. Second, scientific investigations and reading comprehension share meaning-making strategies that can be capitalized on for the mutual benefit of literacy and science. Finally, both science and literacy educators support the use of talk for learning in firsthand investigations and from texts. The following section provides a description of these synergies between science and literacy.

Words as Concepts

As the responsibility for literacy instruction is spread throughout subject areas as a result of the CCSS-ELA, subject-matter vocabulary is set to receive more instructional attention. Under the new standards, students are to determine the meaning of key terms and recognize relationships between targeted vocabulary words. This approach to vocabulary development moves beyond just knowing the definition of a word to more robust vocabulary knowledge that includes seeing how key terms relate to each other. The treatment of conceptual learning in the Seeds/Roots model parallels this goal as it is outlined in the CCSS-ELA.

Considering vocabulary development as conceptual learning requires some unpacking. When literacy educators refer to *robust* vocabulary learning, there is an expectation that students are exposed to the key terms several times (Beck, McKeown, & Kucan, 2002) and through multimodal experiences (Bravo & Cervetti, 2008), with opportunities to use the terms both in talk and through writing (Armbruster, 1992). There is a similar level of expectation when science educators expect key science concepts to be acquired by students (Osborne & Patterson, 2011). This similar goal can be capitalized on for the benefit of vocabulary growth and science understandings. The emphasis in robust vocabulary learning is not to focus on definitional aspects of word learning, but rather to recognize that the terms are part of a conceptual network of concepts that define areas of science study.

To treat vocabulary learning as science concept learning, only a limited number of generative and discipline-specific concepts/vocabulary words can be targeted, given that students require multiple exposures to the target words through different modalities. Students must also be given opportunities to see the relationship between concepts. Carmen, our third-grade teacher, created a diagram (Figure 10.2) with the Earth science vocabulary

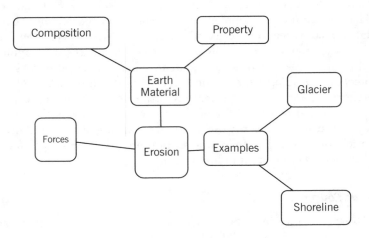

FIGURE 10.2. Vocabulary network.

found in the unit she was piloting. As each term was introduced in the curriculum, she reviewed the meaning of the term with students and would place each term on the word wall, eliciting from students how they had seen or used the term during science lessons. Then she explained how these terms related to each other—whether they were examples of other concepts or part of a larger category. Carmen pointed out these terms in the science books (they appear multiple times in the book) and science notebooks, and explained to students that they should refer to the diagram to use these terms during science discussions and when writing in their science notebooks.

While there is reason to believe that carefully crafted science/literacy instruction can have particular benefits for the development of academic vocabulary, it is also believed that additional supports are needed in order obviate some of the linguistic obstacles that emergent bilingual students may face in science/literacy curriculum. Visual representations such as T-charts, Venn diagrams, and concept maps are useful tools that help abstract concepts become more concrete for emergent bilingual students; they help students better see the relationship between different parts of a concept as well as limit the cognitive load that abstract concepts place on emergent bilingual students who are trying to understand the concept through a language they may not fully command.

One example of a visual representation that can be used to facilitate students' understanding of the nuanced meanings of science vocabulary is a science/everyday word chart. In our efforts to develop active control of science vocabulary through the Seeds/Roots curriculum, we propose to teachers who have emergent bilingual students in their class to write on a T-chart the science terms that students may be familiar with and the specialized way the scientific community represents those concepts. Figure 10.3 shows a T-chart for a second-grade Earth science unit.

As these words show up either in science texts or in preparation for a firsthand investigation, discussions about the similarities and differences between the word pairs would be provided. Students receive an explanation

Everyday word	Science word
Vitamins	Nutrients
Dirt	Soil
See	Observe
Guess	Predict

FIGURE 10.3. Science/everyday word chart.

about the fact that scientists use words that can be similar, but not identical, to words students may know already. As students provide the synonym for the science word, teachers explain the nuanced meanings that distinguish the word pair. For example, the word pair *predict* and *guess* would be explained as both referring to what might happen in the future, but the science version supports the claim based on scientific evidence, whereas the everyday term is supported by personal experience.

Emergent bilingual students are afforded the chance to see the relationship between the words in the word pair as well as their uniqueness when these concepts are represented visually. Explaining these nuanced differences in meaning solely through talk could lead emergent bilingual students, especially newcomers and beginners, to a cognitive overload. The T-chart provides enough of a scaffold that the nuanced meaning of these words can be accessed. (See Crosson, Chapter 5, this volume, for additional recommendations on teaching vocabulary to emergent bilingual students.)

Shared Strategies

When students read, they apply comprehension strategies to make sense of information presented in a text (Palincsar & Brown, 1984; see also Boardman & Jensen Lasser, Chapter 6, this volume). Similarly, when conducting scientific investigations, students apply inquiry strategies to make sense of the natural world. Both science and literacy utilize strategies to make meaning from texts and investigations that are very similar in form and function. Consider the following strategies. Do they belong to science inquiry or to reading comprehension?

- Making inferences
- Posing questions
- Setting goals
- Making predictions
- Visualizing and using mental models
- Synthesizing information from multiple sources

It can be argued that all of these strategies belong to both science and literacy. The cognitive process used in both domains is extremely similar. Helping students see the transportability of these strategies as they are doing science and during reading tasks provides an opportunity for students to "double-up" on practicing these strategies and subsequently services both literacy and science inquiry learning goals.

To activate these common cognitive processes, the Seeds/Roots curriculum targets common reading comprehension and science inquiry strategies and devotes explicit and systematic instruction to point out not only the similarities between the meaning-making strategies, but also the differences. For example, when making predictions, the nature of the evidence to support the prediction offered is different in science than in reading comprehension. Whereas in reading comprehension predictions can be substantiated by prior school learning experiences and those rooted in personal experiences, with inquiry-based science the nature of the evidence in predictions posed must have a closer connection to science-based sources of knowledge. Opportunities to reflect on how the strategies are used in similar and different ways in the context of science and literacy presents students with a metacognitive awareness of the strategies that can be lead to deeper understandings of their use.

Reading science texts with emergent bilingual students requires special attention to their prior knowledge. When considering how to activate or build students' prior knowledge before reading, the common approach has been to concentrate on the content of the text without considering the way in which language is used in science texts and students' prior knowledge regarding these discourse markers. The absence of attention to the language of science in texts is especially impactful to emergent bilingual students. The presence of multiple-meaning words (e.g., *force, behavior, current*), nominalization (e.g., *investigate–investigation, observe–observation*), visual representations (e.g., images, symbols, diagrams, figures, tables), long adjective–noun phrases (e.g., *supportive scientific community, initial chemical reaction*) in science texts require instructional attention in preparation for reading science texts.

Visual representations—not to be confused with the reading comprehension strategy of *visualization,* whereby students construct mental images of what they read—for example, are important sources of information in science texts that often extend what is available in the printed word. Photographs, diagrams, and tables are included in science texts to show relationships and communicate ideas that cannot be captured just with words. These visual representations can illustrate processes such as the water cycle and afford students another modality to solidify their understanding of key science ideas. Yet this requires explicit examples of the process for making sense of visual representations. Preparing emergent bilingual students to read science texts can be done by pointing out the various visual representations in a science text they will read and explaining the role each visual representation plays. These roles might include providing examples of an idea in print (exemplifying), showing where something happens (contextualizing), illustrating a concept that is hard to explain with words (clarifying), or adding new information (extending). Providing this explanation, examples before reading, and opportunities for emergent bilingual students to find other examples of visual representations and match them with the appropriate role will better prepare these students to comprehend science texts.

Ways of Talking

Both literacy and science instruction promote discussion to enhance the learning of abstract ideas, whether they originate in text or in firsthand science investigations. Discussions about text and firsthand experiences promote students' sharing of understandings and create occasions for them to rethink, negotiate, and clarify their own thinking (Osborne & Patterson, 2011). Yet, here too there are distinct ways of talking in literacy and science that also have natural convergences.

Evidence in support of the unique forms of discussion in science can be seen in the way in which scientific argumentations take shape. In formulating arguments, scientists employ a shared knowledge of the natural world in order to communicate and evaluate science claims (Osborne, Simon, Christodoulou, Howell-Richardson, & Richardson, 2013) and provide explanations supported by empirical evidence. These discourse conventions illuminate the centrality of language in doing science. In fact, some suggest that learning science means learning the language of science (Lemke, 1990). This specialized way of talking is used to make sense of the natural world but is often ambiguous and unclear to students (Lee, Maerten-Rivera, Penfield, LeRoy, & Secada, 2008). Talk in science can be one approach to demystifying its language by making it more explicit for students. Consider the following transcript as Carmen, our third-grade teacher, facilitates a science discussion about oil spills. Prior to this discussion about oil spills, students learned about shoreline organisms and their habitat as well as the human impact on shorelines (e.g., marine litter, oil spills). In Figure 10.4, Carmen's students learn not only about ways of talking in science—leveraging evidence from investigations they have conducted regarding shoreline organisms—but also of the nature of science—the fact that scientists come together to discuss and argue their positions based on evidence.

Discussions in literacy are used to help students build a coherent understanding of text information by developing and connecting to the ideas of the text with others (see also Brisk, Kaveh, Scialoia, & Timothy, Chapter 8, this volume). In questioning the author, Beck, McKeown, Sandora, Kucan, and Worthy (1996) suggest that discussions about a text are an opportune time for students to actively share in the investigation and co-construction of meaning from the text. Teachers draw attention to important understandings in the text voiced by students by making such statements as "That's a critical point" or "You are on to an important idea in the book." Teachers also use discussion time about texts as opportunities to model reading processes, allowing students to clearly see ways of interacting with the text to ensure comprehension, including making links between the text and their own experiences.

Oil was an important discovery for people.	
Teacher:	Okay. You've gathered your evidence for and against the topic. Who would like to present their case first?	*Students have investigated and read about oil spills in the previous 2 weeks, especially how difficult it is to clean up oil spills on a beach, and now use this knowledge to understand science ways of talking.*
Student 1:	Our group thinks it was not a good discovery.	*The student's initial response does not have the evidence-based claims the teacher is looking for.*
Teacher:	What is your **evidence**? Remember, our explanations in science have to be supported with evidence.	*Note the teacher's redirection of the student's contribution to include support for his claim.*
Student 1:	. . . Because oil has caused a lot of damage to organisms on the beach, like what we read about.	*The student here leverages evidence and calls attention to the origin of his knowledge*
Student 2:	I agree that oil has caused damage, but it has done more good. Oil makes cars run and we can get to places faster now than before.	*A second student's counterargument compares the strength of the evidence.*
Teacher:	Everybody, notice how evidence is being used. Scientists often get together to talk about their findings just like we are doing right now.	*A metaconversation by the teacher makes available the science ways of talking for the entire class.*

FIGURE 10.4. Carmen's discourse circle.

These common and unique *ways of talking* in both the scientific and literacy enterprises address another key emphasis in the CCSS speaking and listening standards. Anchor Standard 1 (NGO & CCSSO, 2010) states that students should have experiences wherein they "prepare for and participate effectively in a range of conversations and collaborations with diverse partners, building on others' ideas and expressing their own clearly and persuasively" (p. 22). Discussions in science about science texts that have been read or firsthand science investigations are a great context in which to sharpen ways of talking, as students would have multiple sources, both first- and second-hand investigation, from which to develop expertise in talking science. The models for ways of talking presented across both science and literacy increase the likelihood of students understanding the similar and unique ways of talking across disciplines.

The explicit instruction on ways of talking in science is particularly helpful for emergent bilingual students. Yet, as others have pointed out, without the proper scaffolds, the language demands of science can compromise these students' science understanding (August, Branum-Martin, Cardenas-Hagan, & Francis, 2009; Buxton, Salinas, Mahotiere, Lee, & Secada, 2015). Learning the specialized way of talking about science requires that emergent bilingual students see the discourse of science modeled for them. This includes learning the form and function of scientific argumentation and explanation from their teacher and native English-speaking peers. The task becomes more difficult for emergent bilingual students if their teacher's rate of speech is too fast or too slow, is not loud enough, is not enunciated sufficiently, or includes the use of unfamiliar figurative language.

One element of speech—idiomatic expressions—make emergent bilingual students, particularly those at beginning levels of English proficiency, cringe. Idioms suggest one idea when interpreted literally, but actually have a unique meaning based on common usage in everyday contexts. Lazar, Warr-Leeper, Nicholson, and Johnson (1989) noted in their study that one-third of teacher's talk contains an idiom. Moreover, teachers are largely unaware of the frequency with which they use idiomatic expressions (Nippold, 1991). Although students will likely learn the appropriate meaning of idioms as they see them in print and hear them used in conversation, teacher explanation of idioms they use will ensure that emergent bilingual students are appropriately interpreting the teacher's intent.

Idiomatic expressions are not exclusive to English. They exist across languages and this fact could help emergent bilingual students come to understand English idioms if probed to explain some that are common in their language. The teacher could also explain common expressions in English, such as *feeling like a fish out of water*. Students can be probed to discern if the intended meaning is feeling scaly, like a fish, or to feel out of place. Students could then be asked to confirm the intended meaning and allowed to explain an idiom in their language and the two possible meanings. As a class, attempting to guess the intended meaning can offer an experience that prepares emergent bilingual students for the idiomatic expressions they may hear in the classroom. The teacher can reflect with students on how paying attention to idioms can help them better understand important ideas the teacher is attempting to get across. Students should be encouraged to ask for clarification of idiomatic expressions they hear their teacher using. Explanations of idioms help emergent bilingual students become more familiar and comfortable with English.

Lessons learned from the Seeds/Roots research group can offer some suggestions that teachers of emergent bilingual students can utilize as guidance when considering integrating science and literacy. First, capitalizing on the context of science to teach vocabulary as a network of related concepts is advantageous. Second, introducing informational books related to the science themes being addressed is beneficial to both science and literacy learning, as it provides emergent bilingual students with authentic reasons for reading these text types. Third, it is critical to take advantage of the NGSS's promotion of discussion in science. Emergent bilingual students need opportunities to talk in order to build their English proficiency; they just need explicit instruction of the particular *ways* of talking in science.

The nature of science vocabulary, science texts, and the specialized ways of ways of talking in science require pedagogical considerations that amplify emergent bilingual students' experience in the science classroom. Multimodal experiences such as the use of visual representations enhance and deepen understandings of science concepts while emergent bilingual students develop their English proficiency (e.g., academic vocabulary, speaking). Likewise, activating or building students' prior knowledge about the way language is used in science in preparation for reading science texts optimizes their comprehension of science ideas while building a metalinguistic awareness of how the English language works in the context of science. Finally, teachers' willingness to modify their talk for emergent bilingual students will increase the likelihood of these students' participation in science discourse activities. These types of adaptations are necessary to fully reap the benefits of integrated science and literacy instruction provided to emergent bilingual students.

Putting literacy to work in the service of science learning has been illustrated to be academically fruitful for students (Palincsar & Magnusson, 2001; Vitale & Romance, 2011), especially emergent bilingual students (August et al., 2009; Bravo & Cervetti, 2014; Lee, Buxton, Lewis, & LeRoy, 2006; Lara-Alecio et al., 2012). Yet, additional measures have to be taken for emergent bilingual students to further optimize their learning from integrated science and literacy instruction.

Conclusion

Science presents a rich context in which young bilingual students can sharpen their language skills, particularly those outlined by the CCSS-ELA (NGO & CCSSO, 2010). The authentic use of literacy to make sense of the natural world around us (e.g., reading science texts, use of precise science vocabulary) makes for a compelling and often amplified language experience for young bilingual students. However, additional support is needed to fully exploit the integration of literacy and science. In this chapter, a case was made for the potential of capitalizing on the synergy between science and literacy by focusing on the "sweet spots"—those natural convergences that exist between these enterprises. Various scaffolds were presented to illustrate the necessary adaptations that will further enhance this student populations' dual responsibility of sharpening their literacy skills and gaining subject-matter knowledge. Taken together, this work provides evidence that emergent bilingual students learn more science when inquiry is supported by literacy activities, and they make gains in literacy when literacy learning is embedded in meaningful content and surrounded by rich language and inquiry experiences.

REFERENCES

Armbruster, B. B. (1992). Vocabulary in content area lessons. *The Reading Teacher,* *45,* 550–551.

August, D., Branum-Martin, L., Cardenas-Hagan E., & Francis, D. J. (2009). The impact of an instructional intervention on the science and language learning of middle grade English language learners. *Journal of Research on Educational Effectiveness, 2,* 345–376.

Beck, I. L., McKeown, M. G., & Kucan, L. (2002). *Bringing words to life: Robust vocabulary instruction.* New York: Guilford Press.

Beck, I. L., McKeown, M. G., Sandora, C., Kucan, L., & Worthy, J. (1996). Questioning the author. *Elementary School Journal, 95,* 395–414.

Bravo, M. A., & Cervetti, G. N. (2008). Teaching vocabulary through text and experience. In A. E. Farstrup & S. Samuels (Eds.), *What research has to say about vocabulary instruction* (pp. 130–149). Newark, DE: International Reading Association.

Bravo, M. A., & Cervetti, G. N. (2014). Equitable science instruction for English language learners. *Equity and Excellence in Education, 47,* 230–245.

Bravo, M. A., Cervetti, G. N., Hiebert, E., & Pearson, P. D. (2007). From passive to active control of vocabulary. In D. W. Rowe, R. T. Jimenez, D. L. Compton, D. K. Dickinson, Y. Kim, K. M. Leander, & V. J. Risko (Eds.), *56th yearbook of the National Reading Conference* (pp. 164–177). Milwaukee: National Reading Conference.

Buxton, C., Salinas, A., Mahotiere, M., Lee, O., & Secada, W. G. (2015). Fourth-grade emergent bilingual learners' scientific reasoning complexity, controlled experiment practices, and content knowledge when discussing school, home, and play contexts. *Teachers College Record, 117,* 1–36.

Cervetti, G. N., & Barber, J. (2008). Text in hands-on science. In E. H. Hiebert & M. Sailors (Eds.), *Finding the right texts: What works for beginning and struggling readers* (pp. 89–108). New York: Guilford Press.

Cervetti, G. N., Barber, J., Dorph, R., Pearson, P. D., & Goldschmidt, P. G. (2012). The impact of an integrated approach to science and literacy in elementary school classrooms. *Journal of Research in Science Teaching, 49,* 631–658.

Cervetti, G. N., Pearson, P. D., Barber, J., Hiebert, E. H., & Bravo, M. A. (2007). Integrating literacy and science: The research we have, the research we need. In M. Pressley, A. K. Billman, K. Perry, K. Refitt, & J. Reynolds (Eds.), *Shaping literacy achievement* (pp. 157–174). New York: Guilford Press.

Goldschmidt, P., & Jung, H. (2009). *Evaluation of Seeds of Science/Roots of Reading: Effective tools for developing literacy through science in the early grades.* National Center for Research on Evaluation, Standards, and Student Testing, Center for the Study of Evaluation (CSE) Graduate School of Education & Information Studies, University of California, Los Angeles, CA.

Guthrie, J. T., Anderson, E., Alao, S., & Rinehart, J. (1999). Influences of concept-oriented reading instruction on strategy use and conceptual learning from text. *Elementary School Journal, 99,* 343–366.

Lara-Alecio, R., Tong, F., Irby, B. J., Guerrero, C., Huerta, M., & Fan, Y. (2012). The effect of an instructional intervention on middle school English learners' science and English reading achievement. *Journal of Research in Science Teaching, 49,* 987–1011.

Lazar, R. T., Warr-Leeper, G. A., Nicholson, C. B., & Johnson, S. (1989). Elementary school teachers' use of multiple meaning expressions. *Language, Speech, and Hearing Services in Schools, 20,* 420–430.

Lee, O., Buxton, C. Lewis, S., & LeRoy, K. (2006). Science inquiry and student diversity: Enhanced abilities and continuing difficulties after an instructional intervention. *Journal of Research in Science Teaching, 43,* 607–636.

Lee, O., Maerten-Rivera, J., Penfield, R. D., LeRoy, K., & Secada, W. G. (2008). Science achievement of English language learners in urban elementary schools: Results of a first-year professional development intervention. *Journal of Research in Science Teaching, 45,* 31–52.

Lee, O., Quinn, H., & Valdés, G. (2013). Science and language for English language learners in relation to next generation science standards and with implications for Common Core State Standards for English language arts and mathematics. *Educational Researcher, 43,* 223–233.

Lemke, J. (1990). *Talking science: Language, learning and values.* Norwood, NJ: Ablex.

National Governors Association Center for Best Practices & Council of Chief State School Officers. (2010). *Common Core State Standards for English language arts and literacy in history/social studies, science, and technical subjects.* Washington, DC: Authors.

NGSS Lead States. (2013). *Next Generation Science Standards: For states, by states.* Washington, DC: National Academies Press.

Nippold, M. (1991). Evaluating and enhancing idiom comprehension in language disordered students. *Language, Speech, and Hearing Services in Schools, 22,* 100–106.

Osborne, J. F., & Patterson, A. (2011). Scientific argument and explanation: A necessary distinction? *Science Education, 95,* 627–638.

Osborne, J. F., Simon, S., Christodoulou, A., Howell-Richardson, C., & Richardson, K. (2013). Learning to argue: A study of four schools and their attempt to develop the use of argumentation as a common instructional practice and its impact on students. *Journal of Research in Science Teaching, 50,* 315–347.

Palincsar, A. S., & Brown, A. L. (1984). Reciprocal teaching of comprehension-fostering and comprehension-monitoring activities. *Cognition and Instruction, 1*(2), 117–175.

Palincsar, A. S., & Magnusson, S. J. (2001). The interplay of firsthand and text-based investigations to model and support the development of scientific knowledge and reasoning. In S. Carver & D. Klahr (Eds.), *Cognition and instruction: Twenty-five years of progress* (pp. 151–194). Mahwah, NJ: Erlbaum.

Pearson, P., Moje, E., & Greenleaf, C. (2010). Literacy and science: Each in the service of the other. *Science, 328*, 459–463.

Short, D., & Fitzsimmons, S. (2007). *Double the work: Challenges and solutions to acquiring language and academic literacy for adolescent English language learners—A report to Carnegie Corporation of New York*. Washington, DC: Alliance for Excellent Education.

Stoddart, T., Pinal, A., Latzke, M., & Canaday, D. (2002). Integrating inquiry science and language development for English language learners. *Journal of Research in Science Teaching, 39*, 664–687.

Vitale, M. R., & Romance, N. R. (2011). Adaptation of a knowledge-based instructional intervention to accelerate student learning in science and early literacy in grades 1 and 2. *Journal of Curriculum and Instruction, 5*, 79–93.

Wang, J., & Herman, J. (2005). *Evaluation of Seeds of Science/Roots of Reading project: Shoreline science and terrarium investigations*. Los Angeles: CRESST.

PART III

PROFESSIONAL LEARNING

CHAPTER 11

Academic Language and Literacy in Every Subject (ALLIES)

A Capacity-Building Approach to Supporting Teachers in Grades 4–8

Susan P. O'Hara, Robert Pritchard, and Jeff Zwiers

Consider this task from a sample item from the Common Core State Standards (CCSS)-aligned assessment of the Smarter Balanced Assessment Consortium intended for fifth graders (Grade 5 ELA Sample SR Item Form C2 T8):

Which set of words has the same meanings as the underlined words in the sentence in the box?

Scientists <u>pick</u> individual animals and <u>fit</u> them with lightweight, comfortable radio transmitters.

Options:

A. select, equip

B. claim, connect

C. examine, link

D. determine, tame

In this item, students are being asked to identify the academic vocabulary for fairly common words (i.e., *pick*, *fit*). Words such as *determine*, *connect*, and *examine* are more typically used in the texts and talk of classrooms than they are in informal conversations.

Vocabulary is an essential part of academic language, but *academic language* refers to much more than vocabulary. Academic language is also involved in the kind of oral interaction that happens in classrooms. In academic settings, information and directions are presented in complex sentences, as is the case in the directions for the item above. Academic settings also require oral responses beyond a single-word utterance that may suffice in typical conversations. Table 11.1 illustrates some of the differences between the informal language of conversations and the academic language of classrooms and texts.

A lack of fluency in the general academic language (Nagy & Townsend, 2012) serves as an obstacle for many English learners (ELs). The prognosis for school success becomes even more unlikely for ELs when the academic nature of texts and talk occurs with unfamiliar, complex, and abstract content, as is the case in social studies and science classes. *Academic language,* as operationalized in our work, is the set of vocabulary, syntax, and discourse strategies used to describe complex concepts, abstract ideas, and cognitive processes (Zwiers, O'Hara, & Pritchard, 2014). These three dimensions can be broken down further into features that can be observed in lessons and student work. Table 11.2 shows the three dimensions and their associated features and skills.

The task of developing academic language and literacy in ELs is complex and challenging. A major component of this challenge is to develop a system of support for teachers both within schools and across districts that will promote their ongoing learning as part of an integrated professional development (PD) program that can have long-term impacts on student learning. In this chapter we describe a 5-year research and development project—Academic Language and Literacy in Every Subject (ALLIES)[1]—and share the implications of this work for PD approaches designed to meet the need of ELs. The overarching goal of this project was to develop, implement, and test a PD model to build instructional capacity within one school

TABLE 11.1. Informal versus Academic Language

Informal language	Academic language
Repetition of words	Variety of words, more sophisticated vocabulary.
Sentences start with *and* and *but*	Sentences start with transition words, such as *however, moreover,* and *in addition.*
Use of colloquial words.	No use of slang.

[1] This work, a collaborative effort involving universities, school districts, and the Academic Language Development Network, is supported by a National Professional Development Grant from the U.S. Department of Education.

TABLE 11.2. Dimensions and Features of Academic Language

Dimensions	Academic language features	Academic language skills
Vocabulary	• Content terms and collocations • Figurative expressions and multiple-meaning terms • Affixes, roots, and transformations • General academic terms (*aspects, consider, as long as, perhaps, evaluate*)	• Figure out the meaning of new words and terms in a particular message. • Connect to underlying concepts. • Use new words to build ideas or create products. • Choose and use the best words and phrases to communicate the message.
Syntax	• Sentence structure and length • Transitions/connectives • Complex verb tenses and passive voice • Pronouns and references	• Craft sentences to be clear and correct. • Use a variety of sentence types to clarify a message; condense information; and combine ideas, phrases, and clauses.
Discourse	• Organization and text structure • Voice and register • Density • Clarity and coherence	• Combine features to communicate, clarify, and negotiate meaning. • Create a logical flow and connection between ideas. • Match language with purpose of message (clear, complete, focused, logical, and appropriate to the discipline).

district to promote students' academic language and literacy development across disciplines in grades 4–8. The specific goals of the project were:

- To develop a high-quality PD model for mentors to use in supporting teachers' implementation of high-leverage practices for promoting academic language and literacy.
- To build the capacity of mentors who work within six partner schools to support teachers in the enactment of these practices.
- To build the capacity of instructional leadership teams within partner schools to support and sustain this work.

Key Design Principles

The research literature contains numerous examples of PD efforts that have failed to impact student learning or that could not sustain their impact over time (Casteel & Ballantyne, 2010). Although many factors have contributed to these results, we believe that a failure to articulate key design principles on which to base PD is one of the most significant. Determined to avoid this pitfall, we adopted a multi-tiered strategy in developing the ALLIES intervention that attends to four key design principles for building instructional capacity for academic language and literacy development: (1) target the instructional shifts needed to be able to provide a laser-like focus for the work; (2) cultivate a local teacher community wherein mentors and teachers are learning in and from practice; (3) deepen mentors' knowledge in context; and (4) create the conditions necessary for mentors to support teachers in the continuous improvement of teaching and learning.

In this project mentors were teachers identified by the district and school site administrators as exemplary teachers who had the potential to fulfill the role of mentor. All of the teachers who were asked to participate as mentors agreed, and all served in that role at their respective school sites for the duration of the project, with the exception of one who accepted a vice-principal position within the district.

Targeting High-Leverage Practices

Our first design principle addresses the need to focus any instructional improvement process on a set of targeted, high-leverage instructional practices (Windschitl, Thompson, & Braaten, 2013; Fogo, 2011; O'Hara, Zwiers, & Pritchard, 2014). Given the language and literacy requirements of the CCSS and our desire to have a significant impact on EL outcomes, it was particularly essential that we focus on the improvement of a set of high-leverage instructional practices. This design principle is predicated on the importance of providing instructional leaders, mentors, and teachers with a common language around the instructional shifts needed to help ELs meet the challenges of the CCSS, and with time for deliberate practice of new instructional moves that are aligned with CCSS. In the ALLIES project, the Essential Practice Frames (EPFs) articulate high-leverage practices that drive student outcomes and, as such, provide a common language for instructional change.

Learning in and from Practice

The second design principle focuses on the need for mentors and teachers to learn in and from practice. Because learning to enact a complex practice requires the ability to see and understand its underlying components, professionals need opportunities to see vivid examples of the practice and develop ways to distinguish stronger and weaker versions of it (Little, 2003). Video examples become a key resource for learning, because video provides examples of high-leverage practices in action and affords opportunities to examine the elements of these practices as they unfold or are decomposed into their constituent parts. Research suggests that this kind of deliberate and repeated practice of the elements of a complex practice is essential for the development of expertise (Ericsson, 2014). The ALLIES professional learning model was predicated on the importance of providing video examples of teaching, and time for both mentors and teachers to practice new instructional moves aligned with the ALLIES EPF elements.

Mentoring Knowledge in Contexts: Subject, Learner, and Site

The third design principle focuses on the complex knowledge base that mentors need in order to provide teachers with effective support for the academic language and literacy development of ELs within content areas (Achinstein, O'Hara, Pritchard, & Zwiers, 2012). Our design principles build on these three critical areas: (1) discipline-specific mentor knowledge, (2) mentor knowledge of learners, and (3) mentor knowledge of site context. Discipline-specific mentor knowledge includes (a) the specialized content knowledge and pedagogical content knowledge targeted for student learning, and (b) the curriculum and pedagogy for mentoring teachers in the teaching of subject content situated in their classrooms. For example, a mentor must know how to assess the teacher's subject content and pedagogical content knowledge as well as the grade-level content and student performance standards; how to support the teacher in assessing the students' understanding of disciplinary concepts and reasoning; how to use artifacts and prompts in conversations to help teachers unpack content knowledge and reasoning; and when to use an interactive repertoire of approaches from instructive to more facilitative mentoring stances (Luft, Neakrase, Adams, Firestone, & Bang, 2010). Mentors need to consider the contexts within which a teacher works and the classroom and local community contexts in which students are embedded (Achinstein & Athanases, 2010). The ALLIES project was designed to provide mentors with targeted professional learning experiences, both for enacting high-impact instructional practices in their own teaching and for mentoring other teachers to enact them.

Building Capacity to Develop Sustainable Learning

The fourth design principle focuses on the importance of building the organizational infrastructure and the conditions (e.g., knowledgeable leaders and facilitative organizational structures) to grow, sustain, and spread the use of high-leverage practices that support the academic language and literacy development of ELs. Research has also shown that creating the school conditions that are conducive to reform requires leadership and norms of collegiality (Honig, Copland, Rainey, Lorton, & Newton, 2010). Such findings suggest that PD programs that want to have an enduring effect on teaching practice need to engage school leaders strategically in the change process. Furthermore, a growing body of evidence within the leadership literature suggests that the type of existing leadership in a school can have a significant effect on the quality of teaching and learning in that school (Robinson, Lloyd, & Rowe, 2008; Harris, 2009).

This design principle is premised on four central ideas: (1) instructional leadership is most effective when leadership is shared among individuals in a team who have different roles and expertise; (2) a shared understanding of the purpose for and value of academic language and literacy in content area teaching is essential for the uptake of new practices; (3) capacity can be built within a school to stimulate, support, and sustain learning about the use of core academic language and literacy practices; and (4) generating site-based capacity to use core academic language and literacy practices and reflect upon their use creates the conditions for ongoing learning and sustained use of these core practices. In our project we focused attention on building school-based instructional leadership teams to drive the development of the conditions that were needed to support mentors and teachers in enacting the ALLIES instructional practices in their teaching.

Project Design

Essential Practice Frames

We developed the ALLIES EPF and corresponding rubric based on research on effective instruction to foster the academic language and literacy development of ELs (Anstrom et al., 2010; August, Artzi, & Mazrum, 2010; Baker et al., 2014; Brisk & Proctor, 2012; Echevarria, Richards-Tutor, Chinn, & Ratleff, 2011; Jiménez et al., 2015; Moschkovich, 2012; Kibler, Walqui, & Bunch, 2015; Van Lier & Walqui, 2012; Wong Filmore & Filmore, 2012; Zwiers, 2008). This research illustrates the importance of explicitly and systematically building students' academic language and literacy while also teaching content; providing regular, extended, and supported opportunities for ELs to produce oral and written output, engage in academic interactions where they negotiate meaning, and interact with complex texts; fostering ELs' metacognition for language and literacy development; and monitoring and guiding academic language learning throughout instruction.

From the research review, we generated a list of effective practices for the academic language and literacy development of ELs. We conducted a study of expert consensus (Pritchard, O'Hara, & Zwiers, in press; Steurer, 2011) in the field of academic language and literacy to identify high-leverage, essential teaching practices that foster academic language and literacy and to establish content validity of the ALLIES tool (O'Hara et al., 2014). We then analyzed a large number of classroom videos to identify different levels of enactment for each of the elements of each practice (7 core practices and 15 elements).[2]

This study, in combination with our observations of classroom practice videos, revealed not just a list of practices, but ways in which the essential instructional practices support one another. For professional learning purposes we organized the practices into three "frames," each consisting of a high-impact essential practice supported by three crosscutting practices and a foundational practice that are common across the three frames (see Figure 11.1 for an example). The three essential practices identified as high-impact for academic language and literacy development were: (1) Foster Academic Interactions; (2) Fortify Academic Output; and (3) Interact with Complex Text. The three crosscutting essential practices were: (1) Facilitate Acquisition of Academic Language; (2) Foster Metacognition; and (3) Monitor and Guide Language Learning. These are all supported by the foundational essential practice: Design Instruction of Academic Language and Literacy Development.

Perhaps the most challenging high-impact practice is to Foster Academic Interactions, which focuses on structuring, strengthening, and supporting student-to-student interactions that use academic language and literacy. Interaction consists of students responding to one another, building and challenging ideas, and negotiating meaning around subject-matter ideas and concepts (Moschkovich, 2012; Van Lier & Walqui, 2012). The second high-impact practice is to Fortify Academic Output, which focuses on structuring, strengthening, and supporting the quantity and quality of students' production of original, extended, oral and written academic messages that require complex language (Bunch, Kibler, & Pimentel, 2012; Zwiers et al., 2014). The final high-impact practice is to Interact with Complex Texts, which focuses on developing students' overall abilities to practice with and process the language of complex texts. This practice develops students' overall academic language and literacy while also strengthening their disciplinary thinking skills, comprehension habits, and content knowledge of specific texts (August et al., 2010; Wong Fillmore & Fillmore, 2012). These practices, and the ways in which they support one another, were the focus of the PD.

---

[2] The EPF rubric includes four levels for each element. The instrument is designed to rate these elements of instruction over multiple, 20-minute intervals in each class. A generalizability study of EPF suggested that the tool was reliable, and the data showed high generalizability ($\sigma^2 = .90$) and high interrater reliability correlations, $r > .88$.

High-Impact Practice	**Foster Academic Interactions.** • Build conversation skills. • Provide extended and supported opportunities for student-to-student interactions.		
Crosscutting Practices	**Facilitate Acquisition of Academic Language.** • Provide multiple, rigorous, and supported opportunities for students to acquire and use all three dimensions of academic language. • Use a variety of communication strategies to make target academic language understandable.	**Foster Metacognition.** • Visibly enact metacognitive processes students are expected to use in support of academic language learning. • Deconstruct metacognitive strategies that support academic language learning.	**Monitor and Guide Language Learning.** • Monitor academic language learning and adjust instruction, supports, and tasks to meet the needs of students. • Provide written and/or oral feedback to promote academic language use.
Foundational Practice	**Design Instruction of Academic Language and Literacy Development.** • Set academic language and literacy learning targets that are aligned with ELA/literacy CCSS and the target high-impact practice. • Structure and connect tasks that support the academic language and literacy learning targets. • Design supports to help students meet the academic language demands of texts and tasks.		

FIGURE 11.1. Essential Practice Frame.

PD Model

Our PD model involved building foundational knowledge, training mentors and teachers on the ALLIES protocol, and preparing mentors to work with colleagues through professional learning communities (PLCs) to implement ALLIES practices. We launched the program by developing a set of tools, videos, and materials that illustrate the ALLIES practices and facilitate enactment of these practices in math, science, and humanities classrooms in grades 4–8. We also developed a networked website for ALLIES participants and school partners (*aldnetwork.org*). Finally, we developed a PD sequence and curriculum for the mentors.

Phase 1: Establishing Team Roles and Responsibilities

The project team consisted of four people who collectively had a total of 50 years of public school teaching experience in a wide variety of settings, most of which served high percentages of ELs. Each team member had individually developed and delivered PD programs for teachers and administrators in the past, and three members had collaborated on the development of the ALLIES EPF. To ensure that each team member stayed abreast of current developments, we had monthly conference calls, communicated at least weekly via e-mail, and scheduled face-to-face meetings on an as-needed basis.

In terms of responsibilities, each member participated in some aspect of the PD delivery, the specific role depending on areas of expertise. For instance, one member focused on Fostering Academic Interactions whereas another handled the coaching component. Other responsibilities that we divided among team members were facilitation of check-in meetings, communication with district representatives, collection and analysis of data, and content management of website. What emerged as a key ongoing role was the lead coaching person, who observed and provided feedback for lessons, offered one-on-one mentoring, and supported PLC meetings. In addition to these team members, an outside evaluation group supported the work by periodically attending meetings, observing lessons, interviewing participants, and providing us with feedback.

Phase 2: Building Foundational Knowledge

The PD interaction with participants began each year with intensive, 2-day summer institutes designed to build mentor capacity to support teachers in developing the academic language and literacy of ELs in content-area classes. In year 1, the mentors alone were the target group for the summer institute. In subsequent years mentors and their mentees attended together. These sessions focused on the foundational knowledge of both instructional and mentoring practices related to the ALLIES framework. Day 1 activities addressed foundational issues at the student level, including representation of content with a focus on the central role that language plays in content learning; alignment of content and language objectives; components of second-language acquisition; and the broad range of academic and linguistic backgrounds that ELs bring and the implications of those backgrounds for their learning. Mentors also discussed foundational issues at the teacher level, including developing the optimal pedagogy to guide new teachers during coaching sessions in which mentors worked one-on-one with them; learning the needs of teachers in relation to ELs; understanding organizational, sociopolitical, and professional contexts within which teachers work; and mentor and teacher knowledge of self in relation to EL issues.

Activities engaged mentors in authentic tasks of examining student work, lesson plans, and teaching videos, during which they worked collaboratively to build meaning. Institute activities were designed to provide mentors with an introduction to all of the ALLIES elements, which involved developing an understanding of the language of high-leverage practices, providing them with examples at different levels of enactment through video examination and scoring, and supporting mentors in providing teaching feedback based on the elements. We used video excerpts to prompt discussion of specific practices and to develop mentors' abilities to distinguish stronger and weaker versions of a practice. These discussions served to facilitate mentor and teacher understanding of the underlying components of instructional moves associated with a specific practice.

Phase 3: Learning in and from Practice

The next phase of the work occurred during the school year and was focused on mentors learning in and from the practice of mentoring, including working with PLCs to engage in cycles of inquiry around the ALLIES practices. Mentors were given opportunities to develop, reflect upon, and refine their mentoring practices. In order to strengthen mentoring practices over time, mentors were provided with ongoing support, PD, and feedback from project staff on their mentoring practices regarding ALLIES.

In collaboration with mentors, we held a series of 1-day studios for teachers, where one targeted element of ALLIES was introduced, with activities on developing an understanding of core teaching practices of academic language, protocol language, and examples of practice from videos and classroom artifacts (including examples from the teachers' classroom work). As the project progressed, mentors worked with the project team to help plan and lead the studios. Teachers were also provided with "studio time" during which, with the support of their mentors, they could design learning tasks that supported the targeted high-leverage practices, rehearse new instructional practices in a low-risk environment, and innovate and retool their practices.

Mentors followed up these studios in their regularly scheduled PLC meetings. These PLCs included time for classroom observation of instruction, lesson planning and reflecting conferences, analysis of student work, and collaborative work on core practices for developing academic language for ELs. The in-classroom work included iterative cycles of teachers trying out new classroom moves, based on the targeted elements of ALLIES, and then videotaping and sharing these videos with mentors and colleagues in the PLC. In a parallel structure, mentors engaged in their own inquiry work in understanding how their mentoring practices support the teachers in focusing on academic language for ELs.

We also held a series of mentoring check-in meetings at the school sites, scheduled at intervals of approximately 6 weeks. An important insight that emerged during these meetings was that most mentors required more time than we had expected to implement these practices in their own classrooms before they felt confident about mentoring others. Consequently, we created opportunities during these meetings for mentors to revisit knowledge, practices, and tools from the summer institutes and studios and put these into use with their own students.

Mentors also engaged in assessing teachers' progress on the target elements and conducting conferencing (lesson planning to incorporate the element, modeling practices, observing lessons, reflecting conferences, analyzing student work, and reflecting on cycles of inquiry to inform innovations in future instruction). Mentors conducted classroom observations; collected and viewed video excerpts of their teachers' practices; and collected artifacts of teaching, such as student work and lesson plans, associated with their mentoring work. The check-in sessions also included a time for the mentors to collaboratively work with the project team to refine and deconstruct the target elements.

Phase 4: Creating the Conditions to Support and Spread the Work

A major focus of the work was to develop capacity in school-based instructional teams around the high-leverage practices to help our partner local education agencies create the conditions needed to sustain and deepen the work. District- and site-based leaders participated in training on the ALLIES protocol. We utilized the Instructional Capacity Building Framework (Jaquith, 2013) to guide this component of the work. Two areas that are vitally important to the capacity-building design of the model as it has evolved are (1) mentor understanding of and implementation of the ALLIES practices, which we see as a condition related to their serving as leaders for the spread of the practices; and (2) PLCs as contexts for mentors to promote implementation with other teachers, called "focal" teachers. As such, we worked with instructional leadership teams to provide coaches and teachers with the organizational, relational, and instructional supports that would assist their learning as they tried out and refined their enactment of the ALLIES practices.

Establishing site-based instructional leadership teams is one mechanism for developing the organizational conditions that can sustain, deepen, and spread site-specific knowledge regarding the teaching of high-leverage academic language practices in support of the learning of ELs. During the summer institutes, teams that included the instructional leaders from sites and the district participated in the ALLIES training. Principals also attended check-in meetings to keep abreast of progress. In addition, we guided these teams through a process of identifying the site-based conditions needed to support the mentors in *their* support of teachers.

Phase 5: Revising the PD Model

The fifth phase of the project occurred as an iterative process of design and development in response to the needs of the teachers and the contexts of the schools with which we worked. First, during a series of reflective meetings with mentors and the project team, we identified successes and challenges related to building mentors' capacities to support teachers in developing the academic language and literacy of ELs. Then, based on the feedback from these groups and data analysis of the work, the project team revised the model as needed. For instance, after year 1 we refined the ALLIES protocol and other materials; after year 2, we provided more on-site support for mentors. These ongoing reflections, analyses, and adjustments maximized the impact of the project and are a necessary part of any long-term PD model.

Evaluation Design and Measures

The evaluation was designed to collect quantitative and qualitative data with both breadth and depth. Academic language growth of treatment and control groups of students was determined using a measure of academic language proficiency. Surveys of teachers, their mentors, and the instructional leaders were used to document overall program quality and impact over the course of the project. Interviews, focus groups, and observations conducted with participants enabled more fine-grained analyses of participants' perspectives, experiences, and practices. In addition, focal teachers were videotaped at the beginning and end of each academic year to document how and to what extent instructional practices had changed over time, and what the impact of the mentoring component was on teacher knowledge and practice. Finally, audiotapes of each check-in meeting and PLC were transcribed and analyzed to identify themes that emerged during each year of the project.

The following questions guided the project and the data collection process:

- In what ways and to what extent is the project able to provide high-quality PD around academic language and literacy development to teachers, mentors, and instructional leaders?
- In what ways and to what extent do project activities produce participant understanding of key ALLIES concepts and enable them to enact these understandings in their professional roles?
- In what ways and to what extent does project participation build teacher, school, and district capacity to sustain enactment of ALLIES practices as direct support from project leaders recedes?

Findings

Overall, we have seen significant change during the course of the project. We conducted analyses to test the impact of participation in our PD model on the knowledge of 12 treatment mentors and 12 comparison mentors, on the knowledge and practice of 32 treatment teachers and 32 comparison teachers, and on the academic language proficiency (as measured by WIDA [Wisconsin, Delaware, Arkansas] MODEL [Measure of Developing English Language] assessment) of 104 ELs in the treatment group and 96 ELs in the comparison group. The professional development had a positive impact on mentor and teacher knowledge (as measured by the Knowledge-Use Scale) and on teacher practice (as measured by the EPF rubric). Multivariate analysis of variance (MANOVA) was used to compare the ALLIES practices among treatment and comparison teachers. Results showed significant differences between treatment and comparison teachers on the practices ($F = 2.432$, $p = .025$). Results of student academic language data revealed differences in academic language proficiency among students of participating teachers relative to comparison teachers. Using posttest scores as the dependent variable, analysis of covariance (ANCOVA) was used to compare students' academic language growth in the classes of treatment teachers with those in the classes of comparison teachers. Results showed significant positive differences between the treatment and comparison groups ($F = 24.681$, $p < .001$).

These quantitative results are supported by the qualitative data from interviews, observations, and analyses of meeting transcripts. For example, mentors reported that collaboration in the check-in meetings helped them gain greater confidence in implementing the practices because they were able to support each other and share ideas. One mentor said that she was unsure about her efforts to foster academic interactions with her students until she talked to other teachers about the strategies they were trying:

> "I know a lot of us were trying it and we kind of liked it, but we were not quite sure. That is when people started saying, 'Well, this is what I did. I just. . . . '" I think that was a good example of where we were able to see what other people's ideas were and how they maybe tweaked it so that it was more usable for us."

The PLCs were also well received and perceived to be helpful, seeming to evolve organically with input from mentors and focal teachers. One teacher said that in addition to providing time for sharing successes, the PLCs also provided a venue for reviewing the ALLIES concepts and practices introduced at the workshops.

A key support for teachers was that ALLIES complemented existing priorities in the schools, particularly the Advancement Via Individual Determination (AVID) organization and the CCSS. This synchronicity motivated teachers to use the ALLIES practices. Here a teacher explains how the ALLIES practices strengthen both AVID strategies and CCSS expectations:

> "ALLIES actually gives the base of instruction on how to have a conversation and so when you actually do the Socratic seminar [from AVID], the students know how to do it and can do it well. I think the same thing with Common Core. It is as if ALLIES is kind of the scaffolding so that students can do those things."

As the project unfolded and teachers collaborated to adapt the practices to fit their students and shared what they had tried, they gained more facility. The teachers reported that they could integrate the strategies into a lesson because they are effective with students. Even better, teachers said that the strategies are generative in the sense that once the students use them, the teachers can easily think of a variety of ways to adapt them for other lessons. As one teacher reported:

> "[The strategies] were easy and I can use them in a lot of different ways. If it is usable in one place but it is only good there, we are not going to use it."

Teachers also said that they used the strategies frequently once they saw how well their students responded and gained confidence with them. One teacher said that she used them almost daily:

> "I don't think a day has gone by since I really kind of started up with [ALLIES] this year that students didn't have to engage in . . . a more structured conversation with each other, and that would include more than just answering a question, where it had to involve back and forth."

Conclusion

Findings from this study suggest that PD models that are responsive to the needs and interests of the participating teachers, schools, and districts hold great promise for authentic and generative teacher knowledge development. Specifically, models of PD designed around the key, research-based practices of effective PD can positively impact teacher knowledge and practice. As such, our PD model:

- *Was situated in practice.* Teams of teachers from schools came to the PD sessions and worked on curriculum and artifacts of practice from their school contexts. Between sessions and meetings, they implemented new lessons and activities in their classrooms and then they came back together to reflect on implementation and refine these products.
- *Focused on student learning.* The PD sessions were all designed to focus on student learning (i.e., academic language and literacy development, grade-level concepts).
- *Modeled instructional strategies.* The PD team modeled instructional strategies throughout the PD sessions. In addition, teachers modeled various instructional strategies for each other.
- *Engaged teachers in active learning.* The design studio components of the PD meant that teachers were active participants in the PD sessions.
- *Built PLCs.* Many activities in the PD sessions were designed to build learning communities, both among the teams of teachers from each school and among teachers across schools from the same grade level.
- *Was integrated with other aspects of school change.* This initiative was developed in response to the district's emphasis on the CCSS. The PD team met with the district leaders many times to elicit their goals for the PD program and to understand the bigger strategic goals for the district. The PD team then worked to design the PD sessions such that they aligned with district goals.
- *Was sustainable.* The PD program was offered over an extended period of time, consisted of activities that were ongoing and sustainable over time, and provided the opportunity for teachers to engage in cycles of experimentation and reflection. In addition, district instructional leaders participated in the PD sessions so that they would have the knowledge and skills needed to sustain the work beyond this initiative.

Learning how to use ALLIES practices requires expert instruction, explicit modeling, and ongoing support. Learning to integrate these practices into an existing schema for teaching ELs requires time to practice and collaborate with colleagues. This studio model of PD, designed around the key principles of effective PD, provided time for teachers to learn how to use the practices that support academic language and literacy through explicit modeling, individual and collaborative experimentation, and expert and peer mentoring. The PD providers' ability to determine and respond to the needs of teachers, by balancing modeling with appropriate support, were the critical components in what participating teachers reported were

authentic and generative learning experiences that promised to impact positively student academic language and literacy and their understanding of
grade-level concepts.

The Academic Language Development Network (ALD Network) is a
collaborative project focused on the academic success of all students who
need to improve their abilities to use language in school. The Network
focuses on research-based teaching and assessment practices for developing
the complex academic language, literacy, and thinking skills that support
the learning of the CCSS, the Next Generation Science Standards, English language development, and other new standards. We currently collaborate on PD and research efforts in multiple school districts and coun-
ties and provide materials and resources for ALLIES. We will continue to
share updated research and effective PD resources for building systemwide
capacity to meet the instructional needs of academic ELs through the ALD
Network website (*aldnetwork.org*). We welcome new partners into the network and invite interested educators and instructional leaders to visit the
website for more information.

REFERENCES

Achinstein, B., & Athanases, S. Z. (2010). New teacher induction and mentoring for educational change. In A. Hargreaves, A. Lieberman, M. Fullan, &
D. Hopkins (Eds.), *International handbook on educational change* (2nd ed.,
pp. 573–594). New York: Springer.

Achinstein, B., O'Hara, S., Pritchard, R., & Zwiers, J. (2012). Strategic mentoring
for new teachers of English learners. *Journal of Communication and Education, 11*(10), 20–23.

Anstrom, K., DiCerbo, P., Butler, F., Katz, A., Millet, J. & River, C. (2010). *A
review of the literature on academic English: Implications for K–12 English
language learners*. Washington, DC: George Washington University Center
for Equity and Excellence in Education.

August, D., Artzi, L., & Mazrum, J. (2010). *Improving science and vocabulary
learning of English language learners*. Austin, TX: CREATE.

Baker, S., Lesaux, N., Jayanthi, M., Dimino, J., Proctor, C. P., Morris, J., et al.
(2014). *Teaching academic content and literacy to English learners in elementary and middle school* (NCEE 2014-4012). Washington, DC: National
Center for Education Evaluation and Regional Assistance (NCEE), Institute
of Education Sciences, U.S. Department of Education. Retrieved from *http://
ies.ed.gov/ncee/wwc/publications_reviews.aspx*.

Brisk, M. E., & Proctor, C. P. (2012). Challenges and supports for English language learners. In K. Hakuta & M. Santos (Eds.), *Understanding language:
Language, literacy, and learning in the content areas* (pp. 115–122). Stanford, CA: Stanford University.

Bunch, G. C., Kibler, A., & Pimentel, S. (2012). *Realizing opportunities for*

English learners in the common core English language arts and disciplinary literacy standards. Paper presented at the Understanding Language Initiative, Stanford, CA.

Casteel, C. J., & Ballantyne, K. G. (Eds.). (2010). *Professional development in action: Improving teaching of English learners.* Washington, DC: National Clearinghouse for English Language Acquisition.

Echevarria, J., Richards-Tutor, C., Chinn, V., & Ratleff, P. (2011). Did they get it?: The role of fidelity in teaching English learners. *Journal of Adolescent and Adult Literacy, 54*(6), 425–434.

Ericsson, K. A. (2014). Why expert performance is special and cannot be extrapolated from studies of performance in the general population: A response to criticisms. *Intelligence, 45*, 81–103.

Fogo, B. (2011). Making and measuring the California history standards. *Phi Delta Kappan, 92*(8), 62–67.

Harris, A. (2009). *Distributed leadership: Different perspectives.* Amsterdam, The Netherlands: Springer.

Honig, M., Copland, M., Rainey, L., Lorton, H., & Newton, M. (2010). *Central office transformation for district-wide teaching and learning improvement.* Seattle, WA: Center for the Study of Teaching and Policy, University of Washington.

Jaquith, A. (2013). Instructional capacity: How to build it right. *Educational Leadership, 71*(2), 56–60.

Jiménez, R. T., David, S., Fagan, K., Risko, V. J., Pacheco, M., Pray, L., et al. (2015). Using translation to drive conceptual development for students becoming literate in English as an additional language. *Research in the Teaching of English, 49*(3), 248.

Kibler, A., Walqui, A., & Bunch, G. (2015). Transformational opportunities: Language and literacy instruction for English language learners in the Common Core era in the United States. *TESOL Journal, 6*(1), 9–35.

Little, J. W. (2003). Inside teacher community: Representations of classroom practice. *Teachers College Record, 105*(6), 913–945.

Luft, J., Neakrase, J. J., Adams, K. L., Firestone, J., & Bang, E. (2010). Bringing content into induction programs: Examples from science. In J. Wang, S. Odell, & R. Clift (Eds.), *Past, present and future research on teacher induction: An anthology for researchers, policy makers, and practitioners* (pp. 205–220). Lanham, MD: Rowman & Littlefield Education.

Moschkovich, J. (2012). Mathematics, the Common Core, and language. *Teachers College Record, 96*(3), 418–431.

Nagy, W., & Townsend, D. (2012). Words as tools: Learning academic vocabulary as language acquisition. *Reading Research Quarterly, 47*(1), 91–108.

O'Hara, S., Zwiers, J., & Pritchard, R. (2014). Cutting to the Common Core: Changing the playing field, Part 1. *Language Magazine: The Journal of Communication and Education, 13*(5), 24–27.

Pritchard, R., O'Hara, S., & Zwiers, J. (in press). Framing the teaching of academic language to English learners: A Delphi study of expert consensus. *TESOL Quarterly.*

Robinson, V., Lloyd, C., & Rowe, K. (2008). The impact of leadership on student outcomes: An analysis of the differential effects of leadership types. *Educational Administration Quarterly, 44*(5), 635–674.

Steurer, J. (2011). The Delphi method: An efficient procedure to generate knowledge. *Skeletal Radiology, 40*(8), 959–961.

Van Lier, L., & Walqui, A. (2012). Language and the Common Core State Standards. *Commissioned Papers on Language and Literacy Issues in the Common Core State Standards and Next Generation Science Standards, 94*, 44.

Windschitl, M., Thompson, J., & Braaten, M. (2013). Developing a theory of ambitious early-career teacher practice. *American Education Research Journal, 50*(3), 574–615.

Wong Fillmore, L., & Fillmore, C. (2012). *What does text complexity mean for English learners and language minority students?* Paper presented at the 2012 Understanding Language Summit, Understanding Language Initiative, Stanford, CA. Retrieved from *http://ell.stanford.edu/sites/default/files/pdf/academic-papers/06-LWF%20CJF%20Text%20Complexity%20FINAL_0.pdf.*

Zwiers, J. (2008). *Building academic language: Essential practices for content classrooms.* San Francisco, CA: Jossey-Bass.

Zwiers, J., O'Hara, S., & Pritchard, R. (2014). *Common Core Standards in diverse classrooms: Essential practices for developing academic language and disciplinary literacy.* Portland, ME: Stenhouse.

CHAPTER 12

Supporting Linguistically Responsive Teaching

e-Learning Communities for Academic Language Learning in Mathematics and Science (eCALLMS)

Kara Mitchell Viesca, Boni Hamilton, Anne O. Davidson, and the eCALLMS Team

The education of emergent bilingual students overall is not a successful enterprise in the United States (Goldenberg & Coleman, 2010). For instance, students who are labeled *English language learners* or *ELLs* in schools are consistently the lowest-performing subgroup in the United States (Slama, 2014). We refer to these students as *emergent bilinguals* to acknowledge their daily use of varied language practices and multiple linguistic repertoires and registers for success and survival across multiple communities, including home and school. As Slama (2014) highlighted, despite more than 50 years of federal and state legislation requiring emergent bilingual students to have access to high-quality and adequately funded programs (e.g., *Casteñeda v. Pickard*, 1981; *Lau v. Nichols*, 1974), across the country these individuals still struggle to gain access to grade-level curriculum, strong academic language-learning opportunities, and well-qualified teachers (López & Iribarren, 2014). With current accountability and assessment practices not taking into account students' language practices, cultural backgrounds, and developing English proficiencies (Abedi, 2002; Shohamy, 2007; Solano-Flores, 2011), emergent bilingual students may be either over- or underrepresented in special education programs (Artiles, Rueda, Salazar, & Higareda, 2005) and losing access to bilingual education opportunities (Menken, 2013; Menken & Solorza, 2012). Additionally, high-stakes decisions about schools and teachers frequently do not meaningfully account for the linguistic abilities and practices of emergent bilingual students and are based on invalid and unreliable data (Jones, Buzick, & Turkan, 2013; Wright, 2015). In this difficult context, general education teachers, including mathematics and science teachers, are increasingly working with emergent bilingual students but are underprepared for that work (Lucas, 2011; Freeman & Freeman, 2014). Additionally, with new content standards such as the Common Core State Standards (CCSS) and the Next Generation Science Standards (NGSS), as well as increasing use of English language proficiency standards such as WIDA (Wisconsin, Delaware, Arkansas) English Language Development (ELD) Standards, content teachers working with emergent bilingual students need meaningful supports.

e-Learning Communities for Academic Language Learning in Mathematics and Science (eCALLMS) was developed to provide innovative approaches to support teacher learning (from preservice through inservice) that would improve content and language development for emergent bilingual students in general education classrooms, particularly in mathematics and science. This chapter explores the empirical and theoretical foundations, the practices, and the initial outcomes of the eCALLMS project's efforts to improve teaching and learning for emergent bilingual students.

Empirical and Theoretical Foundations

Research on Preparing General Education Teachers to Work with Emergent Bilingual Students

The body of literature examining the preparation of mainstream content teachers to work with emergent bilingual students is relatively small (Lucas, 2011; Freeman & Freeman, 2014). However, multiple conceptual frameworks do exist to guide the practices of teacher educators preparing teachers to work with this population of students. Several frameworks have been summarized in Table 12.1 and described in further depth below.

Starting with Chisholm and Becket (2003), these various frameworks recommend attention to particular aspects of teaching, learning, and language development. For instance, Chisholm and Becket focused on the Teaching English to Speakers of Other Languages (TESOL) Standards, Howard Gardner's theory of multiple intelligences (Gardner & Hatch, 1989) and technology. Herrera and Murry (2005) and Herrera, Murry, and Pérez (2008) focused on how teachers can provide accommodations to multilingual learners as well as teacher readiness to engage in that work. De Jong and Harper (2005, 2008) asserted that teaching emergent bilinguals is more than "just good teaching" and requires particular areas of teacher expertise. They focused on understanding language use in the classroom; accommodating for varying English proficiency levels; understanding the

TABLE 12.1. Frameworks Guiding General Education Teacher Preparation for Emergent Bilingual Students

Authors	Frameworks
Chisholm & Becket (2003)	*Integration framework:* Focuses on integrating TESOL standards, Howard Gardner's theory of multiple intelligences, and technology.
Herrera, Murry, & Pérez (2005, 2008)	*Accommodation readiness spiral:* Recommends a six-step accommodation readiness spiral that focuses on teachers' espoused and practical readiness for diversity. It starts with a readiness for critical reflection on practice, then moves to readiness for students and families, then environmental readiness, to curricular readiness, to programming and instructional readiness, to readiness for application and advocacy.
de Jong & Harper (2005, 2008)	*More than "just good teaching":* Asserts that teaching emergent bilinguals is "more than just good teaching." Teachers need to (1) understand language use in classrooms and how to accommodate the differing levels of English proficiency to make content comprehensible; (2) understand the process of second-language development and create teaching and learning opportunities that reflect these understandings; (3) understand the complexities at the intersection of language, culture, and schooling; and (4) understand that emergent bilinguals are learning language, literacy skills, and content simultaneously, so it is the responsibility of the content teacher to facilitate learning growth in each realm.
Lucas, Villegas, & Freedson-Gonzalez (2008); Lucas & Villegas (2010, 2011)	*Linguistically responsive teaching:* Suggests seven components under two major themes: "orientations of linguistically responsive teachers" and "knowledge and skills of linguistically responsive teachers" (Lucas & Villegas, 2011, p. 57). The seven components include having a sociolinguistic consciousness that encompasses understanding the relationships between language, culture, and identity and the sociopolitical dimensions of language use and education; esteem for linguistic diversity; and an inclination to advocate for emergent bilinguals. Under the knowledge and skills aspect of the framework, they contend that teachers need to know the academic, cultural, and linguistic backgrounds of their students; be able to identify the language demands of classroom tasks; understand and apply key principles of second-language acquisition in classroom practice; and scaffold instruction for meaningful content and academic language development.
Bunch (2013)	*Pedagogical language knowledge:* Asserts that teachers need the "knowledge of language directly related to disciplinary teaching and learning and situated in the particular (and multiple) contexts in which teaching and learning take place" (p. 307).

(continued)

TABLE 12.1. *(continued)*

Authors	Frameworks
Turkan, de Oliveira, Lee, & Phelps (2014)	*Disciplinary linguistic knowledge:* Identifies the knowledge base that teachers need within specific academic disciplines to assist emergent bilinguals in developing understandings of oral and written discourse within those specific disciplines. In particular, they assert that content teachers need to be able to identify linguistic features of their disciplinary discourse and model for emergent bilinguals, through oral and written engagement, how to communicate meaning using expected linguistic codes for the discipline.
Tharp, Estrada, Dalton, & Yamauchi (2000); Teemant, Leland, & Berghoff (2014)	*Standards for effective pedagogy:* Emphasizes critical sociocultural instructional practices in content classrooms to achieve excellence, fairness, inclusion, and harmony. This framework was not originally proposed by the designers as a framework for teacher preparation; however, we assert that it should be considered a framework for pre- and inservice educator development work based on the strong theoretical and empirical foundation of these standards. The standards include teachers' and students' joint productions, language and literacy development, contextualized learning, challenging activities, teaching through dialogic instructional conversation, and teaching to transform inequity.

process of second-language acquisition; understanding the complexities at the intersection of language, culture, and schooling; and accepting responsibility for the learning of emergent bilingual students in content classrooms.

This attention to the role of language in the classroom is a major point of focus for the rest of the frameworks highlighted here. Lucas, Villegas, and Freedson-Gonzalez (2008) suggested that linguistically responsive teacher education demands a focus on three types of pedagogical expertise for general education content teachers: (1) knowledge of the linguistic and academic backgrounds of students; (2) understanding of the language demands of the classroom tasks in which students engage; and (3) the skills to offer the appropriate scaffolding for emergent bilingual students to successfully participate in classroom tasks. In 2010, Lucas and Villegas expanded the framework to include seven total components, and in 2011, organized the seven components under two major themes: "orientations of linguistically responsive teachers" and "knowledge and skills of linguistically responsive teachers" (p. 57). Their work focuses on orientations such as valuing diversity and sociolinguistic consciousness, as well as skills centered on understanding the language demands of classrooms tasks, applying understandings of second-language acquisition to classroom practice, and meaningfully scaffolding learning for emergent bilingual students.

Recently, Bunch (2013) reviewed the research on developing content teachers to work with emergent bilingual students and proposed the notion of "pedagogical language knowledge," or the "knowledge of language directly related to disciplinary teaching and learning and situated in the particular (and multiple) contexts in which teaching and learning take place" (p. 307). Along the same lines, Turkan, de Oliveira, Lee, and Phelps (2014) argued for a knowledge base for content teachers of emergent bilingual students called *disciplinary linguistic knowledge*. They built on the work occurring around systemic functional linguistics (Halliday, 1994) and suggested the content-based language knowledge that general education teachers of emergent bilingual students should attain.

A framework that was not initially proposed for guiding content teacher preparation for emergent bilingual students, but offers a strong pedagogical system relevant to the work of content teachers of these students is the standards for effective pedagogy (Tharp, Estrada, Dalton, & Yamauchi, 2000). These standards were originally created by the Center for Research on Education, Diversity, and Excellence (CREDE) and have been expanded recently to include "Critical Stance" (Teemant, Leland, & Berghoff, 2014), a standard focused on teaching to transform inequity. These standards are grounded in critical sociocultural theory and have a strong empirical base demonstrating their effectiveness in supporting high learning outcomes for students from diverse backgrounds, particularly emergent bilinguals (Doherty & Hilberg, 2007; Estrada, 2005; Hilberg, Tharp, & DeGeest, 2000; Padron & Waxman, 1999; Teemant & Hausman, 2013).

Each framework offers a particular perspective on optimal teacher attitudes and beliefs regarding working with emergent bilingual students as well as what teachers should know and be able to do to support high-quality teaching and learning these students. However, all the frameworks draw from a similar research base and, for this reason, overlap, particularly in a focus on language use and support in classroom contexts. Each framework presents ways to bring language to the forefront of teacher education for content teachers.

Although impacted by each of these frameworks and the body of literature they were drawn from, eCALLMS was designed with a particular focus on the linguistically responsive teaching (LRT) framework that has evolved over time (Lucas & Villegas, 2011). The LRT framework represented the latest thinking and most comprehensive framework at the time eCALLMS was initiated in 2011. The more recent frameworks from Bunch (2013) and Turkan et al. (2014) have impacted the work of eCALLMS, bringing awareness to the language demands of content classroom tasks and the responsibilities for teachers.

eCALLMS has also been guided since its inception by the standards for effective pedagogy (Tharp et al., 2000) including the sixth "critical stance" (Teemant et al., 2014) standard. Before eCALLMS began, the standards for effective pedagogy had been adopted as the guiding pedagogical framework in the university's teacher preparation program. The leaders of the eCALLMS project also felt that this critical sociocultural framework with a strong empirical foundation was consistent with the project goals and likely to be able to assist in meeting the desired outcomes of eCALLMS, specifically to improve content teacher preparation for emergent bilingual students.

Teacher Professional Learning

eCALLMS has multiple initiatives focused on teacher professional learning (including online eWorkshops and face-to-face coaching) that were developed around the research evidence regarding high-quality and impactful professional learning for teachers. We drew extensively on the findings from Desimone, Porter, Garet, Yoon, and Birman's (2002) longitudinal study that determined which characteristics of professional development programs were most likely to effect change in teacher practices. Through their review of the existing literature and their own research, six key aspects of high-quality professional development programs were established: (1) reform type (more than just sitting in a lecture); (2) duration (the longer the better); (3) collective participation (as many from the same school community as possible); (4) active learning (doing rather than listening); (5) coherence (making connections to teachers' professional lives); and (6) content focus (more than just pedagogy). K. E. Johnson (2006) supported this alternative to the traditional professional development model for having similar approaches to teacher learning and professional growth as that put forth by Cochran-Smith and Lytle (1999, p. 250; 2009). These researchers discuss creating teacher learning communities involving "knowledge-*of*-practice," where "the knowledge teachers need to teach well is generated when teachers treat their own classrooms and schools as sites for intentional investigation at the same time that they treat the knowledge and theory produced by others as generative material for interrogation and interpretation" (1999, p. 250). eCALLMS professional learning initiatives, targeted to impact teacher preparation through improving the classrooms where preservice teachers are trained, were built upon the ideas that stakeholders in a school community should have opportunities to be engaged in generating and sharing their own knowledge, and at the same time, interpreting and critically engaging with outside knowledge sources. In order to create high-quality professional learning opportunities for teachers of emergent bilingual students, eCALLMS has explored the research and practice of using online approaches.

Online Teacher Professional Learning

Since the late 1990s, teachers have been using networked technologies to develop their professional skills and knowledge (Barnett, 2002; C. M. Johnson, 2001). As Internet and technology tools have become more affordable and reliable, the opportunities for online teacher professional development (OTPD) have burgeoned (Reeves & Li, 2012; Smith, 2014). Districts find OTPD more cost-effective than traditional face-to-face offerings because online delivery eliminates transporting teachers to central locations, paying for classroom substitutes, and disrupting the workflow in schools (Carr, 2010; Roskos, Jarosewich, Lenhart, & Collins, 2007). Teachers value opportunities to choose professional development topics that are relevant to their current needs, engage in professional development at times convenient to themselves, embed new practices into their classrooms immediately, and collaborate with peers across distances (Russell, Kleiman, Carey, & Douglas, 2009; Smith, 2014). Additionally, OTPD seems to be at least as effective as face-to-face coursework (Carr, 2010; Fishman et al., 2013). Researchers have found that OTPD has had positive effects on teachers' instructional practices and content knowledge (Borko, 2004; Cady & Rearden, 2009; Cavanaugh & Dawson, 2010; O'Dwyer et al., 2010; Russell et al., 2009). Because OTPD delivery is "time-independent, text-based, and dialogic" (Smith, 2014, p. 448), teachers have opportunities to engage in critical reflective thinking about teaching, learning, and the consequences of teaching decisions through asynchronous conversations with peers (Sung, 2009).

However, what works successfully in face-to-face teacher professional development cannot be transferred to online instruction without modification (Roskos et al., 2007). For instance, participants in OTPD usually do not see or talk to one another in real time, so online designs must include ways for participants to get acquainted (Smith, 2014; Sung, 2009). In order to safely share ideas, opinions, and experiences, participants need to be comfortable with online discussion tools; understand the expectations for when, where, and how to respond to prompts; and, most important, build a sense of trust with their online peers (Carr & Chambers, 2006; Carter, 2004; Smith, 2014; Sung, 2009). Some researchers have reported low participation and completion rates (Reeves & Pedulla, 2011). Online learning must offer a mix of engaging materials—text video, sound, graphics, images, and learning activities—that motivates learners to commit to ongoing participation (Carter, 2004). Consistency in format and content within OTPD has helped increase teachers' success and motivation (MacKenzie & Staley, 2001).

Technological expertise may influence teachers' satisfaction with OTPD. Participants may struggle with limited connectivity, inexperience with technology, or unfamiliarity with web-based courseware, although these problems are decreasing as technology use among teachers grows more common (Atkinson & O'Connor, 2007; Reeves & Li, 2012; Sung, 2009). One online design question that has yielded mixed results is whether facilitation is necessary for OTPD (Carter, 2004; Hanraets et al., 2011; Henderson, 2007; Russell et al., 2009).

Despite the growing body of literature about OTPD, very little has been written about it for inservice teachers working with emergent bilingual students. Smith (2014) designed and organized OTPD for K–12 teachers of emergent bilingual students. She expanded the community of inquiry (CoI) framework (Garrison, Anderson, & Archer, 2000), of *teaching* presence (instruction and facilitation), *social* presence (social interactions), and *cognitive* presence (knowledge construction and meaning making) as a basis for her design to include *learning* presence (self-regulation of monitoring and reflection). Kibler and Roman (2013) studied two teachers' in-class support for students' use of native languages after OTPD preparing California teachers for state endorsement to teach emergent bilingual students. The two monolingual teachers demonstrated positive changes in their perspectives, but the timing and impetus for the growth differed.

Overall, although OTPD has been increasing in availability, much more research is needed to identify best practices in online design for promoting teacher change and student achievement (Dede, Ketelhut, Whitehouse, Breit, & McCloskey, 2009; Fishman et al., 2013; Moon, Passmore, Reiser, & Michaels, 2014). Our work on eCALLMS is beginning to contribute to this research.

Overview of eCALLMS Project: Practices and Initial Outcomes

eCALLMS was designed to better prepare teachers of emergent bilingual students within the Urban Community Teacher Education (UCTE) program at the University of Colorado Denver. We proposed to substantially improve curricula and enhance existing networks and relationships by focusing on two levels of initiatives (preservice and inservice) that are intertwined and sustainable through the continued development of both face-to-face and online learning and collaboration opportunities. An overview of the initiatives of the grant is provided in Table 12.2.

Although certain initiatives were designed and implemented to have a major effect on either pre- or inservice teachers, they were also conceived of as impacting each other and collectively for the purpose of improving initial licensure. Figure 12.1 illustrates these connections.

TABLE 12.2. eCALLMS Initiatives

Targeted group	Initiatives
Preservice teachers	1. Professional development of preservice faculty in regard to instruction that supports emergent bilinguals' acquisition of language, literacy, and content knowledge. 2. Inform teacher education through district-based innovation in practice. 3. Cohesive curricular alignment across initial licensure courses and internships in regard to preparing preservice teachers to engage in instruction that supports high levels of learning for emergent bilinguals.
Inservice teachers	1. The creation of substantial high-quality online professional development focused on research-based instruction for emergent bilinguals, particularly in science and math, intended for every member of the teacher education community (clinical teachers, graduates, faculty, district partners, etc.). 2. Increased capacity of clinical teachers and program graduates to utilize instruction that supports high levels of learning for emergent bilinguals.

Essentially by improving the work of inservice teachers to teach emergent bilingual students, preservice preparation can be improved by offering preservice teachers better student-teaching placements. The online learning eWorkshops as well as the CREDE Practitioner Institute, two distinct yet related initiatives, offer opportunities for pre- and inservice teachers to learn collaboratively as well as to bring the latest thinking and work of the teacher preparation program into meaningful alignment with the practices and skills of the inservice teachers hosting teacher candidates.

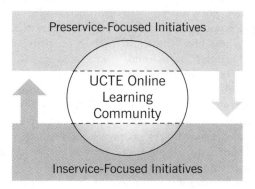

FIGURE 12.1. Graphic representation of relationship of eCALLMS initiatives.

Online Professional Learning eWorkshops

The eCALLMS eWorkshops are designed to be dynamic and interactive multimedia resources that support groups of inservice teachers in meaningful collaboration toward the goal of becoming more linguistically responsive (Lucas & Villegas, 2011) through their joint investigations of teaching practices for emergent bilinguals in their classrooms. Designed by a collaborative multidisciplinary team of university professors (science and mathematics [STEM; science, technology, engineering, and math] educators, second-language acquisition faculty, and instructional technology experts), the eCALLMS eWorkshops build the capacity of inservice teachers (K–12) to attend to emergent bilinguals' growth in both grade-level content knowledge and language development related to the register and discourse of content discipline.

Purposeful design of the eWorkshop environment provides a consistent look and feel, which has enhanced teachers' learning experiences. eCALLMS eWorkshops are housed on a password-protected learning management system (currently, Canvas) where teachers interact in small groups with the resources we have created. Each eWorkshop has six units and requires approximately 2 hours of work per unit. As flexible online resources, groups of teachers may pace their work through the eWorkshops collaboratively, selecting the start time, duration, and collaborative path on which they engage with the eWorkshop content. This means that each group that engages with an eCALLMS eWorkshop is essentially taking its own unique "class." This class is housed in a password-protected space on a learning management system, so that teachers' work and ideas area visible only to those with access to that course shell (usually, just the other members of the learning community and eCALLMS project management personnel). As a unique class, the members of the learning community may make important decisions about their collaborative learning paths.

For instance, some groups choose to engage in the eWorkshop fully online, whereas others choose to add face-to-face discussion time (sometimes over Happy Hour!). Additionally, some groups choose to go through the six units in 6 weeks, whereas other groups take 2 weeks per unit, thus extending the overall length of the eWorkshop. All groups select when they start, which eWorkshop they would like to take, how they would like to organize themselves, etc. This flexibility is an important commitment of the eCALLMS project as we seek to provide relevant, meaningful professional learning opportunities that work for teachers with their busy schedules and varied learning goals and desires.

The eWorkshops were not designed for individual self-paced participation, but rather to engage three or more teachers simultaneously in learning communities. Frequently, these learning communities already exist within schools and districts. However, eCALLMS eWorkshops also provide meaningful opportunities for new teacher communities to be developed across schools and even districts. Because eCALLMS eWorkshops are not facilitated, the learning communities interact dynamically to support one another as they explore and try new ideas. However, districts taking on eCALLMS eWorkshops as professional development have frequently provided facilitators to guide their learning communities and ground the learning in local district perspectives, initiatives, and practices.

Most teachers access these eWorkshops through district-led efforts such as a district coach leading an eWorkshop for interested teachers. Some districts have even provided financial incentives to teachers for participating and completing eCALLMS eWorkshops. However, groups of interested teachers have also created their own opportunities to engage with these eWorkshops. Anyone interested in the eWorkshops (district leaders, principals, instructional coaches, teachers, etc.) can contact the eCALLMS project (see *http://ecallms.ucdsehd.net*) and within 2 weeks can be launched successfully into his or her own flexible, meaningful, learning opportunity grounded in online resources. These eWorkshops have been sustainably designed to remain low-cost and freely available, even beyond the funding of the eCALLMS grant. Therefore, it is our hope that their use will continue to grow and expand for years to come. Table 12.3 presents the publically available eWorkshops at the time of press.

eWorkshop Design

Prior to beginning the work of any eCALLMS eWorkshop, participants get acquainted through a Meet and Greet prompt such as "What memorable science experiences do you recall from your K–12 education?" Responses to questions like these posted in discussion threads asynchronously break the ice, promote collegiality, and trigger reflective thinking about the content of the eWorkshop.

The learning cycle of each eWorkshop follows a standardized pattern: *Explore, Make It Work,* and *Share.*

- In *Explore,* participants learn by watching videos, reading practitioner-friendly material, and studying examples tightly focused on a single idea (requiring about 30 minutes of a teacher's time). They also may begin an online discussion of the week's learning with their online learning community in the "class." Collective participation and intensive focus conform to good professional development practices (Desimone et al., 2002).
- In *Make It Work* (MIW), participants practice what they learned (requiring about an hour of a teacher's time). Given three or four possible practical applications of the week's focus, including the

TABLE 12.3. Available eCALLMS eWorkshops

eWorkshop title	Essential question
Language Development for Bilingual Learners (grades K–12)	"How can I create meaningful contexts that support strong multilingual language development in schools?"
Language Grouping Strategies (grades K–12)	"How can I maximize opportunities for all learners in a multilingual setting?"
Learning through Two Languages (grades K–12)	"How can I build on students' linguistic and cultural assets to foster bilingualism?"
Language and Concept Development (grades K–12)	"How can I provide bilingual learners with the greatest opportunities to acquire both the knowledge and the language needed to be successful in my classroom?"
Math Functions (grade 8)	"How can I support multilingual students in learning the mathematical language and concepts of functions?"
Math Ratios and Proportions (grades 5–8)	"How can I support multilingual students in learning the mathematical language and concepts of ratios and proportions?"
Math Fractions (grades 3–5)	"What is the language of fractions and how can all students have access to it?"
Math Numbers and Operations (grades K–2)	"How can mainstream elementary teachers purposefully plan and deliver mathematics instruction that combines rigorous mathematics content with attention to language development and learning strategies?"
Language in the Multilingual Science Classroom (grades 3–5)	"How can I create a culturally and linguistically rich classroom environment in a science unit?"
Science Inquiry: Engaging Bilinguals in Scientific Questioning (grades 4–8)	"Why does inquiry science especially benefit bilingual learners?"
The 5E Science Model for Multilingual Students (grades 3–5)	"How can I use the 5E Science Model to improve my science instruction to engage multilingual students more meaningfully in the development of science knowledge and language?"
Writing in Science (grades 3–12)	"How can I teach academic writing through meaningful STEM activities?"

option to design their own, teachers apply the new ideas to their teaching practice as active, job-embedded learning focused on the content they teach (Desimone et al., 2002; Wayne, Yoon, Zhu, Cronen, & Garet, 2008).

- For *Share,* participants return to the online discussion to reflect on the MIW experiences, analyze the effects on their practice, upload examples, and/or ponder next steps (requiring about 30 minutes of a teacher's time).

The first five sessions of the eWorkshop follow the pattern described above, and then during the sixth unit, teachers synthesize their learning from the previous five units. This approach not only reactivates reflection, but also builds coherence across the eWorkshop (Wayne et al., 2008). Within the eWorkshop, teachers also access documentation that aligns eWorkshop work with teacher professional standards. eWorkshop completion equals 12 hours of continuing education.

eWorkshop Development

Cross-disciplinary work requires close collaboration and shared knowledge. STEM educators were keenly aware of content concepts that teachers struggle to master, but often less familiar with integrating meaningful language practices (García & Wei, 2014) into content instruction. On the other hand, bilingual/multilingual education professors were not necessarily strong in mathematics and science content knowledge. Content experts paired with language development experts to develop mathematics and science eWorkshops, but it was a challenge to find the right balance between deepening teachers' content knowledge and developing teachers' understanding of language development. Newly released standards such as the CCSS, the NGSS, and the WIDA ELD Standards provided a valuable platform for interdisciplinary collaboration as well as ensured that our work would be relevant to the curricula and the contexts in which eWorkshop users work.

Additionally, eWorkshop authors realized that mathematics and science have different curricular structures. Mathematics concepts often span 3 or more years (e.g., fractions are taught in multiple consecutive grades), but science concepts are assigned to particular grade levels (e.g., in Colorado energy is taught in fourth grade and not again until middle school). Therefore, whereas mathematics eWorkshops could focus on specific concepts, science modules needed to address broader topics, such as science inquiry or writing in science. The language development eWorkshop strand was expanded to include equity topics such as race awareness and bilingualism advocacy.

A major challenge for all eWorkshop authors has been narrowing the scope of the learning within an eWorkshop to one or two ideas in each unit that collectively contribute to one key concept for the eWorkshop. Participants spend approximately 30 minutes in the learning phase of *Explore* and the remaining professional learning time trying something out in the MIW phase and writing online in discussion boards with their peers. Each eWorkshop's narrow focus means that the changes in teachers' thinking, instructional strategies, or student advocacy are small but powerful.

All eWorkshops undergo testing at least once before they are revised and released for public use. Testers complete feedback surveys for each unit and give posttesting interviews. Tester feedback assists eWorkshop authors in making revisions and improvements in their material.

As of this writing, 12 eWorkshops have been released for public use (see Table 12.3) and 18 are in the design phase. More than 200 teachers in Colorado, Germany, and Finland registered for at least one eWorkshop in the 2014–2015 school year, the first year our eWorkshops were publicly available. One eWorkshop has been translated into German and is currently being translated into Finnish. Overall, the completion rate for eCALLMS eWorkshops to date is over 75%, a high rate for free, online courses.

Effectiveness of eWorkshops

eWorkshop testers have acknowledged that their participation has sensitized them to the language development and language practices of emergent bilingual students that they had previously overlooked. The eWorkshops provide useful strategies for building academic registers, promoting an assets-based view of emergent bilinguals and their families, and highlighting the importance of attending to the language practices of students within a classroom.

The following post by a middle school science teacher after an *Explore* phase demonstrates how new information can trigger reflective thinking about a classroom practice:

"I have a hard time with teaching vocabulary in my lessons and making it interesting. I have often felt that it is the student's job to learn the vocabulary, but after this week's Explore lesson, I don't feel that way anymore. I need to try and come up with good ways to teach science vocabulary and expose students to it every day."

Sometimes an MIW option leads to new insights as well. A middle school teacher participating in an eWorkshop on grouping strategies that support emergent bilingual students wrote:

"I took particular notice of the article detailing the assignment of group roles and personality grouping. I reviewed my groups and rated every student as a *1, 2,* or *3*—with *1* being passive, *3* being outgoing as each appears in my small-group setting. I then highlighted all of my ELL students. Everyone was a *1*. I made a couple of changes to groups where there was only one 1 and several 3's to even things out. I then assigned stronger roles to my 1's and more passive roles to my 3's. I have only had one session, but I definitely noticed more confidence in my 1's. I intend to continue this role assignment for at least a month to observe the results."

After participating in six units, teachers sometimes indicate a changed perspective toward emergent bilingual students. A fourth-grade teacher said that identifying the WIDA language proficiency levels in reading for students in each of her two science classes (almost every student was an emergent bilingual) made her aware that the classes had significantly different language proficiency profiles, which she had not been accommodating. The name charts are a strategy she continues to use:

"One of the first activities was putting the students on the WIDA continuum of reading [language proficiency levels] on the name charts. I actually have those and pull them out and use them because when I'm trying to make groups for science, I'm like, these guys need a different book. I can just grab the list and use it. So, just the awareness of where my students are and using that so that it's not something that they're penalized for because the assignment is inaccessible."

This teacher's awareness of how WIDA name charts could help her plan accommodations enabled her to support her emergent bilingual students more effectively in her classroom.

Overall, from tester data and examining users' data within the eWorkshops, we feel confident that eCALLMS eWorkshops are providing valuable learning opportunities for content teachers as they improve how they work with their emergent bilingual students. Therefore, we suggest that interested schools, principals, districts, and teachers use these easily accessible, high-quality resources in their efforts to support improved teacher practice for emergent bilingual student populations. However, more research is needed (and will be conducted over time) to understand the impacts of eCALLMS eWorkshops on student learning outcomes as well as on long-term educator development.

Because the eCALLMS grant targets support across an entire initial licensure teacher education program, in addition to the online modules, a practitioner institute was developed to support inservice teachers who host teacher candidates through a collaborative partnership between the university and local, urban schools.

CREDE Practitioner Institute

The practitioner institute focuses on the standards for effective pedagogy mentioned previously. The CREDE Practitioner Institute (CPI) was developed to support inservice teacher participants in enacting culturally and linguistically responsive practices within their diverse, inclusive classrooms. By targeting classroom teachers who host teacher candidates during their internships, the CPI leveraged inservice teachers' development to improve preservice teacher learning.

The CPI was originally offered to K–12 teachers in schools across three diverse urban school districts that partner with the university in a professional development school (PDS) network that supports preservice teacher training. Interested inservice teachers were invited to a 1-week summer training to explore the CREDE standards and then engage in monthly conversations with a "thought partner" (coach) or CREDE coach to deepen their practice around the CREDE standards across the school year. During the first year of the CPI, participants self-selected into the project, with some teachers choosing to continue for the second year and even recruiting school peers to join the project. One school site has found the CPI to be particularly beneficial and will be the sole site for the third year of the CPI (the final year of the eCALLMS project), with a focus on every K–3 teacher in the school. During this final year of the CPI, teachers are engaging in both online modules and face-to-face coaching opportunities.

Across the first 2 years of the CPI, each practitioner was given an iPad, video lens, external microphone and tripod to capture CREDE practices in the classroom. Practitioners were encouraged to set personal goals for their CREDE classroom development and meet approximately monthly with university-connected thought-partner collaborators. In addition, teachers had opportunities to collaborate across the CPI community during specific, limited, out-of-school sessions. Session formats varied in response to reflective feedback from participants.

Inservice teachers shared their videos of instructional practice with their peers for collaborative reflection. The teachers identified the instructional context of their videos and a goal or inquiry for their own development of CREDE practices. The participants reported that these collaborative reflections were insightful, enabling them to explore new ideas for their practice, even when reflecting on the video of a peer. Although teacher practitioners valued the video reflection experience, they also encountered challenges creating the video clips. It was difficult to capture video of instruction while attending to the classroom and students' learning and then to edit their video into short, easily sharable clips. Broadband issues also proved difficult for sharing videos through online resources.

The coaching model varied across participants and years of the project. The CPI participants who found the CREDE standards most aligned with their districts' evaluations practices and in-school initiatives gained the most from participating in the CPI. These participants were eager to schedule meetings with their CREDE thought partner and engage in all aspects of the project, whereas teachers in schools with conflicting efforts and district initiatives reasonably found ongoing participation difficult.

Teachers reported benefit from engaging with a thought partner to debrief lessons, co-teach, and co-plan, and they also greatly appreciated the opportunity to visit other CPI participants' classrooms and learn from one another's practice. Scheduling such visits presents its own challenges, including the reality that with increasing high-stakes decisions attached to teacher performance and student learning, teachers found it difficult to voluntarily leave students in order to pursue their own professional learning.

Overall, the work on the CPI has provided excellent opportunities to collaborate with district partners who host the university's teacher candidates. We have also learned important lessons regarding working with teachers on professional learning initiatives through coaching/face-to-face endeavors. First, the CPI was successful when the work was aligned with other aspects of a teacher's life (e.g., evaluations, principal expectations, district-mandated curricula) and when there was substantial administrator buy-in and support. Second, asking teachers to share their classrooms and practices presented both affordances and challenges. Video can capture practices for sharing and reflection, but the process of creating, editing, and managing video for sharing and reflective conversation is logistically difficult and practically unmanageable to sustain. Tools and resources that might simplify the process are often expensive. Teachers valued long-established approaches (i.e., taking substitute days to visit one another's classroom) for professional growth, but found scheduling challenging. Third, being responsive to teachers individually and collectively has great merit. Teachers reported that the highly individualized and contextualized nature of their participation in the CPI was valuable and supportive of their professional growth.

Conclusion

Grounded in theoretical and empirical research, the eCALLMS project is striving to support teachers in the current context of new standards, new assessments, and new accountability frameworks. Initial evidence from our project suggests that this work is proving extremely useful for teachers and emergent bilingual students. However, more research is needed to understand the relationships between engaging in eCALLMS-related professional learning and the outcomes in terms of teachers' practices and their emergent bilingual students' learning.

Yet, despite the future research still necessary, there is a great deal that teachers, teacher educators, professional developers, and administrators can learn from and use based on eCALLMS efforts. First, the eWorkshops are free of charge into the foreseeable future. eCALLMS eWorkshops are already supporting teacher development internationally and can grow in their reach within the United States as well. Anyone interested in the eCALLMS eWorkshops may contact the authors or visit our website (*http:// ecallms.ucdsehd.net*). Further, the work of the CPI can be replicated and expanded into other contexts, where appropriate. We especially encourage those interested to engage with the six standards of effective pedagogy and responsively support groups of teachers to develop this pedagogy. Essentially, the work of the eCALLMS grant can provide important supports for teachers across many contexts, through both online and face-to-face initiatives, to engage meaningfully in the new context of education with new standards and assessments. Through these efforts, we seek to meaningfully support teacher development aimed at improving emergent bilingual students' language, literacy, and grade-level content development.

ACKNOWLEDGMENTS

eCALLMS is a National Professional Development grant from the federal Office of English Language Acquisition, Award No. T365Z110177. The co-principal investigators on eCALLMS are Kara Mitchell Viesca, Jacqueline Leonard, Honorine Nocon, and Cindy Gutierrez. Significant collaborators on the eCALLMS project currently and historically have included Christopher Carson, Nancy Commins, Anne Davidson, Susan Detrie, Helen Douglass, Polly Dunlop, Carlos Garcia, Bonita Hamilton, Colin Hueston, Kim Hutchison, Joy Barnes-Johnson, Elizabeth Mahon, Cheryl Matias, Sally Nathenson-Mejia, Roberto Montoya, Naomi Nishi, Aysenur Ozyer, Luis Poza, Nicole Joseph, Valencia Seidel, Nancy Shanklin, Sheila Shannon, Lee Tran, Geeta Verma, Gama Viesca, and Brent Wilson. Many local practicing teachers and other collaborators have also tested our work and provided extremely valuable feedback. Without all of these collaborators, the success of eCALLMS would not be possible.

REFERENCES

Abedi, J. (2002). Standardized achievement tests and English language learners: Psychometrics issues. *Educational Assessment, 8*(3), 231–257.
Artiles, A. J., Rueda, R., Salazar, J. J., & Higareda, I. (2005). Within-group

diversity in minority disproportionate representation: English language learners in urban school districts. *Exceptional Children, 71*(3), 283–300.

Atkinson, T. S., & O'Connor, K. A. (2007). Establishing professional development partnerships. online: Reaching out to veteran teachers. *Tech Trends, 51,* 21–29.

Barnett, M. (2002, April). *Issues and trends concerning electronic networking technologies for teacher professional development: A critical review of the literature.* Paper presented at the meeting of the American Educational Research Association, New Orleans, LA.

Borko, H. (2004). Professional development and teacher learning: Mapping the terrain. *Educational Researcher, 33*(8), 3–15.

Bunch, G. C. (2013). Pedagogical language knowledge preparing mainstream teachers for English learners in the new standards era. *Review of Research in Education, 37*(1), 298–341.

Cady, J., & Reardon, K. (2009). Delivering online professional development in mathematics to rural educators. *Journal of Technology and Teacher Education, 17*(3), 281–298.

Carr, N., & Chambers, D. P. (2006). Cultural and organizational issues facing online learning communities of teachers. *Education Information Technology, 11,* 269–282.

Carr, V. B. (2010). The viability of online education for professional development. *AASA Journal of Scholarship and Practice, 7*(3), 6–16.

Carter, K. (2004). Online training: What's really working? *Technology and Learning, 24*(10), 32–36.

Castañeda v. Pickard, 648 F.2d 989 (U. S. Ct. App. 1981).

Cavanaugh, C., & Dawson, K. (2010). Design of online professional development in science content and pedagogy: A pilot study in Florida. *Journal of Science Education Technology, 19,* 438–446.

Chisholm, I. M., & Beckett, E. C. (2003). Teacher preparation for equitable access through the integration of TESOL standards, multiple intelligences and technology. *Technology, Pedagogy and Education, 12*(2), 249–275.

Cochran-Smith, M., & Lytle, S. L. (1999). Relationships of knowledge and practice: Teacher learning in communities. *Review of Research in Education, 24,* 249–305.

Cochran-Smith, M., & Lytle, S. L. (2009). *Inquiry as stance: Practitioner research in the next generation.* New York: Teachers College Press.

Dede, C., Ketelhut, D. J., Whitehouse, P., Breit, L., & McCloskey, E. M. (2009). Research agenda for online teacher professional development. *Journal of Teacher Education, 60*(1), 8–19.

de Jong, E. J., & Harper, C. A. (2005). Preparing mainstream teachers for English-language learners: Is being a good teacher good enough? *Teacher Education Quarterly, 32*(2), 101–124.

de Jong, E. J., & Harper, C. A. (2008). ESL is good teaching "plus": Preparing standard curriculum teachers for all learners. In M. E. Brisk (Ed.), *Language, culture, and community in teacher education* (pp. 127–148). New York: Erlbaum.

Desimone, L. M., Porter, A. C., Garet, M. S., Yoon, K. S., & Birman, B. F. (2002).

Effects of professional development on teachers' instruction: Results from a three-year longitudinal study. *Educational Evaluation and Policy Analysis*, 24(2), 81–112.

Doherty, R. W., & Hilberg, R. S. (2007). Standards for effective pedagogy, classroom organization, English proficiency, and student achievement. *Journal of Educational Research, 101*(1), 24–35.

Estrada, P. (2005). The courage to grow: A researcher and teacher linking professional development with small-group reading instruction and student achievement. *Research in the Teaching of English, 39*(4), 320–364.

Fishman, B., Konstantopoulos, S., Kubitskey, B., Vath, R., Johnson, H., & Edelson, D. (2013). Comparing the impact of online and face-to-face professional development in the context of curriculum implementation. *Journal of Teacher Education, 64*(5), 426–438.

Freeman, Y. S., & Freeman, D. E. (Eds.). (2014). *Research on preparing preservice teachers to work effectively with emergent bilinguals.* Bingley, UK: Emerald.

García, O., & Wei, L. (2014). *Translanguaging: Language bilingualism and education.* New York: Palgrave Macmillan.

Gardner, H., & Hatch, T. (1989). Multiple intelligences go to school: Educational implications of the theory of multiple intelligences. *Educational Researcher, 18*(8), 4–9.

Garrison, D. R., Anderson, T., & Archer, W. (2000). Critical inquiry in a text-based environment: Computer conferencing in higher education. *The Internet and Higher Education, 2*(3), 87–105.

Goldenberg, C., & Coleman, R. (2010). *Promoting academic achievement among English learners: A guide to the research.* Thousand Oaks, CA: Corwin.

Halliday, M. A. K. (1994). *Introduction to function grammar.* London: Edward Arnold.

Hanraets, I., Hulsebosch, J., & de Laat, M. (2011). Experiences of pioneers facilitating teacher networks for professional development. *Educational Media International, 48*(2), 85–99.

Henderson, M. (2007). Sustaining online professional development through community. *Campus-Wide Information Systems, 24*(3), 162–173.

Herrera, S. G., & Murry, K. G. (2005). *Mastering ESL and bilingual methods: Differentiated instruction for culturally and linguistically diverse (CLD) students.* Boston: Allyn & Bacon.

Herrera, S. G., Murry, K. G., & Pérez, D. R. (2008). Classic: Transforming hearts and minds. In M. E. Brisk (Ed.), *Language, culture, and community in teacher education* (pp. 149–173). New York: Erlbaum.

Hilberg, R. S., Tharp, R. G., & DeGeest, L. (2000). The efficacy of CREDE's standards-based instruction in American Indian mathematics classes. *Equity and Excellence in Education, 33*(2), 32–40.

Johnson, C. M. (2001). A survey of current research on online communities of practice. *The Internet and Higher Education, 4,* 45–60.

Johnson, K. E. (2006). The sociocultural turn and its challenges for second-language teacher education. *TESOL Quarterly, 40*(1), 235–257.

Jones, N. D., Buzick, H. M., & Turkan, S. (2013). Including students with disabilities and English learners in measures of educator effectiveness. *Educational Researcher, 42*(4), 234–241.

Kibler, A. K., & Roman, D. (2013). Insights into professional development for teachers of English language learners: A focus on using students' native language in the classroom. *Bilingual Research Journal, 36*(2), 187–207.

Lau v. Nichols, 414 U.S. 56 (1974).

López, F., & Iribarren, J. (2014). Creating and sustaining inclusive instructional settings for English language learners: Why, what, and how. *Theory Into Practice, 53*(2), 106–114.

Lucas, T. (Ed.). (2011). *Teacher preparation for linguistically diverse classrooms: A resource for teacher educators.* New York: Routledge.

Lucas, T., & Villegas, A. M. (2010). The missing piece in teacher education: The preparation of linguistically responsive teachers. *National Society for the Study of Education, 109*(2), 297–318.

Lucas, T., & Villegas, A. M. (2011). A framework for preparing linguistically responsive teachers. In T. Lucas (Ed.), *Teacher preparation for linguistically diverse classrooms: A resource for teacher educators* (pp. 55–72). New York: Routledge.

Lucas, T., Villegas, A. M., & Freedson-Gonzalez, M. (2008). Linguistically responsive teacher education: Preparing classroom teachers to teach English language learners. *Journal of Teacher Education, 29*(4), 361–373.

MacKenzie, N., & Staley, A. (2001). Online professional development for academic staff: Putting the curriculum first. *Innovations in Education and Teaching International, 38*(1), 42–53.

Menken, K. (2013). Restrictive language education policies and emergent bilingual youth: A perfect storm with imperfect outcomes. *Theory Into Practice, 52*(3), 160–168.

Menken, K., & Solorza, C. (2012). No child left bilingual: Accountability and the elimination of bilingual education programs in New York City Schools. *Educational Policy, 28*(1), 96–125.

Moon, J., Passmore, C., Reiser, B. J., & Michaels, S. (2014). Beyond comparisons of online versus face-to-face PD: Commentary in response to Fishman et al., "Comparing the impact of online and face-to-face professional development in the context of curriculum implementation." *Journal of Teacher Education, 65*(2), 172–176.

O'Dwyer, L. M., Masters, J., Dash, S., De Kramer, R. M., Humez, A., & Russell, M. (2010). e-Learning for educators: Effects of on-line professional development on teachers and their students. Available at *www.intasc.org.*

Padron, Y. N. & Waxman, H. C. (1999). Classroom observations of the five standards of effective teaching in urban classrooms with English language learners. *Teaching and Change, 7*(1), 79–100.

Reeves, T. D., & Li, Z. (2012). Teachers' technological readiness for online professional development: Evidence from the US e-Learning for Educators initiative. *Journal of Education for Teaching, 38*(1), 389–406.

Reeves, T. D., & Pedulla, J. J. (2011). Predictors of teacher satisfaction with online professional development: Evidence from the USA's e-Learning for Educators initiative. *Professional Development in Education, 37*(4), 591–611.

Roskos, K., Jarosewich, T., Lenhart, L., & Collins, L. (2007). Design of online teacher professional development in a statewide Reading First professional development system. *The Internet and Higher Education, 10,* 173–183.

Russell, M., Kleiman, G., Carey, R., & Douglas, J. (2009). Comparing self-paced and cohort-based online courses for teachers. *Journal of Research on Technology in Education, 41*(4), 443–446.

Shohamy, E. (2007). Language tests as language policy tools. *Assessment in Education, 14*(1), 117–130.

Slama, R. B. (2014). Investigating whether and when English learners are reclassified into mainstream classrooms in the United States: A discrete-time survival analysis. *American Educational Research Journal, 51*(2), 220–252.

Smith, S. U. (2014). Frameworks shaping an online professional development program for K–12 teachers of ELLs: Toward supporting the sharing of ideas for empowering classroom teachers online. *TESOL Journal, 5*(3), 444–464.

Solano-Flores, G. (2011). Assessing the cultural validity of assessment practices: An introduction. In M. D. R. Basterra, Trumbull, & G. Solano-Flores (Eds.), *Cultural validity in assessment: Addressing linguistic and cultural diversity* (pp. 3–21). New York: Routledge/Taylor & Francis.

Sung, L. C. (2009). *Online professional development for K–12 inservice teachers from views of Online Learning Forum (OLF) designers.* Paper presented at the Information Technology: New Generations, 2009—Sixth International Conference on Information Technology, Piscataway, NJ.

Teemant, A., & Hausman, C. S. (2013). The relationship of teacher use of critical sociocultural practices with student achievement. *Critical Education, 4*(4), 1–20.

Teemant, A., Leland, C., & Berghoff, B. (2014). Development and validation of a measure of critical stance for instructional coaching. *Teaching and Teacher Education, 39,* 136–147.

Tharp, R. G., Estrada, P., Dalton, S. S., & Yamauchi, L. A. (2000). *Teaching transformed: Achieving excellence, fairness, inclusion, and harmony.* Boulder, CO: Westview Press.

Turkan, S., de Oliveira, L. S., Lee, O., & Phelps, G. (2014). Proposing a knowledge base for teaching academic content to English language learners: Disciplinary linguistic knowledge. *Teachers College Record, 116,* 1–30.

Wayne, A. J., Yoon, K. S., Zhu, P., Cronen, S., & Garet, M. S. (2008). Experimenting with teacher professional development: Motives and methods. *Educational Researcher, 37*(8), 469–479.

Wright, W. (2015). What has No Child Left Behind accomplished for students designated as English language learners? What do the Common Core State Standards and accountability requirements change? In G. Valdés, K. Menken, & M. Castro (Eds.) *Common core bilingual and English language learners: A resource for educators* (pp. 11–13). Philadelphia: Caslon.

Index